Inconvenient Adventures

By

Helen Cadd

An adventure is an inconvenience rightly considered.
An inconvenience is an adventure wrongly considered.
G.K. Chesterton

Helen Cadd
Ps. 138 -2-3
(Living
Bible)

www.xulonpress.com

Other books by Dick and Helen Cadd:

Never to Forget, 1977, by Helen Cadd

Four Flats and a Pitchpipe, 2003, by Dick Cadd (with comments "I Married a Quartet" by Helen Cadd)

The Madri-Gals and Guys, 2010, by Dick and Helen Cadd

Thank You!

No words are adequate and there is no way to express my thanks to:

My oldest daughter, **Carolyn Cadd Brannon**. If I tried to list the ways she came to my rescue, it would almost make another book! She sacrificed weeks of her precious time struggled to teach me how to put this book on the computer, as well as constantly preparing delicious meals for me.

LuAnne Cadd, my youngest daughter, worked tirelessly on a new cover when I changed the name of the book. This took place while she was traveling around the world in her job as Roving Senior Communications and Media Officer for Mission Aviation Fellowship (MAF) International. She is based in Kenya, so all of our ideas had to be planned and discussed by Skype and email. Because of the different time zones, this was not always easy.

Lorrie Parker apologized for not helping me more, but besides doing research, getting permissions and helping edit the book, she kept my garden alive by watering each day and then picked my berries for me. That's along with driving me places, cleaning my house and running errands for me, just so I could write.

I received encouragement from many different places: **Family and Friends** who prayed for me, loved me and told me they were waiting to read this book.

Most important is still my husband, **Dick Cadd**, and my other children: **Jon, Steve and Yvonne**. Without them, I wouldn't have had most of these adventures. Their files were constant companions.

My relationship with **GOD** through **JESUS CHRIST** will always be the most important part of my life. We are told to always give thanks, and that is what I want this book to be about. **THANK YOU, LORD!**

Contents

CHAPTER 1

INTRODUCTION

I can't remember daydreaming of great adventures as a child. In fact, I was probably more cautious than many children and even fearful of serious adventures. But then, I fell in love and married Dick Cadd. It didn't take long to discover that I was actually married to an adventure. Although it wasn't always easy, my attitude had to change! I learned that pouring a glass of cold water on Dick to wake to him up so we wouldn't be late for our college classes, ended with a cold shower for me with all my clothes on. If I playfully threw a pillow at him while we were making the bed, he playfully put me back in bed.

These were simple little "get-acquainted" adventures. In every kind of adventure, an attitude reveals itself, either good or not good. Dick and I had a choice to have an attitude of fun or of anger. We chose fun! However, I didn't always have the right attitude in very important issues, and it took some serious help from the Lord to change. I'm convinced my attitude could have ruined our lives, but instead, with God's help, we had the most fabulous and fascinating life imaginable for 58 years!

I have felt that the Lord was asking me to tell some of my stories, and I actually thought seriously about doing it in 2007. But writing is not easy for me. It's hard work! I'm not comfortable with my writing, so I would prefer to mop the floors. There are always too many other jobs to do and I have problems with managing my time and priorities. Then I woke up one morning thinking about a story Dick and I used to tell in our meetings before we went to the Philippines.

There was a shopkeeper who hired a girl to help take care of things when he went on a trip for a few days. He gave clear instructions about what he wanted her to do while he was gone, which was to unpack some boxes of canned goods and put them on the shelves where they belonged. However, the girl thought she should dust and clean and sweep first. Then she noticed some of the counters really needed paint, so she did a nice job of painting. But time ran out before she could unpack the boxes, and the shopkeeper came back. She was excited to show him everything she had accomplished. "See, I cleaned and dusted and even painted the counters. Doesn't everything look nice?" He replied, *"Yes, but you didn't do what I asked you to do!"*

I had not thought of this story for years, but when I was praying in bed recently, it came very vividly to my mind. Since I felt that the Lord had asked me to do some writing again, I wondered if maybe this could apply to me. *"But Lord, I'm really confused. There are so many other things to do. I can't begin to get everything done, and there simply isn't time to write. What do I leave out? And how can I get more energy to do what needs to be done? I am feeling overwhelmed. I'm 87 years old and I can't do everything I used to do."*

I have been reminded of the story in Exodus 35 when God chose two men to do a specific and important job. These were ordinary men and not qualified for this work, but the Lord gave them every skill, ability and knowledge they needed in order to do what He asked them to do. When God asks us to do something, He makes it possible.

Although God gives the ability, there is still a lot of hard work involved. There are many places in the Bible that speak about work. One verse from I Chronicles 28:20 has spoken to me several times: **"Be strong and courageous and get to work. Don't be frightened by the size of the task, for the Lord my God is with you. He will not forsake you. He will see to it that everything is finished correctly."**

My greatest desire is to honor and obey God and bring glory to Him. I want others to know Him personally, to trust Him, to obey Him, to love Him and to let Him use them in any way He desires. God works with each of us individually and in entirely different ways, but it is an exciting adventure with Him when we are willing to let Him lead and be in control and when we have the right attitude!

This is not a book of "Do, Don't, and How To." It is simply stories in my life of adventures and the results of an attitude change. Stories are not in chronological order, but I assure you that all of these experiences really did take place.

I have already given you the key to opening your life's adventures: the right attitude. **"Your attitude should be the kind that was shown us by Jesus Christ."** (Philippians 2:5) **"Your attitudes and thoughts must all be constantly changing for the better. Yes, you must be a new and different person, holy and good. Clothe yourself with this new nature."** (Ephesians 4:23) You may think that you can't change your attitude, but with God's help, I assure you it is possible. The choice is up to you.

—⁓—

One of our unusual experiences in recognizing the importance of attitude came as we welcomed a group of sailors. Suddenly, someone shouted "ATTITUDE CHECK!" Before we had time to think, a thunderous shout rang out, "PRAISE THE LORD." We looked to see if the roof was still on! Our family of seven was spending the summer working at the Christian Servicemen's Center just outside the U.S. Naval Base at Subic Bay in the Philippines. We soon found that the men on one of the big ships had discovered this was a way to find other Christian guys. Or if they were searching for a friend, they would call out "Attitude Check!" When they got the response, "Praise The Lord!" they knew they had found a friend. It was also a way to check someone's attitude that day. Were they lonely, sad, angry, depressed and discouraged; or happy and excited? We liked this idea!

Yes, as a family we liked this idea. . .most of the time. I don't remember why I was so upset and angry one day, but I was driving somewhere with my teenage son, Steve. I was venting my anger when Steve interrupted with "Attitude Check, Mom." I was in no mood for this and said, "I can't do it Steve. Don't ask." But my son was persistent. "Just try and say it Mom. It will make a difference." So he repeated "Attitude check!" I groaned and barely whispered, "Praise the Lord." Steve wasn't satisfied and insisted we do it again, with a little more enthusiasm. It wasn't easy, but I discovered something that day. It is virtually impossible to praise God and stay angry. I also learned that children can often help and teach their parents. And I had a great lesson on the importance of attitude – also on humility and obedience! Of course, attitude makes the difference; it can turn a disaster into a great memory. It can turn tragedy into triumph. We can learn important lessons and even change disappointments into fun or real joy.

Charles Swindoll gives us an excellent article on attitudes. (©1981, 1982 by Charles R. Swindoll, Inc. All rights are reserved worldwide.)

ATTITUDES

The longer I live, the more I realize the importance of choosing the right attitude in life.
Attitude is more important than facts.
It is more important than your past;
More important than your education or your financial situation;
More important than your circumstances, your successes, or your failures;

More important than what other people think or say or do.
It is more important than your appearance,
your giftedness, or your skills.
It will make or break a company.
It will cause a church to soar or sink.
It will make the difference between
a happy home or a miserable home.
You have a choice each day regarding the
attitude you will embrace.
Life is like a violin.
You can focus on the broken strings that dangle,
Or you can play your life's melody on the one that remains.
You cannot change the years that have passed,
Nor can you change the daily tick of the clock.
You cannot change the pace of your march toward your death.
You cannot change the decisions or reactions of other people.
And you certainly cannot change the inevitable.
Those are strings that dangle!
What you can do is play on the one string that remains –
your attitude.
I am convinced that life is 10 percent what happens to me
And 90 percent how I react to it.
The same is true for you.

I remember a time when Steve's family went on a long-anticipated vacation. They had a new tent and planned carefully. They even took their house girl and the dog. This was to be a terrific outing, and it was a very memorable time. The tent blew down, the dog ran away, a suitcase was stolen, it rained, and just about everything that could possibly go wrong did just that. But Steve kept telling the family, "We had an adventure—something special to remember!" He turned a disaster into a fun memory to talk about. So it's time to remember some of my life experiences, and the attitude change that turned them into adventures.

CHAPTER 2

ADVENTURES WITH
THE PIANO

I never really wanted to play the piano. I wanted to excel on the trumpet, but my parents said, "No piano. No trumpet!" I was not happy about this, and my piano practice was almost non-existent. My piano teacher almost gave up on me, but she liked my mom who was a piano teacher, too. My mom was also wise enough not to try and teach me! However, I soon learned that playing the piano was useful for my trumpet. I had learned about rhythm and timing, and even though I couldn't sight-read anything on the piano (it was too many notes to see all at the same time), I discovered that I could easily read one line for the trumpet. This made it much easier to get first chair in the trumpet section because I could read the music better than those who didn't have piano lessons.

I still didn't like the piano, but while I was in high school, all that suddenly changed. I went to a summer music camp. You could only go to this camp if you had 1st or 2nd chair in your section of the band or orchestra. There were very few girls who played the trumpet, so that was probably in my favor and I tied for first chair. The guy who tied with me was a handsome blond who was fantastic on the piano as well as on the trumpet. All the girls were after him, but I had a great advantage because I sat next to him for hours every day in both band and orchestra. Bob's major piano piece was "Polonaise Militaire" by Chopin, which was my type of bombastic music. My whole attitude changed toward the piano. And yes, Bob and I dated during the camp.

When I went home that summer, I immediately began learning "Polonaise Militaire." Up to this point, I was still playing about 3rd grade music, and Chopin's music was considered difficult. When I went back to my piano teacher and played it for her, she immediately called my Mother and said, "I don't know what happened to Helen. Someone obviously challenged her this summer, which I have never been able to do. I can't teach her anymore." I don't think Mom knew the challenge was a boy friend.

I also learned "Malagueña" and so I knew two very impressive pieces of music on the piano. But I still couldn't play a song out of the hymnbook or play anything without learning it from written music. And then I went to college. I was very happy to show off my two great songs on the piano. This was my downfall. The Bible mentions about pride going before a fall. I began dating Dick Cadd, the wonderful bass singer in the Four Flats Quartet. He often sang solos and asked me to accompany him. If I had the music long enough and could practice for hours, I could usually get through a song, so I was able to bluff my way for a while. Dick was also an outstanding song leader, the kind that went from one song to another with no music to follow. And he was the director for Newberg's Youth for Christ Rally.

By now I was falling in love, so when Dick asked me to go with him, it didn't matter where we went. I always said, "Yes!" One night we went to a big Youth for Christ Rally and Dick was to lead singing. When he discovered that the piano player didn't show up, he rushed over and grabbed me to take me to the piano. Of course he didn't have any music, and I couldn't have played it anyway. I had never in my life even thought about playing by ear. I assured him that I couldn't do it as he was pulling me toward the stage. This had the same effect on me as if I was forced to play at Carnegie Hall for a full house. It was time for the meeting to start and Dick totally ignored my pleas. He was convinced I could play anything. I won't go into great detail about how my hands became paralyzed, my brain went numb, my heart almost thumped out of my body, and my lungs refused to get a breath.

I cried myself to sleep that night and never wanted to see anyone again. I knew Dick probably wouldn't speak to me, and I didn't ever want to see him either—except that I was still hopelessly in love. As soon as I had time the next day, I found a large hymnal and sneaked into the music hall to find an unused piano. I practiced for hours. I memorized, sight-read over and over and made my first attempt to play without music. Dick must have really loved me too, because he asked me to marry him. His belief in me changed my life. However, my attitude needed a lot of help.

Except for my two "show-off" songs, I was always afraid to play the piano in public, especially if I couldn't practice ahead of time, or when I knew someone in the audience played better than I did. Dick always liked me to play for him, just because I was his wife and he liked to do things together as a couple. This wasn't a big problem during quartet days, because the Four Flats didn't use an accompanist. But then we went to the Philippines as missionaries. No more quartet. It was just Dick, and he needed an accompanist. I really wanted to accompany him, and I was jealous when someone else did it instead of me, but we often had a major problem. If Dick was going to sing a solo in a church service, he wanted it to fit into the theme of the meeting. I often didn't know what he was going to sing until minutes ahead of time. This meant that I didn't know what to practice, and many times the church pianist was far better than I was.

Fear and pride caused other strong emotions. I felt angry, stubborn, resentful, rebellious and irritated. My stomach was tied in knots; my hands were cold, clammy and shaky. My mind was so confused with negative thoughts that even if I could see the music clearly, I couldn't begin to read it. Consequently, I was always at my worst. Dick had learned that when he led singing, it was wise to give me some kind of warning of his plans. But he didn't always stick to the plans. I usually had plenty of practice for his choirs, and so most people thought I was pretty good on the piano. I didn't want my reputation destroyed. I also played for our children who had become quite popular in Manila. They were being asked to sing for all kinds of affairs, and I accompanied them. But I knew what I was doing and had practiced, although I was never very comfortable in big auditoriums or on radio and television.

Many times I emphatically told Dick, "Have the church pianist play for you; she can sight read better than I can!" He lovingly explained, "Honey, I want you to play for me. There is something special about a married couple working together as a team. Even if the music isn't the best in the world, I still prefer you." But the time came when my attitude was so deplorable that Dick's patience began to give out. Finally he exploded, "OK I'll get someone else! But why don't you face the truth! It's all your pride. You aren't playing for me or the Lord. You just want people to think YOU are good!" I was furious! Of course I knew he was right, but I wasn't about to admit it. And the idea of him getting someone else made me jealous and angry.

I didn't tell Dick, but I did begin to pray constantly, "Lord, please help me to have the right attitude in playing the piano for Dick." I know the Lord tried to help me in gentle, tender ways, but I guess pride and fear were too strong. God finally got through to me though! It happened unexpectedly, with no warning, no time to think, no music, and no involvement from Dick; so I couldn't blame him.

—⁓—

There's a lot of talent in the missionary community, and I think I wanted to impress this group of people more than anyone else. Probably the biggest gathering of missionaries in one place was for Faith Academy's baccalaureate and graduation. They used the largest auditorium available at that time and people came from all over the Philippines. I often played for Faith Academy affairs because I worked with Dick in the music department. But this time they were using recorded music for the graduates' processional and Dick was in charge of that part so he needed to be right up front. Since I was not involved, I chose to sit in the back so I could read our mail.

After reading the mail, I decided to look at the program. I was horrified to see my name at the very top of the program. It read: "Prelude – Helen Cadd." No one had said one word to me about this, but by this time, I probably could have played for 10 minutes without a lot of trouble. I hurried to show Dick the program and ask his advice. He was surprised too and told me it was time to get started with the processional, so just forget it. I went back to my secluded spot and carefully searched the program to make sure I wasn't listed any other place. I breathed a sigh of relief. My name was nowhere else on the program.

By now the seniors were in their places on the platform. Someone gave the invocation and Mr. Poppinga, Superintendent of Faith Academy, said, "Please remain standing while we sing together 'A Mighty Fortress is Our God.' Will Helen Cadd please come to the piano?" I was much closer to the back than I was to the platform. I seriously considered making a mad dash for the exit, but I knew I'd never get away with it. While everyone waited, I walked all the way to the front, up the steep steps, across the stage and sat down at the piano, in full view of everyone.

Dick was nowhere in sight to clue me in on the proper key for the song. My brain was so muddled I didn't even think about using my favorite key of C, which would have been correct! Instead, I chose the key of F. Even with music and practice, 'A Mighty Fortress' was difficult for me. I could play simple songs without music now, but certainly nothing so complicated. Had I tried anything near the key of C, the audience might have been able to sing and help cover my mistakes. But I managed to pick a key that no one could sing. Consequently, everyone just stood and listened to me play.

I have never played worse in my life! Every chord was wrong, and I couldn't even pick out the melody. It was as though I had never touched a piano before that night. At the end of the first verse, Mr. Poppinga turned to me and asked (so all the audience could hear), "Helen, would you please play in a different key?" And so, without thinking, I began in G, which was probably worse than F. "Why, oh why didn't I think of C and just play the melody in octaves? Why didn't someone ask me ahead of time or at least bring music? Why did this have to happen to me?" I completely ruined a dignified, solemn and special occasion. I felt like I made a fool of myself in front of the huge special audience that I wanted to impress.

I stumbled off the back of the stage that led to the outside. Had it been possible, I would have taken the first plane to some desert island where I'd never have to face anyone again! Through hot tears of anger and resentment, I demanded, "God, what are you doing to me?" There in the shadows, He lovingly and clearly spoke to me: "I'm answering your prayer. I want your fear and your pride. You can't handle them." I told the Lord in no uncertain terms that I did not expect Him to do anything awful like this, and He very patiently informed me, "I tried to help you in less drastic ways, but you wouldn't respond. Now that everyone knows your ability; you don't ever need to attempt to impress people again. You no longer have to be bound by your pride and fear. Just accept my freedom."

It wasn't easy, but I finally handed the whole mess over to Jesus. I was still embarrassed and didn't want to see anyone, but the Lord didn't let me off that easily. Graduation came a few days later and this time I knew I was to accompany one of Dick's choirs. I wished to be sick, but unfortunately, no matter how hard I tried, I was in perfect health! And so, once again, I played the piano in front of the same audience. That was the biggest hurdle.

21

It's hard to break an action or an attitude that is deeply ingrained, but if I ever begin to think in my old ways, God says, "Helen, do you need another lesson?" My reaction is swift, "No thank-you, Lord! I'll do it for YOU!" The results have been amazing. Since I don't have to worry about what people think of me, I am usually no longer tight and tense. There are still occasions that affect me, but it has automatically helped me relax and enjoy playing. I still didn't have that wonderful natural ability to be able to play anything or sight-read music easily, but I practiced more. I wanted to give Jesus (and Dick) my best but my best didn't have to compete with anyone else. This was choosing the right attitude.

I didn't realize how much God hates pride and to what extent He will go to help us get rid of it. I probably read it in the Bible many times without letting it influence me. It has top billing on the list of seven things God hates in Proverbs 6. It's listed even before murder. The Bible also states, "Proud men (and women) end in shame. . .Pride disgusts the Lord. . .Proud men (and women) shall be punished. . .Pride goes before destruction. . ." I'm thankful the Lord is patient enough to keep teaching me and helping me change my attitude. I can't say I've always had the perfect attitude and that I have never failed, but it did change my life.

My piano experiences don't end there. In fact, I have had some very interesting times since God helped change my attitude. I had the privilege of accompanying Dick's special group, The Madri-Gals and Guys. This meant concerts in many different countries, as well as radio, television and recording sessions. We performed for the American Embassy and were even asked by Mrs. Marcos to sing for a gala affair she was putting on for all the foreign ambassadors and their wives. Unfortunately, school was out for the summer and the students had already gone to their homes all over the Philippines and the U.S. We were frequent guests at the U.S. Military Bases in the Philippines, as well as several in Europe. When we brought the group to the United States, we not only sang in churches, but also were invited into high schools, colleges and service clubs. In almost every school, we received a standing ovation. I would never have survived if my attitude hadn't changed.

Another situation bothered me. It was always difficult for me to play the piano when a certain woman we knew was in the audience. She was not only beautiful, but was a professional accomplished pianist. She had given concerts in Carnegie Hall as well as equally prestigious auditoriums in Europe and several countries in Asia. Her piano playing was absolutely fabulous. She attended our church in Manila where I played the piano when Dick led the singing in the early, contemporary service and she directed the choir for the later, more formal service.

One adventure with this talented woman happened when our family was invited to sing for the Presidential Prayer Breakfast in Manila. By this time our children were grown and we used recorded accompaniment with whoever in the family happened to be in Manila. I even sang with the family. We were more nervous than usual because this was a really big affair and President Aquino was attending, as well as nearly every senator and important person in the government, business, and entertainment world.

But then the unbelievable happened. This beautiful concert pianist came rushing to me and in panic said, "Helen, please, will you play the piano for the audience singing? I'm supposed to play, but the song leader wants to do choruses and he doesn't have any music. I can't play without music! Please!!" I don't know if you can feel what went through my whole body. It was like a bolt of lightning, and I began desperately looking to see if there was someone else she could ask. It was time for the program to begin and I wanted to refuse, but the Lord was saying, "Helen, remember what I taught you?" There really wasn't anyone else around that I could suggest.

Probably the worst part of all was that it wasn't Dick who was leading the singing. Dick knew what I could and what I couldn't do, so I was quite comfortable with him leading, but not a total stranger. I didn't really have a choice, and I told the Lord that He would have to help me. I wasn't sure that I knew the songs being sung, or if I could get through them at all. And then I also had to sing with the family later in the program. I guess everything went OK because I didn't pass out and Dick was proud of me. Although my stress level was off the charts, I had a grateful friend and I gained a new dependence and appreciation for my Lord. I also discovered that even professionals can have fears.

There was also a Chinese lady who could sight-read anything. She accompanied several choirs around the city and was amazing. I still was terrible at sight-reading. I needed to practice hours if I couldn't play it by ear. She came to me one day and asked me if I would teach her how to play without music. Although she could read any music, she had no idea how to play any other way. Since I had no natural ability this way and had to teach myself the basic chords, it was easy to show her what to do. She was such a superb musician that she picked it up immediately, but she thanked me every time she saw me for teaching her this way to play the piano. Again, I had to thank the Lord for changing my attitude.

—m—

I have been privileged in so many ways and had such fun adventures playing the piano over the years after my devastating experience, talk with God and attitude change at the Faith Academy Baccalaureate Service. I have played all kinds of "pianos" in a variety of places. In some of the provincial areas, because of the humidity, most of the piano keys would stick or not play at all. There were times when there wasn't a real piano, but an unusual substitute.

In the National Prison, they had a small pump organ. The prisoners wanted to do something special because we were coming, so the night before, they painted their tiny pump organ a beautiful blue. They also waxed and polished the floor. Because of the humidity, the paint didn't dry, so I had blue paint on my hands and on my legs and clothes. And because the floor was polished so nicely, as I pumped the pedals, my chair began to slide back away from the organ. I actually had to stop in the middle of a song and pull my chair back up to the organ. It was such a small keyboard that I couldn't begin to play the music like it was written, and if I forgot to keep pumping there was no sound.

Although I was a mess, we had one of the most wonderful services I have ever been in. Two inmates, who had been leaders of rival gangs and had been responsible for killing 10 people while in prison, had accepted Jesus as their Savior. They had actually tried to kill each other, but now they stood together and gave their testimonies and then served us Communion. I thought that if I never saw or heard another testimony, I couldn't help but believe in Jesus. Nothing and no one can change lives like that. But if my attitude hadn't been changed, I'm sure I would have missed a great blessing. I would have been too upset about the blue organ, but now I could laugh and enjoy the experience. The adventure here really was an attitude.

One other piano adventure I must mention was when we gave our final concert in one of the best and newer auditoriums in Manila. Dick was checking out the pianos for the concert. He wasn't very happy with the one they showed him, but then he spotted a huge grand piano in a dark corner. He told them that this was the piano he wanted to use for our concert. They informed him that this was a very special piano Mrs. Marcos had bought for Van Cliburn when he came to Manila. No one else had ever played that piano. It was the biggest and best Steinway grand piano that could be found and had been flown to the Philippines for one person to play.

This marvelous piano had been sitting there for several years, and Dick really wanted to use it. Since Dick had made friends with the officials of the auditorium, they finally consented to let us use it for the concert. So I got to play this one and only piano that no one else had ever played except Van Cliburn. It felt like I was playing a symphony orchestra — the sound was so awesome that it sent chills down my spine.

—⁓—

Just think of all the "adventures" I almost missed when I had the wrong attitude. But the best part was God's blessing and the marvelous relationship Dick and I had working together as a couple. It changed our lives. We became a real team. And the final confirmation from God that He was pleased with my attitude change came when Faith Academy got the new auditorium they were praying for. They named the building for both of us! *The Dick and Helen Cadd Fine Arts Center.* This is the article as it appeared in Faith Academy's story of the Auditorium Project.

For nineteen years Faith had dreamed of having an auditorium where concerts and plays could be held. Faith's dream began on December 11, 1989 when Dr. Dennis Vogan proposed a campus development plan for a multipurpose Fine Arts building.

Construction on Phase 1 began on December 28, 1998. This three-story building housed the maintenance shop, two science classrooms, a middle school computer lab, two sixth grade classrooms and a seventh and eighth grade English and Bible classroom. The second Phase focused on the fine arts classrooms, including vocal music, band, drama, video production and a general music classroom. It also included a lower floor that was designed for future classrooms.

"God's work – done in God's way – in God's time – will never lack God's supply." These motivating words were hung in front of the proposed auditorium site to remind people to pray for the funds that were needed for the completion of Phase 3.

On January 29, 2006, Faith Academy received word from the Ttokamsa Home Mission Church that they had decided to fund the auditorium project. The ground-breaking ceremony for this third phase occurred on April 7, 2006. Classes continued in the midst of the chaos of construction, but God was faithful and the dedication of the Fine Arts Center was celebrated on October 8, 2008.

This Fine Arts facility was named in tribute to Dick and Helen Cadd and their long and fruitful ministry at Faith Academy. Dick and Helen and their five children came to Faith Academy in 1962. Dick directed all the bands and choirs at Faith. His ministry ranged from Elementary to High School. One of the Cadds' dreams became a reality when the Madri-Gals and Guys were formed. This premier singing group toured the Philippines and did three international tours (1970, 1974, and 1976) in Europe and the United States as well as releasing three records.

Dick and Helen were incredibly creative and combined their love for music, students and the Lord in a powerful way. Desiring excellence, they motivated students to push themselves to be their best. Dick and Helen impacted thousands of lives and lived up to Dick's standard that "there is no better way to invest your life than to invest it in the lives of others for Jesus' sake." The Dick and Helen Cadd Fine Arts Center stands as a tribute to their musical excellence and fruitful ministry.

"Lift Him Up" was the dedication's theme and this was literally done as the High School Band opened the celebration with a beautiful prelude from the new orchestra pit. Helen Cadd and Don Chang, from the Ttokamsa Church, cut a ribbon draped across the front of the 50-foot stage. Don MacKay, campus pastor, welcomed over 900 students, faculty, staff, alumni, former teachers, guests and dignitaries. Tears came to many eyes as Steve Cadd's PowerPoint tribute to his parents' ministry was shown. Steve Schwarze synopsized God's faithfulness as he detailed construction events of the past few years. The High School Chorale lifted up Christ in song and Glen Mate, a construction worker gave a gripping testimony of rededication to the Lord as a result of Chaplain Pong's ministry. The moving service ended with ten prayers spoken by varying people from all walks of Faith's life.

I was able to attend the dedication of the new auditorium, but Dick had gone to be with Jesus in 2005. When asked to say a few words I wrote this so I could read it, because I only had a minute or two and I wasn't sure I could get through it without crying. Steve stood beside me in case I couldn't continue to the end. Even though I did cry some, I managed to finish. I wanted people to know Dick, and this is what I said:

Have you ever had a dream, so incredible, so exciting, so unbelievable, that you don't want it to end? I think this is how I feel right now. This is so amazing it's hard to believe. I keep waiting to wake up. Of course, the one person who should be here is gone.

I have been trying to imagine Dick's reactions if he was here. I know he would be totally overwhelmed and wonder why he was being honored this way. He never had a clue that he was special in any way, or that he had ever done anything unusual. Maybe that's one reason he was so great.

Dick was the best husband and father anyone could ever have. He was fun (sometimes crazy). He knew how to play and pray and worship and laugh. He made our family life fun and exciting. He included us as much as possible in every part of his life and ministry. He especially included me, and even though he could have had a far better accompanist, he wanted us to be a team—he wanted to work together. And that gave us the most wonderful life possible and the reason I've been included in his honors.

Our son Jon, who works with MAF in Uganda, sent me an email and gave a perfect description of Dick: "Dad had the ability to touch people's lives and change them for the better, to take the wayward ones and show them the way, to encourage the average to greatness and the great to go even higher."

All of my children wanted to come, but because of work, distance, finances and cancer, it was impossible. But Jon's son and his wife from Kenya (Josh and Audra) are here to help represent the family along with Steve and Mayen.

I lived with Dick for 58 incredible years and I knew him better than anyone—he was not only my husband and lover, but he was my best friend. Of course he wasn't perfect (no one is), but I can honestly tell you that more than anything in the world, he wanted to be all the Lord desired him to be and to live a life that brought glory to God. His favorite Bible verse was Galatians 2:20, **"I have been crucified with Christ; it is no longer I who live, but Christ lives in me, and the life which I now live in the flesh I live by faith in the Son of God, who loved me and gave Himself for me."** (NKJV)

I'm sure Dick would say with me: We trust and hope and pray that this beautiful building will always bring honor and praise and glory to our indescribable, incredible, powerful, awesome GOD thru JESUS CHRIST our LORD!! I guess there is just one more thing to say. THANK YOU!

It took a painful, embarrassing experience for the LORD to get through to me, but with His help and Dick's patient love, my attitude did change and it made a difference in the rest of our lives.

I accompany the family on the piano at a church meeting in Medford, Oregon.

I played the piano for all of Dick's school choirs at Faith Academy.

Dick and I review some choir music with two of our students.

Steve and Mayen Cadd and friends attended the dedication of the Dick and Helen Cadd Fine Arts Center on October 8, 2008.

The Dick & Helen Cadd Fine Arts Center includes a 900-seat auditorium.

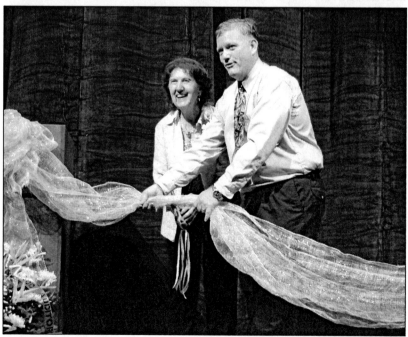

I spoke and cut the ribbon at the dedication of the new Fine Arts Center.

CHAPTER 3

ADVENTURES WITH CHRISTMAS

Everyone has some sort of Christmas memories, and they usually begin very early in life. I remember the time when I wanted a certain doll more than anything in the world. I was really too old for a doll and this one was extra expensive. I knew it was foolish; so when I found it behind the big chair on Christmas morning, after all the other packages had been opened, I was hilariously happy and completely surprised! I still have that doll, and it remains a special reminder of my wonderful parents.

Another Christmas I vividly recall was in California, about two years before we went to the Philippines. Our five children had received so many toys and gadgets that we almost needed another house. Of course, they were thrilled with everything—for about three days. By that time, many of the items had broken and those remaining were boring. Cardboard boxes were again the favorite toys. Dick and I were totally disgusted and felt that as a family we had missed the whole beautiful Christmas story of Jesus and sharing with others. We weren't teaching our children the proper emphasis. But what could we do about it? Television convinced all of us that we really must have "things" in order to be happy.

After much discussion and prayer, we came up with an idea. Instead of heaping gifts on the children at Christmas, we decided to have a Family Gift Exchange Day every three or four months throughout the year. Since anticipation is important, we set the date several weeks in advance. This gave us time to talk about and plan our special day. We only gave the children one gift each time, but a lot of planning went into that gift. I found adorable dolls on sale for the girls once—dolls I could not have afforded at Christmas. Roller skates proved to be lots more exciting to receive in the spring when they could be used immediately; and when the children longed for a large plastic swimming pool in the heat of summer, our gift-giving day was a perfect time to present it.

The advantage became obvious. Financially, it was far easier to spread our spending over the year; sales were more prevalent, with larger discounts; we bought things the children could use immediately; they had greater appreciation for one special gift than for so many all at once; and excitement abounded throughout the year. Each package was gift-wrapped and we tried to make the day extra special in many ways, with favorite foods, nice clothes, kind actions toward others, a party atmosphere and remembering Jesus.

We decided not to give each other gifts on Christmas day, but the whole family would concentrate on helping someone else. Each gift-exchange day we prayed that God would give us a special family for Christmas: a family who needed help, one with whom we could share and love. We envisioned a family similar to ours and we could hardly wait to invite them to spend Christmas day in our home. All year we put aside money and gifts for our Christmas family, but as Christmas drew near, we still had no family. Dick and I began to worry. How would our children react if we found no one? We knew God must have someone for us, but we didn't know how to find them. As a family, we learned an important lesson that year. God does answer prayer, but not always to our specifications or expectations.

Following a rehearsal of the annual church Christmas program, I sat waiting in our car for the children to come. It's vague in my mind as to the exact details, but I was introduced to a young lady who lived a few blocks from the church. Someone had invited her to attend our services. She had two small girls and a strong German accent. In the course of the conversation, I found that they had just moved to California and her husband had gone back east to bring their meager household belongings. Except for her children, she knew no one and was hesitant about trying to make friends because of her speech. She didn't expect her husband before Christmas, lived in an almost empty house and was out of money.

When I heard her story, I was elated. Here was our family! But to our dismay, someone else had already invited her to spend Christmas day with them. After a full year of anticipation and excitement, it seemed like our plans fell apart and we were disappointed. And yet, when our family talked about the situation, we all felt compelled to help them. Even though we couldn't share our home on Christmas day, we presented them with gifts of food, clothes, toys, jewelry and miscellaneous items.

Back at our home, we concentrated on Jesus and the meaning of His birthday, and there was a small gift exchange from relatives and friends. We learned first hand what God meant in Isaiah 55:8, **"For my thoughts are not your thoughts, neither are your ways my ways, declares the Lord."** Isaiah 55:9 goes on to say, **"For as the heavens are higher than the earth, so are my ways higher than your ways, and my thoughts than your thoughts."** (NIV) I understood verse 8, but in this case, I questioned how God's ways could be higher than ours, when He didn't even allow us to carry out our magnificent plans to help someone and to teach our children a valuable lesson at the same time.

Christmas passed and our disappointment faded, but we all lost interest in continuing this practice. However, one day I felt urged to phone the German girl and was alarmed to find her destitute and dejected. Her husband had met with an accident and was detained for several weeks. She still had no money for food, rent and other bills. At that time the Four Flats Quartet had disbanded and we were all going our separate ways. We still didn't know what the Lord had in mind for us, so we were between jobs and didn't have any regular income. However, we knew we had to help her. I searched my kitchen and freezer for anything I could spare and then collected from the other quartet families in the same way.

For the next few months we literally fed this family at a time when we ourselves had very little. I took her places, paid for medicine, and all the time I talked about Jesus. Her response was anything but encouraging when she informed me, "I don't want to hear about God and Jesus. My husband's family is religious, but live bad the rest of the week. Don't talk to me about God!" Ordinarily, that word of discouragement would have stopped me instantly, but for some reason I kept right on talking about Jesus. Even after her husband arrived in California, they remained penniless. He couldn't find the kind of work he wanted and wasn't content with menial tasks. He went away early, came home late and left her to face the stream of bill collectors. She eventually refused to answer the door.

Early one morning, our telephone rang and it was my German friend. Her voice quivered as she told me of her desperate, hopeless, depression. And then she stated, "Helen, you've always talked to me about God, and I have refused to listen. I got out of bed this morning, went into the kitchen, and turned on the gas stove. I was going to end my miserable life. But then I began thinking about some of the things you told me about Jesus, and I decided to give you one chance to talk to me. If you can't help me, I'm going to kill myself and my girls!"

No one had ever talked to me like that before and I was scared. Dick happened to be home that day, so immediately I went to her home, brought the children back to Dick for babysitting and took Gundy out for lunch where we could talk without any interruption. She listened as if her life depended on it, while I simply explained how, **"God so loved the world (and her personally), that He gave His only Son, that whoever believes in Him should not perish, but have everlasting life."** (John 3:16) (NKJV) I told her how He had changed my life and assured her that she could trust Him no matter what the circumstances. Over a cup of coffee, my troubled friend asked Jesus into her heart and life as her personal Savior. Although her problems remained the same, with God's help she could now face them and trust Him.

Before long we moved to Idaho, and I received a letter from Gundy telling about a miraculous inheritance she received from Germany. One paragraph read, "Helen, where I got this money handed out — all I could think of was you — how many time you have told me God listen to you prayer — or He is answering — and when you need the most — He will help. . .we do thanked God. . ."

Now, of course, I understood how God's ways are so much higher than ours. He gave us far more than just "a family for Christmas." Once again, even though my attitude wasn't all it should have been, God gave me the best adventure it's possible to have: helping someone find Jesus as their Savior. Again, it required obedience when things were not going as I had planned. But that's not the end of the story.

Over the years, we lost track of Gundy and her family. We were living in the Philippines and had no idea what had happened to her and the children. One day when I was going through some old mail, I found a letter I had received from Gundy when we were in Idaho. She mentioned living with relatives in the Black Forest in Germany at one time when her parents were trying to protect her from the Nazi influence. I kept the letter, and when we were going through Europe on our way back to the U.S. for a year, I got the bright idea of trying to find Gundy's relatives and hoping they could help us find her.

Since we didn't have any exact schedule at that time, and we had heard so much about the Black Forest over the years, the family agreed it would be an interesting experience.

Looking back, I can't imagine we thought it would be possible. It was almost harder than "looking for a needle in a haystack." We didn't have an exact address or name, we didn't speak any German, we had never been in this place before, and there seemed to be dozens of small villages scattered throughout a large area. All we had to go on was an old letter and a couple of names.

We didn't have too much trouble finding the Black Forest area. But from that point on, we weren't quite sure what to do. We finally decided to just stop along the way and ask questions. Only we really couldn't ask questions, because we didn't speak their language. So, when we saw someone, one of the kids or I would approach them and show them the letter. Most of the time they would just shake their heads and that was the end of our "conversation." We did pray about finding Gundy, but then we also began to think about how impossible this was. This had been an all day adventure, and now we were ready to call it quits. There was one more place up ahead, so we decided this would be our last inquiry. I don't remember who took the letter to show the people standing outside of their house. Instead of heads shaking negatively, there was a sudden burst of excitement, arms waving, shouting and motioning for all of us to come to them. They recognized Gundy's name.

These were Gundy's relatives, and of course they knew where she was: she was in a small city only a few miles away. They had the exact address and a phone number. We really hadn't expected her to be in Germany. We had just hoped to find where in the world she did live. Now they wanted to feed us and give us gifts and food. We were so excited to find that Gundy was close enough to see, all we could think of was going and surprising her. This drama was all taking place without being able to understand each other. But we were communicating. With clear instructions and lots of hugs, we were on our way again, hardly believing what had just happened. We could only come to one conclusion: the Lord wanted us to contact Gundy. It was really a miracle.

We couldn't wait to find Gundy's home. We were also apprehensive. Would she know us? Would she be upset at being surprised this way? We were about to find out!

I don't think there is any way to adequately describe Gundy's reactions when she saw us. She laughed and cried and jumped and hugged, but what she said over and over again was what broke my heart. "I can't believe you are here for me. No one has ever cared this much for me. Did you really come just to see me? I can't believe you cared that much!" When we told her how long we had been looking for her, she started all over again, overwhelmed that we would do that for her. Once again we reminded her how much God loved her. He loved enough to give His son.

Then Gundy told us stories about paying bills, buying groceries, clothes and other needs with the inheritance she had received. Things were better as long as the money lasted, but her husband still wouldn't work unless he had exactly the job he wanted, so before long the money was gone. After that, the family slept in parks, or in office buildings after everyone else had left. But they had to leave before people came back to work. They often had nothing to feed the children.

Gundy finally decided to go back to Germany with her children. She had family and friends in her own country, and she could get free medical care. When we met her, she had a good job working for the U.S. Army at an American hospital. She was living in an apartment with her children, and they seemed happy, but they hadn't seen her husband for quite some time. I'm not sure they knew where he was, and they had heard that he was sick and had some form of cancer. We wanted to keep in touch with Gundy, but she moved back to the U.S. to work in a similar job that she was doing in Germany, and we lost track of her again. I'm so thankful the Lord doesn't lose track of people. He knows where they are; He knows their names and their needs; and He loves them! There's a chorus that I think is so appropriate: "He knows my name; He knows my every thought; He sees each tear that falls and hears me when I call."

I can still pray for this family, even if I don't know where they are, and maybe someday we will find them again. I still think of them as our special Christmas family, and when God had bigger plans than we ever dreamed of. A different kind of attitude was involved here: an attitude of acceptance when disappointment that our best laid plans didn't work out our way.

—∿—

From the birth of our first child, we had family traditions, such as opening one package on Christmas Eve. Early Christmas morning Dick put on our favorite Reader's Digest marvelous version of "Joy to the World" and turned the volume so high that the whole house became a speaker. Then we sat on the floor around the softly lit tree, read about Jesus' birth from Luke 2, sang "Happy Birthday" to Jesus, complete with a lovely Angel Food Cake. (When Steve was small, he asked if we could "throw the birthday cake up to Jesus.")

We opened our individual "Christmas Breakfast Boxes." This was my idea in order to save time in preparation, cleanup and dishes. I wanted to get breakfast out of the way before the big mess of opening packages, and the children looked forward to special foods they usually didn't have. Many times in Manila, we had "extra family": Faith Academy boarding students who couldn't go home to another country, single teachers, or guests from other countries. Twice we didn't get to be home for Christmas Day because we sang for banquets and programs on the U.S. military bases. And one year the children were on TV every week of December before Christmas.

—∿—

Although we had many memorable Christmases, probably the one I remember most vividly was one that started out totally wrong. It was many years later, after our children were grown. We lived in a large house near Faith Academy, which we usually shared with some of our now-married children, but none of them were in the Philippines that year. Nearby was also a "squatter village." It was traditional for the local people to go caroling for weeks before Christmas and expect to get money for their singing. It was a way for groups to raise money for a project and also a way for people to get extra income.

Every evening, sometimes almost the whole night, people were singing, yelling, using homemade drums and banging on our gate until we got up and gave them something. It seemed like on every corner in town was a policeman stopping cars to demand a "Merry Christmas" for themselves. At each stoplight our car was surrounded by children, all wanting a gift. We felt overwhelmed, tired from lack of sleep, lonesome for our family and disgusted with the whole "system." I guess you could say we forgot the true meaning of Christmas that year.

One day, as Dick and I were walking, we started discussing our attitude. We were beginning to hate the most wonderful season of the year and even resent the people we had come to serve. As we talked, we decided it was time to pray and ask the Lord to change our attitude and show us how to cope. It actually was more a selfish prayer. We were thinking of ourselves and our feelings. We decided that maybe we could post a big notice on our gate saying that we would give a gift on one certain evening between limited hours, but no other time. That wasn't exactly a change in attitude, just an idea for our benefit. But the Lord did answer our prayer and gave us a unique idea, one that we couldn't do by ourselves. We wanted to have a neighborhood party for the squatter village.

Our mission organization had many Christian movies, so we enlisted the help of our Filipino staff. They could show a film and even share Christ in the local language. Another group had Bible stories in a comic book form in the local language. They made these available for us. This could be our gift to the people, along with a small bag of candy. We would have entertainment, share Christ and give a gift, all at the same time. Our dead-end street and large vacant lot were big enough to accommodate many people. And so we posted notices on our gate and various places around the community.

I don't know how many people came that first year, but it seemed like a lot. And we didn't have people pounding on our gate the rest of the season. It felt good and right. It must have been special for the people in the village, because they were friendlier and asked if we were going to do that again. As our attitude changed, we began to be excited about planning another Christmas party. Other missionaries in the community, as well as students in nearby boarding homes, wanted to be partners.

Each year our parties got bigger and better, with many more people attending. *700 Club* gave us large plastic buckets filled with household, medical and food supplies. (The buckets alone were a valuable item for the families.) After the buckets were filled, we then poured rice into them until every inch of space was used. Each family got a bucket, and we also gave them New Testaments in their language. Some of our adult children were back and became a vital part of the celebration.

I don't remember how many parties we held, but each Christmas that we lived in that house we had one. We took nice invitations to each family in the village closest to us. Then other villages wanted to come. In order to get the men to come and also so that each family would get one bucket, the man in the family had to bring the invitation to pick up their family gift. Eventually, the people themselves wanted to be involved too. So each barrio decorated part of the vacant lot, and they participated in the program. We got donations from some large businesses for food, and the last year we were there, we fed over 1000 people a meal—not just candy. We began early in the afternoon and had games and even a small horse to ride. We still had the movie and a short salvation message. The large bucket gifts were given at the end of the party, so everyone stayed to the finish.

We never again had people begging at our gate. We were now friends, and if someone had an important need, they would come and ask for help, but it wasn't the same as the begging before. We often took them to the doctor, or bought medicine for a sick child. Yvonne, who was a nurse, held a baby clinic and taught them how to stay healthier through cleanliness. A group of people from a larger church in town began a Bible Study in the village, which later became a small church. Students in the boarding homes learned the joy of helping others.

Sometimes it seems like we can change our attitudes by ourselves, but usually we can't do it. Only God knows what it will take to make that change. When seeking God's help and following His ideas, what started out as a very bad attitude was turned into an adventure for years of friendships, service, ministry, joy and people coming to know Jesus as their Savior.

—◆—

We also needed to find a way to work with the children who gathered around our car at every stoplight in the city. Sometimes it was hard to move ahead when the light changed, and we were afraid we might hit someone. Although the city officials discouraged it, this was a tradition and a time when children could expect some sort of gift.

I don't know where we got the idea, but we began making hundreds of small packets to hand out. We bought colorful plastic bags and filled them with various foods. We tried to find something that would give the children some nourishment, but we also included some candies as a special treat. We put in an attractive Christian booklet or tract in the local language that was made especially for children, and we often added a few coins. When the packets were filled, we tied them with colorful ribbon and then we felt ready to face the traffic of children. Sometimes, when policemen saw us giving out the packets to the children, they came to get one too.

One time, after the Christmas season was over, Dick and I walked out of a new pizza place after stuffing ourselves.

I became aware of someone walking beside me. He began softly speaking and saying "I am hungry." When I turned to look at him I saw a teenager whose only clothes were a pair of ragged shorts.

He was barefoot and his body was covered with sores. I remembered that we had a few of the Christmas packets left in the car. So I invited him to come with us, but by the time we reached the car two more boys had joined the first one. We only had four of the food packets left, so I gave them each a bag. But one of the boys who didn't speak English kept insisting he wanted the extra one. I didn't think it was fair to give him two when the other boys only got one each. So I said "No!" But as we started to leave, he reached into the open window and grabbed the bag from my hand and took off running across the street. I was angry and expressed to Dick how ungrateful he was.

Because of the bumper-to-bumper traffic, we were sitting where we could clearly see the boy as he ran away. The scene that took place was devastating. The young boy stopped where a small girl was sitting on the curb holding a baby. The boy gave her one of his packages of food, but as he started to leave, a much older and larger young man grabbed the package away from the boy and ran off. Now I was even angrier. I was angry with myself for not understanding why he wanted the extra package and I was even more upset that he now didn't have anything.

I continue to be bothered, and I have lots of questions: What could I do? What should I have done? Could I have changed anything? What would Jesus have done? What should I do next time? I have prayed: "Father, I have an awfully hard time handling this kind of thing. Please show me what You want me to do in situations like this. I know you love these 'jungle children' so please send help!"

Christmas certainly means many things to different people, depending on background, where we live and previous experiences. But the true meaning of Christmas is still all about God's unfathomable love and His gift to humanity:

Jesus Christ. God's love is perfect, He doesn't make mistakes, and He wants us to spend eternity with Him, so He made it possible through Jesus.

Carolyn helps choose our first Philippine Christmas tree, a white painted branch.

Christmas always included guests, often boarding students who couldn't go home at the holiday to see their family.

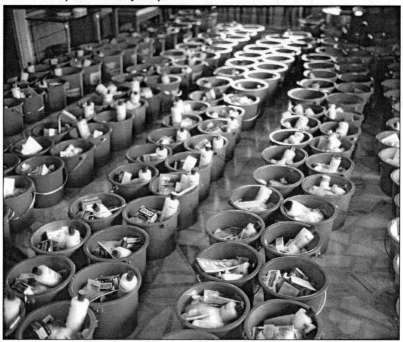

As part of the large Christmas party held for the squatter village, plastic buckets filled with household, medical, and food supplies were given to each family.

Yvonne, a registered nurse, held a clinic during the Christmas party for the neighborhood squatter families, and held baby clinics during the rest of the year.

The last year we were in the Philippines, the annual Christmas party had grown to the point where we fed a meal to over 1000 people.

Large businesses donated food for the Christmas party, which also included games, a program, a Christian movie, and a time to share the salvation message.

CHAPTER 4

ADVENTURES WITH POVERTY

Poverty is not a pleasant adventure, but it is an unpleasant fact of life. We never got used to the poverty and the begging in the Philippines—and especially the street kids. There was no way to avoid it, but there didn't seem to be any way to help much. Dick always gave to the blind, prayed for them and thanked God for being able to see. But there were times when we found ourselves getting cynical and "hard" toward beggars. There are people with tremendous needs, but there are also "professional" beggars, and it's almost impossible to tell the difference. Mabini Street downtown was known as the tourist area, because it was near the hotels and stores filled with beautiful Filipino carvings, paintings and embroidery work. Beggars frequented the area because tourists gave more money than anyone else.

When we had guests, we usually took them to this tourist area, since it was often the only place they could buy souvenirs, and we almost always saw someone with a blind baby. She was so pathetic and so obviously blind, that most people gave something to the person carrying her. We learned that different people "rented" this baby so they could use her for begging, and they always seemed to be getting money. Then one day a doctor who was an eye specialist and surgeon saw the baby and felt he could give her some sight, which he offered to do for free. This offer was rejected, because they could make so much more money from the baby being blind. We heard many similar stories, and soon we began to resent the beggars rather than wanting to help them. And once again, we needed God's help to change our attitude.

There were genuine needs. In fact, they could be overwhelming. One day, when I came home from school, I found a woman sitting outside our gate. She was nursing a tiny baby and she had another small child with her so skinny you could see her bones! The mother wanted something for her children to eat, and I wanted to give her food. I told her to wait while I went inside to get some canned milk, rice and whatever else I could find. But she evidently didn't understand me and when I came back with the food she was gone. I was sad, and I didn't know what to do.

Once when I was shopping in a busy downtown area, a tiny girl (probably six or seven years old, but the size of a four year old) came up to me and asked for money. She was carrying something in her arms and when I looked closer, I honestly couldn't believe my eyes! She had a baby and his head was about the size of a tennis ball. He was alive, but surely couldn't live long. I tried to talk to the child, but she didn't understand me, and no one around seemed to care at all. I wanted someone who spoke the local language to help me communicate with the little girl, but they didn't want to be involved. I had extremely mixed emotions. I wanted to help the children, but I was furious with the adults who allowed this kind of thing. Were they professional beggars or a desperate family? Maybe they were "sacrificing" a baby who couldn't live anyway so other children could survive. This haunted me for days. I wanted to help, but how? I couldn't make myself understood. What should I have done? What could I have done? This is something we hadn't had to face in the U.S., and I didn't know how to handle it.

Another time, we were very tired as we drove home late. Out of the corner of my eye I saw something move by the side of the road. I said, "Honey, I think maybe that was a person lying near the curb." All we wanted to do was to get home and go to bed, but since there was no traffic that time of night, Dick stopped the car and backed up. I was right. It was a person, only we weren't sure he/she was alive. We both got out and discovered a very old woman who seemed to be asleep. She was curled up, barefooted and quite dirty. At least she was still breathing. We really didn't know what to do, but we knew we couldn't leave her there. She could easily be hit when traffic started up in the morning. We gently picked her up and put her in the back seat of our car, and of course, this woke her up.

Trying to communicate was very difficult, because she not only didn't speak English, but our Tagalog was extremely limited. Once again, it was a dilemma. What should we do? We could take her home and find a place for her to sleep, but did she wander off and have a worried family looking for her? She was very confused and so were we! We tried in every way to see if she knew where she lived. She began pointing in a certain direction, so we went that way. She tried telling us something, but we didn't understand. After driving around for about an hour, we came to one area and she thought she lived nearby, but wasn't sure where. So when we came by a police station, we stopped and went in to inquire if anyone had reported her missing. They immediately told us to bring her in and leave her with them. They would find where she lived. All the way home we wondered if we did the right thing. The police were not noted for their compassion, but Filipinos did respect the elderly! At least they could understand what she was saying. Experiences like this always left us with the question of whether we made the right decision.

I'm not sure exactly when it happened, but I remember standing at a counter waiting to buy something when a child came and asked me for money. My first reaction was to say an emphatic "No! Go away!" But I really believe I heard Jesus say, "I see your heart, and it's better to have the right attitude and lovingly give, even if you make a mistake and give to the wrong people." It was a wakeup call!

It's easy to forget lessons you have learned in the past — at least it's easy for me. When we were in Israel, we loved visiting all the places we had heard about in the Bible, and yet it seemed like every place we went, someone had their hand out to receive payment just to be able to look. So when a little boy came up to me and tapped my arm, I wasn't very friendly. He had a small bouquet of flowers he had picked and tried to hand them to me. I didn't take them, but rather harshly said, "I don't have any money!" This adorable child softly replied, "I don't want money. I just wanted to give you some flowers." I was totally ashamed of myself and knelt down beside him. I put my arm around him, took the flowers and truly thanked him. I don't think there is ever a time to be rude, but I still need the Lord's help in this area.

———

It's inevitable. You can't avoid seeing poverty in the Philippines. It's everywhere! We were driving through a nice part of town one day and on the edge of the sidewalk next to a tall wall, a mother and several children were making their home in cardboard boxes.

The plight of street children around the world is so critical that Newsweek predicted it would become the number one problem in the world if something wasn't done about it. We worked with Action International Ministries for several years, and street kids were their greatest passion. Besides homes for various age groups, several different types of training programs were initiated: watch repair, mechanics, sewing, making furniture, carpenter work, etc. Camps became popular, and the children were always introduced to Jesus, along with good food and new clothing. But it's difficult to understand and comprehend just how serious and sad life is for the majority of children worldwide.

Years ago as Dick and I were making a documentary about street kids, we happened to turn on television and watched, in horror, a news report about what was happening in Brazil. The country was expecting a large International Convention about environment, so they wanted to clean up their city. They went out in the morning and dug graves on a hillside, and then in the evening they killed street children and buried them in the graves. This was their way of clearing the problem of street kids. We also interviewed a young man who had been a street kid, and he told about "salvaging." The police arrested boys and then at night they took them to a secluded place and shot them. He personally saw two of his friends "salvaged," but he managed to escape before he was killed. He later came to one of Action's homes and turned his life over to Jesus. Now he was committed to working with these kids.

—*m*—

For many years Manila had the reputation of having one of the top ten largest garbage dumps in the world. It was even pictured on the front cover of the National Geographic Magazine. There was a village at the base of the dump with thousands of people living there and using what they could gather from the garbage. Unfortunately, the garbage collectors had already gone through everything they had picked up and taken anything that seemed useable. Homes were a patchwork of every conceivable material they could make work: tin cans, cardboard boxes, old tires, broken boards, plastic and glass bottles, pieces of cloth and plastic, etc. There was no running water available, so they carried in bottles of water from other areas.

The city tried to clean out the village and move the people to a better location, but it didn't work very well because the poor needed what they could collect from the garbage. There were no jobs, no running water, no place for a garden, and no electricity in the new area. It was away from the city and left the people with nothing to do and no place to go; so they moved back to their homes among the garbage. Different mission groups went in and tried to make the dump more livable and give the people some dignity. A beautiful sign was erected, giving the area a new name called "Smokey Village." A well was drilled so water became available. Other organizations set up a medical clinic and makeshift school. There was still the huge mountain of garbage with all the filth and smells, but it did give one of the most important ingredients to life: HOPE! Christians who loved Jesus donated all of these improvements.

Dick and I were asked to come and make a documentary. That evening, we were invited to a big dinner at a home in the wealthiest area of Manila. I wasn't sure I could handle the contrast — from the poorest to the richest. The other guests were the people who had been helping with the improvements at "Smokey Village." I made an important discovery that evening. When the rich love Jesus and become aware of the tremendous needs of others, they can be a great financial help in projects for the poor. An attitude of Jesus' love makes the difference.

Some of these Scriptures found in Romans 12 are applicable: **"So in Christ we, though many, form one body, and each member belongs to all the others. We have different gifts, according to the grace given us. . .Love must be sincere. Hate what is evil; cling to what is good. Be devoted to one another in love. Honor one another above yourselves. Never be lacking in zeal, but keep your spiritual fervor, serving the Lord. . .Do not be proud, but be willing to associate with people of low position. Do not be conceited. . .Do not be overcome by evil, but overcome evil with good."** (NIV)

You can't avoid seeing poverty in the Philippines, and the plight of street children is especially distressing.

At night the parks in Manila are filled with homeless adults and street kids who have nowhere else to sleep.

A young girl picks through garbage to find anything salvagable to sell or use. Street kids gather near traffic lights, or hang out near tourist shops and attractions to beg for money.

The "Smokey Mountain" garbage dump in Manila was at one time one of the largest in the world, where scavengers made their living from picking through the landfill's rubbish.

A man searches through a mountain of garbage at the Manila garbage dump that once held two million tons of trash.

CHAPTER 5

ADVENTURES WITH MY TRUMPET

My trumpet adventures actually began with a violin. When I was in sixth grade, I decided I wanted to play an instrument—something besides the piano, which I didn't like at all. My older sister thought she wanted to play the violin, so my parents bought her one, but she gave it up rather quickly. The rest of the family probably tormented her because of the awful squeaks. It does take time to learn to play any instrument. Since this violin was just sitting in the closet, I took it to school and informed the teacher I wanted to join the orchestra. However, I was told that the violin was too big for me and I should tell my parents to get me a smaller one.

This didn't go over with my Dad at all, but he brought out his World War I cornet and said I could try for the band. I really liked this cornet, even though the keys stuck so bad that I had to pull them up every time I pushed them down. I became so fast at pulling up the keys that I could keep up with the rest of the band. That's when my Dad decided I was serious about playing an instrument, so he bought me a very used trumpet. I thought it was wonderful and so did the band director until he discovered that it could only be tuned one way. There was a knob to turn that made it either A or Bb—nothing in between. So the band had to tune to me. When I finally got an instrument where the keys came up normally, I discovered that I could finger really fast.

When I was in Jr. High, the U.S. Navy Band came to Nampa, Idaho and put on an unforgettable concert. I had visions of being the first girl invited to be their guest soloist. I taught myself to triple tongue and since I could sight-read because of playing the piano, I could almost always get first chair in the trumpet section, which was mostly boys. In high school, I was asked to play for all kinds of affairs, from Taps on Memorial Day to the opening trumpet call at the Boise Valley Easter Sunrise Service.

However, when I went to a small college, there was no band to play in. But when I met Dick and discovered that he was a drummer and loved to play in the band, it helped start our friendship. I decided to major in music just to be in the same classes with Dick. But that meant we had to give a senior recital. Since we were married our last two years of college, I managed to get pregnant early in my senior year. After talking to our music professor, it was decided that we should give an early joint recital: Dick would sing, and I would play the trumpet. Hopefully, it was early enough so that no one could tell I was expecting a baby. During this time, I managed to teach trumpet and played professionally.

After our first baby, four others arrived over the next eight years. It wasn't long before my vision of playing with the Navy Band disintegrated into years of changing diapers, mopping floors, wiping strained spinach off the windows and picking up toys scattered over the house and yard. I totally forgot my Navy Band dream. Once in a while I would see my trumpet case in the back of the closet and take it out to dust it off. I even tried to play it occasionally, but it wasn't the same. And then we went to the Philippines as missionaries. That's when the unbelievable happened.

The extraordinary chain of events had its beginning one lovely Sunday afternoon when we treated ourselves to an army band concert in Rizal Park, the largest, most beautiful area in downtown Manila. The performance was superb and we wanted the director to know how much we enjoyed and appreciated his band. We found Colonel Carino to be remarkably friendly, and when he learned we taught choir and band at Faith Academy, he offered to bring his group for a concert — no charge!

Now somehow, Colonel Carino heard that I played the trumpet. Women trumpet players were exceedingly rare in the Philippines, so he came up with the bright idea of featuring me as his guest soloist the next time they performed in the park. That would have been my dream a long time ago, but sometimes dreams turn into nightmares. I knew it was utterly impossible! It had been too many years since I really played. I went five years without even taking my trumpet from the case; the remaining 11 years had been hit and miss - mostly miss! So I graciously declined. I was pretty certain he didn't actually mean it anyway.

I was wrong! A few days later Colonel Carino phoned, and again I explained that playing was impossible. It had been too many years since I had practiced, and the concert was only a few weeks away. He firmly informed me, "In the army you don't say no!" I meekly replied, "But sir, I'm not in the army." I thought he was convinced and that was the end of it. But the next morning when I answered a knock at our door, a soldier shoved a stack of music into my hands and announced, "Your first practice with the band will be next Thursday at 2:00 p.m. Come to Colonel Carino's office on the base." (Incidentally, though Colonel Carino was the Commanding Officer of a large military base in Manila, directing music was his first passion.) I opened my mouth to refuse, but nothing came out and the soldier was gone.

When Dick came home and we talked it over, we decided maybe we should ask for God's direction in this touchy situation. Dick sympathized with me because he knew I hadn't played for ages. (He was probably as scared as I was!) When we finally asked the Lord, He made it quite clear this was His plan. I was not to fight it any longer or try to get out of it. I argued with God until He assured me He would be with me to perform the impossible. Philippians 4:13 promises, **"For I can do everything God asks me with the help of Christ who gives me the strength and power."** I expressed my feeling to God, "If you want me to do this, then I want to enjoy it. I want it to be fun, not terrifying! And I want you to use it in some really special way." I guess I didn't need to add that last remark; why else would He have me do it?

God's promise of help was reassuring, but it didn't mean I could sit back and do nothing. I began to frantically practice. Since my teeth were not formed for trumpet playing, after a few days of intense practice, my lip began to swell and bleed and it became so sore I cried most of the time while practicing. But it finally healed and hardened, and then I enjoyed playing.

Colonel Carino knew a Filipino woman who also played the trumpet, and he asked her to play a duet with me. She was an exceptionally topnotch trumpeter, and this far surpassed playing alone. One day I was glancing through a Manila newspaper and almost fainted when I saw a large picture of me playing the trumpet. According to the article, this Filipino lady was to represent the Philippines and I was representing the U.S.A. The photo had been taken at a practice. I thought I was afraid before, but now I was simply terrified!

Some days sounded fine as I practiced and other days I could hardly make a noise. I managed to memorize one song, and then just three days before the concert, Colonel Carino wrote an arrangement of a Filipino folksong for us to play. Sounds simple? At that time, Colonel Carino was the only non-American who was honored as one of the ten top band directors in the world. He was a fabulous arranger, and his song included many variations of runs, triple tonguing, double tonguing and unusual rhythms. This new music only added to my panic.

All during church the next morning, I kept reminding the Lord of His promise to help me. But my faith was weak and powerless. I'm thankful God is faithful to His promises even when we fail in faith. When we arrived at the huge Rizal Park Stadium, it was packed with people everywhere. It was estimated that at least half a million people strolled through this big park area every weekend, especially on Sunday. To me it seemed like twice that many people. Several strangers approached me, remarking that they had seen my picture in the newspaper and had come to hear me perform. That was really not comforting!

After the band played several numbers, introductions began. At first I simply wanted it to be over so I could relax. Then suddenly, it dawned on me what a tremendous experience I was having. This was actually my dream come true, only bigger and better! When I saw those thousands of people and realized where I was and what was happening, I became so excited that all fear left me. I know it was God answering my prayer and changing my attitude, and it was a miracle. Colonel Carino introduced our whole family to the audience and his band members presented us with garlands of flowers. Dick was interviewed, with questions that led to a testimony about Jesus and why we were in the Philippines. It was a beautiful, unforgettable experience! It went way beyond my wildest dreams.

Earlier, I had been far more fearful than my Filipino companion, but when we stood to play, she was visibly shaking. I know she didn't understand the change that came over me—the excitement and yet peace—but I think it helped her. She was fantastic as we played, and even I remarkably surpassed my present ability. The audience gave us a tremendous response, and my biggest disappointment was that my Dad and Mom weren't there to enjoy it. Dad had always been my biggest fan and he would have been thrilled.

I obeyed God—although reluctantly—and He not only gave me my dream, but changed my attitude. I had the privilege of playing in a featured trumpet trio number with the army band two other times. Many smaller community bands invited our family to attend their concerts as special guests. We became acquainted with so many people we never would have met otherwise.

There were many new experiences that resulted from our friendship with Colonel Carino. Since he was in command of the army base, he allowed not only our family, but also our mission organization access to the facilities. Up to this point, it was impossible for us to go onto the base. But now we were given total freedom to come and go whenever we wanted. We were treated like celebrities, and we could use their bowling alley, tennis courts, chapel, etc. One of our missionaries began going every Sunday to have Bible Studies, show Christian films and interact with the soldiers. Besides all that, Colonel Carino and his wife became our very special friends, which led to many more unusual experiences.

After being in the United States for furlough, we had just returned to the Philippines when we received a phone call from the top Admiral in the Philippine Navy. This man was a special friend of Colonel Carino, and he informed us that the Colonel had suffered both a heart attack and stroke. He was confined to the intensive care unit of the Veteran's hospital. He was asking for us and we were requested to visit him. The Admiral wanted us to come as soon as possible. We dropped everything and headed for the hospital. All the signs posted said, "No visitors allowed in this area," but we were immediately taken to his bedside. Because of his serious heart condition and partial paralysis from the stroke, we couldn't carry on a two-way conversation, but he knew we were there. We had time to pray for him, read from God's Word and assure him of God's love and our love for him. We visited him often and were always welcomed when we went to the hospital. One day Dick had the opportunity to ask the Colonel if he wanted to trust Jesus as his Savior and he said, "Yes!"

We were honestly afraid Colonel Carino might not pull through when we first saw him in the hospital, but God raised him up, and he called himself, "The Walking Miracle." He told people it was because we prayed for him and God answered. When he retired from the armed forces, Mrs. Marcos invited him to direct the Rizal Park Band. Any band Colonel Carino directed was the best; he wouldn't settle for anything less. The Rizal Park Band practiced every day and performed each evening in the beautiful park near the bay. His group never just sat and played. He had them enacting all kinds of marches and actions while playing the music to perfection. They not only sounded great, but also were fun to watch. The Colonel was invited to the United States to accept big band awards, at the same time as being a guest conductor of some of the most important bands in the U.S. Wherever he went, his lovely wife was by his side. We felt so honored to be their friends.

God always fulfills His promises. One of my favorite verses in the Bible is found in Psalms 138:2-3. ". . .**For your promises are backed by all the honor of your name. When I pray, you answer me, and encourage me by giving me the strength I need.**"

When my attitude changed from fear to trusting God, it gave me one of the most exciting adventures of my life, and it was even better than my youthful dream. God not only used it to open many doors that had been closed, but He shared His love and opened hearts to Jesus.

Colonel Carino directed the army band at Rizal Park in Manila where I played the trumpet alongside a talented Filipino woman for a special performance.

The park was packed out with thousands of people for the special performance. It was a dream come true for me.

When Colonel Carino's band performed at Faith Academy, I played in a trio with two other teachers.

Our children performed together for most of their childhood, and the oldest three became quite good on the trumpet.

CHAPTER 6

ADVENTURES IN EASTERN EUROPE

D oing anything with my friend Sally Begbie was always exciting. Sally looked like Julie Andrews, so we encountered stares, requests for autographs, whispers and special attention wherever we went in the Philippines. Sally not only looked like Julie, but she was from Australia and had a similar accent. She also sang. Although I am old enough to be Sally's mother, we instantly bonded as special friends and age never mattered. Sally is married to a great man named Malcolm and they have two wonderful sons. This adventure story is about our trip into Eastern Europe immediately after the Iron curtain went down. There were six of us: Sally and her two teenage sons (David and Josh), and Dick and me with our grandson Jesse (also a teenager). We lived in the Philippines at the time, but our adventures began in England where a remarkable lady, Chris Fox, planned our trip, furnished a van and loaded it with just about everything but the kitchen sink.

This trip actually started out quite differently for me. In fact, to quote me, "We left rather leisurely for the airport and arrived more than an hour before the ticket counter even opened. Steve took us." In case you are wondering why this was different, I am rather famous for never being ready to leave and even finishing my packing on the way to the airport. One time, we even had to make a quick stop on the way to buy another suitcase because I had misjudged and couldn't stuff everything into the one I had with me. I'm not talking about a few items I would have to leave behind, but half of what I needed. I have a terrible reputation for always being late. Dick said he prayed for patience, and the Lord gave me to him. He claimed that I was born with a faulty time clock that was beyond repair, so he learned to always carry a Newsweek magazine wherever we went.

We met Sally and her boys in London and then headed for Eastern Europe. Here is the story of our trip, as told by Dick, Sally and me in letters to family and reports to the mission.

Dick

Helen and I just returned from a four-week trip into four countries of Eastern Europe: Poland, Czechoslovakia, Hungary and Romania. We were invited to take supplies, Bibles and food to pastors and Christian workers in these countries. We were also scheduled to interview people on video in each place we visited.

We traveled under the most Spartan conditions, some of us sleeping in the van and a couple of the boys using a small tent for most of the trip. We ate many of our meals at the side of the car, heating whatever we could on a tiny gas burner. We stayed in campgrounds when we could find them, but this was not always possible. Roadside rest stops in that part of the world have no toilets and no running water. The weather was cold and rainy much of the time. (Helen and I feel like we have triumphed and can now face many more adventures.)

Helen

I've never really liked camping unless it is in a completely contained RV. You know the kind — small kitchen with stove, refrigerator, sink, bathroom, table and beds, heat, privacy — simply the modern conveniences. On this trip I had to change my attitude in a hurry, or I wouldn't survive.

After traveling what seemed like forever in the crowded van, we were finally in Poland, and Sally was sure she knew where we were supposed to go. They were expecting us and would have beds ready. But it was dark, and Sally finally realized she was lost. Of course, we were lost with her. The most urgent task now was to find someplace where we could park our van and try to sleep until daylight and then find out where we were and where we should be. There were no such things as motels, hotels, etc. in those days. In fact, there wasn't much in the way of places to eat or even grocery stores. We drove around looking for someplace with privacy off the main roads.

We finally thought we found the perfect location. Although it wasn't the most comfortable, it seemed to be away from people and cars. We were all so tired; we didn't even care about eating. It's a little hard to remember, but I think Dick and I "slept" in the front seat of the car, sitting up, of course. Sally and one of her boys did the same in the second seat, and the other two unlucky guys tried to slip in between the packed back of the van and the ceiling. There was very little space to move, and the luggage under them was anything but smooth and comfortable. They couldn't turn over and I think even breathing was difficult. We were too tired to set up our little tent. In trying to find someplace to use as a toilet area, we discovered our car was in the middle of a gravel pit or rock quarry, but at least it should be private.

I guess we were worn out enough to sleep pretty soundly. It took a while for us to realize the noise we were hearing came from cars passing by. When we finally became conscious, we discovered our "private hideaway" was right next to a major highway and we were totally exposed to the public. As quickly as possibly, we left and eventually found our way to our original destination in a beautiful farming area in the hills. The people were expecting us and had prepared a special meal, as well as clean, warm beds.

Dick

After crossing the channel from England our trip eventually began and ended in Poland, where we had our best contacts and where the evangelical gospel has a firm foothold. We had good contacts in the four countries we visited. We were able to videotape various evangelists, pastors and Christian workers to get their stories of life under Communism and tell us the present needs of the church from their perspective. We were often in tears during these interviews as we listened to the hardships, deprivation and sometimes torture and beatings. We made an effort to get their point of view, especially when it came to hearing what they felt was their most urgent and greatest need now.

Helen

The language was different, but we soon discovered other differences. The coffee was served in glasses, and cream was a total luxury. Since I was still learning to like coffee, I mostly drank it for the cream and the fellowship. The most unusual part of the coffee was all the black stuff in the bottom of the glass. This turned out to be the coffee grounds, which were part of the drink. We discussed among ourselves whether we were supposed to actually drink the coffee grounds or just leave them. We didn't want to offend our hosts. As I recall, we did try to drink them, but finally were told that it wasn't necessary.

Although we discovered many little differences in the way we did normal activities, and we couldn't understand each other's language, we certainly did understand the language of love. We were bathed in love and appreciation. Even though we had gifts to leave every place we went, we always left with far more than we were able to give them. It's very hard to remember all the people we met on this trip, but every one of them was awesome and had exciting stories to tell.

As I said, the people were amazing, but this was so soon after the collapse of the Soviet Union, that conditions were anything but ideal. We tried to eat at a restaurant, but they had nothing to serve us. I don't believe we ever found a bakery that had anything to sell. Unless you were there very early in the morning—and often the lines were a block long—you had no chance of getting a loaf of bread. People were extremely generous and we were treated like royalty, even though they hardly had enough for their own family. In one of the countries, we were served tomatoes and cucumbers, while in another it was potatoes and cabbage. These foods were usually found in small outdoor markets where people brought things to sell, or exchange, from their gardens.

In all of the places we went, we had contacts we were supposed to meet. We had brought foods, literature, medicines and a variety of items to give to the families we met with. Some of the countries seemed worse off than others. One of the things we had trouble adjusting to were the rest stops with no toilets. The provision was a forest of trees. Just about the time I thought I had found a private tree, some man would walk by. But usually there was no such thing as privacy, and it was hard to find a place that hadn't already been used too many times. However, we soon discovered that these "rest stops" among the trees were far more acceptable than the public rest rooms in city parks. We often stayed in parks and set up a small tent. With this tent, the small kerosene burner, sleeping bags and the van, we could eat and sleep. We often had to find a bush to use as our toilet, because the public toilets were full and running over.

Dick

As we traveled farther east into Romania, conditions became worse and worse. It was like stepping back in time. Horse drawn carts were everywhere. Crops were harvested with the ancient scythe. Food was even scarcer. The grocery stores were barren, often only with five or six items. Fruit (when available) was sold in glass jars. Bread lines were long, with bread only available in the early morning.

Aside from the staggering backwardness and lack of material things, the spiritual darkness was even greater. There was a heaviness and oppression in the air itself. We often saw drunkards staggering down the roads, even in the middle of the day. Liquor is available everywhere and alcoholism is the plague of these countries.

Helen

We probably were most impressed with Romania, because we saw so many signs of Communist influence and heard personal stories of tragedy and torture. Many buildings, especially the huge apartment houses, were like big boxes — all alike and all the same dull color. One area we visited had several blocks of the big tall identical apartment buildings, and nearby was one of the biggest buildings I had ever seen. This old beat-up place furnished the heat for all of the many apartment buildings in that area. The people had no control over heating their homes. The heat all came from this one huge plant. And if the government was unhappy with them, they might not get any heat at all, no matter how cold it was. It seemed like the communist leaders controlled everything in their lives. There was no room for individuality.

The smaller villages escaped some of this and were very charming, but the cities were depressing. The roads were narrow, full of holes and shared equally by cars and horse-drawn wagons filled with hay. This was especially treacherous after dark, because the wagons were still on the roads, but with no lights.

Romania is a beautiful country and at one time had plenty of food and products for everyone. But their leaders began sending the food to other countries until there wasn't enough for their own citizens. The people had nothing to say about what was happening, and their leaders were becoming extremely rich, building mansions for themselves while the ordinary citizens were becoming poor and hungry.

We visited Pastor Cornel and his wife Sanda, in the town of Timisoara. The events that occurred here were instrumental in beginning the revolution against the communist government in Romania. Cornel gave us a vivid account of what happened as he showed us their lovely town square. Timisoara had a large beautiful park-like area with small businesses around most of it and a large church at one end.

When conditions became unbearable, hundreds of students gathered for a peaceful demonstration in the Timisoara town-square. The young people had nothing to fight with, but the government sent in their army with plenty of ammunition and began shooting into the crowd. Looking for safety, the kids began running for the church. They believed it would be a shelter, but this was a State church. Immediately the doors were locked before anyone could find refuge inside. The peaceful protest ended in mass murder, much of it on the steps of the church. Nearly every building around the square was riddled with bullet holes, which were very evident when we were there. However, the government's response to the rally backfired, and Romania had a real revolution. The country became free and their leaders were executed.

As I mentioned earlier, one of the purposes of our trip, besides delivering special things for their use, was to do interviews with pastors and other Christians who had lived and worked under Communism. These interviews would be used in video documentaries. Every person we had contact with had a story to tell, and each one was special. Dick and I did the video part, and Sally interviewed the people. They were so happy to see us that no matter how little they had, they always managed to find something to share with us. They were also very glad to tell their stories. We were truly humbled in their presence.

Dick

Observations. I believe we heard the same concerns consistently from each country.

1. In nearly all the countries we visited the feeling of those we spoke to was that there is little hope for the generations who were steeped in Communist atheistic teachings. They are the "lost generations." They have now traded Communism for Materialism. The hope is in the children and the youth. Here is where the evangelistic and training efforts need to be concentrated right now!

2. They all stated that their greatest need from the West is PRAYER. Since the fall of the Communist ideology in Eastern

Europe, Western Christians have slacked off in their giving and concern. The great battle is now only beginning. Prayer and concern are urgent.

3. As far as help is concerned from the West, they want people who can TRAIN THEIR PEOPLE, especially children's workers and those who can teach apologetics. Universities and seminaries are wide open for those who can "defend the faith."

4. There is much more suffering ahead before these countries can get on their feet economically and make the change to a market economy. We should not forget their physical needs during this period.

Sally's memories of Romania

One area we were in was Moldavia, and it is stunningly beautiful. We wondered if we'd somehow stumbled upon Austria or Switzerland when first we found it. Little wooden huts atop glorious mountain ranges, goats and cows with bells echoing in wooded valleys; it was truly *Sound of Music* stuff. But traversing the roads through this breathtaking scenery was to prove nightmare material.

Romania's roads are notoriously dangerous. Nearly all are bumpy, narrow and poorly marked. The greatest hazard on them, however, is the traffic. One can be driving steadily at 130 km per hour, only to round a corner and find one's nose in the back of a huge load of hay, pulled by a toothless farmer and his worn-out horse. It's all very picturesque, but absolutely terrifying. To me, Romania's roads were something between riding the big dipper and driving the dodgems all at one time. I think everyone in that van was most grateful to know that others were praying for our safety.

Sometime it would be fun to backtrack and see at what particular times someone felt a greater than usual need to pray. A certain Sunday in Moldavia would be highly likely to come up on such a list. We had met a man whose character is as colorful as the country is grey. His name is Pavel. His friends call him "No Problem Pavel!" or, for short, simply NPP, because nothing is ever a problem for this man. KGB? Securitate? Opposition from the Orthodox Church? No money? No problem!

We had driven for 14 hours on Romania's roads to reach NPP's home the night before. "No problem! You sleep this night and then, tomorrow, we will have wonderful evangelistic meeting. You will see. It will be wonderful!" Where was this meeting? "Beyond my church." Where was his church? "150 kilometers from my house. Yes, I drive it every Sunday, but it's no problem!" Where, exactly, was the meeting? "150 kilometers beyond my church!" Hmm, a round trip 300 km on Romanian roads just to attend the meeting we were to videotape? "But it's no problem. You'll sleep now and tomorrow we will have such wonderful time together, yes! You will see!" Pavel gesticulated with large hands and spoke with a booming voice that somehow imbued us all with his confidence.

Bright and early, we headed out behind NPP's car to travel the first 150 km. The trip was breathtaking in beauty and in speed, for a time. NPP had been told of a short cut through the forest that would reduce our distance to 15 km instead of 150. Sounded ideal. We turned confidently off the main road but, before long, our legs had turned to jelly.

The road (that really was too generous a word for it) was a relic from World War II. It consisted mainly of two very deep ruts which themselves contained giant holes filled, at times, with sloshy mud or horribly black water. What did Pavel think? You already know, "No problem!" He drove ahead waving and smiling all the time despite the violent side-to-side lurching of his car. We tried to follow, grimacing as the bottom of our van scraped who-knew-what underneath us. Dick did a valiant job. He avoided the ruts as best he could, but usually this meant driving on the edge of the downside slope, an exercise somewhat precarious in itself. We jolted on, wondering if, at any minute the van would simply die completely, and possibly we would too.

That moment seemed very nearly to realize. Dear NPP suddenly found his car swimming in a giant pool of the black water. It was going nowhere. He revved like crazy, steering left and right, prayed and revved again. The wheels pointlessly spun in the liquid mud. He revved again. They gripped. Suddenly, defying all laws of probability he was out of the pool, his car waltzing wildly on the ancient road. He finally parked up ahead leaving sufficient space for our van to come through. This time, though, he walked solemnly toward us and said the unthinkable for NPP. "I think this situation is impossible, no?" Coming from anyone else, that would have been one thing. But, coming from the indomitable NPP, it left us feeling almost defeated.

What, though, were we to do? It seemed we couldn't go on, but we couldn't go back either. And we certainly couldn't drop a coin in a nearby phone box and call some friendly automobile service that would drive on down to that Moldavian valley and tow us all home.

Romania is probably 25 years away from even considering such a facility. We prayed till we were dry-mouthed, then laid branches on the road for traction and watched, in awe, as Dick the wonder-driver came at speed toward us. He told us later he was praying and, perhaps, simply heard God's voice in a special way in that moment. NPP kept telling him to go slowly. Dick thought the opposite. He felt sure the van needed momentum in order to traverse this ooze. He drove, therefore, in a hurry. I remember watching the nose of the van dip as the front descended into one of the submarine depressions.

What, I wondered, if it proves too deep, and the van simply summersaults? Could we lose Dick over this? I agonized and hardly knew how to formulate a prayer, so thankful that the Spirit prays for us when we can't. All at once, the van was up again and bouncing, mud flying everywhere. Suddenly all was fine. Dick was through the pool, parking the van and walking toward us with a big smile. The relief was almost inexpressible. I tried to laugh along with everybody else but actually, wanted to go away and cry. I really had been afraid we might lose Dick and couldn't quite believe the moment of danger was past. We really depended on people's prayers, but most of all on God's protection.

Helen

Dick had made his decision: everyone was to get out of the van and he would make a wild run to try and get through the mess. All we could do was pray and then of course, we had to find a way ourselves to get to the other side. Dick backed up to get some speed and then raced into the mud lake. The van lurched back and forth and looked like it was going to tip over, but it did get through. Those of us left behind eventually found our way through the bushes and trees, with the only damage being very dirty shoes.

We had fascinating meetings with interpreters and then fantastic fellowship while eating a delicious meal. This was a very out-of-the-way village and so hadn't been bothered as much by the communist government. They still had their individual homes and raised most of their food, so they had much more than the cities. It was hard emotionally to leave these new friends, knowing that we probably would not see them again until we meet in Heaven. Needless to say, we did not try any more shortcuts on the way home, even though it was much farther to go the normal way.

After spending a few days with Pavel (and especially seeing the way he drove on these already dangerous roads, which he contributed to their danger), we decided he must have a legion of broken and bruised angels following him wherever he went. But we all fell in love with Pavel. He told us his story of being taken to police headquarters and questioned about everyone he knew. Who were the Christians? Who had a Bible? Who had not joined the Communist Party? He was offered a chance to go to the U.S. if he would give them a list of names. Since he was not cooperative, they put him on a steel table, spread his hands out flat and pounded them until they were like pulp. They continually tortured him, but he always responded, "No problem!" Instead of "breaking him," it took away all fear of them, and it became "no problem."

None of our teenage boys were old enough to drive a car in the Philippines, so they had no license and had never driven yet. That left Dick doing most of the driving except a few times when Sally or I would relieve him—and I'm not sure that really was a relief to him. The roads were terrible: narrow and with many holes. I don't remember any freeway-type highways. Sally and I were responsible for directions, until the boys decided they wanted to take turns doing that job. No matter who was in charge, we almost always got lost at times.

We had specific people we were supposed to contact in each country, and since we didn't speak the language, it was a challenge, whether it was in reading the maps or asking people questions. Although some people spoke English, there were many more that did not know our language. Sally was superb, because she did speak some French and that would often supply us with what we needed to know.

Sally

In Hungary, our time was limited and we knew very little about the people we were to meet and interview. We parked in the middle of Budapest and walked right up to the address, only to discover, you guessed it, there was no such name on this building. It was a big apartment block, with a list outside. Our contact was not to be found. We had no one to turn to. There was no second point of reference. Just this address. Had we wasted our time? Were we to come out of Hungary empty-handed? We began talking to the Lord. We told Him we had no idea how to find this couple and we asked for His help.

The Lord obviously took over. We pushed someone else's button on the security panel. The door opened and we entered the building to find a kindly old couple shuffling out to meet us. To our delight, they spoke French, so we could communicate. To our even greater delight, they knew the wife of the couple we sought. Her brother lived in the building. We were warmly welcomed at his place and were soon speaking by phone to the couple we needed. The next day we were able to interview them at length, before leaving Hungary for Czechoslovakia. These seem like little things, it's true, but we didn't want to miss the hand of the Lord. If the old couple had been out; if they had not wanted to let us in; if they hadn't spoken French; if they never heard of our couple; so many little "ifs" could have resulted in a dead end. God truly guided.

Helen

This was not a new experience for Sally and her boys, because they had worked with Brother Andrew in Eastern Europe years before. They often went into a city to deliver Bibles without knowing where to go, and it was too dangerous to ask questions. This was when there was a strong Iron Curtain and it wasn't safe for them or the people they were to meet. Many times the Lord was their only guide, but He never failed them. And He never failed us.

It was a new thing for people to be able to talk to us so freely. At first some of them were hesitant, as though they expected to be arrested at any moment. They seemed to be afraid that they weren't really free yet. I think my attitude about being free took on a whole new meaning as we traveled these countries and heard stories from people who had lost their freedom—even their right to worship God.

Although the people in these countries had very little in the way of material things and foods, they were always extremely friendly and generous. They gave, like in the Bible when Paul told about the people in Macedonia. **"Though they have been going through much trouble and hard times, they have mixed their wonderful joy with their deep poverty, and the result has been an overflow of giving to others. They gave not only what they could afford, but far more, and I can testify that they did it because they wanted to."** (II

Corinthians 8:2-3.) It was this way every place we went, even in the most unexpected places.

One day when we were traveling, we came upon an unusual scene. A large bird (I think someone said it was a stork) had built a nest on top of a tall light pole. When we stopped to take some photos, a lady came from a house nearby and invited us to come in and take pictures from her second floor balcony, which had a beautiful close-up view. She offered us something to drink and then began collecting lovely ceramic flowers, special embroidered pieces of material and whatever she thought we might like from her house. All this was from a total stranger, and I am reminded of her generosity every time I look at my pair of colorful ceramic flowers.

Although we were close to the Russian border, we chose not to try and go there. We wanted to go to Yugoslavia, but they were beginning to have trouble in their country and we were running out of time. Shortly after we left, the hate war broke out between the Serbs, Croats and Muslims there. One man was basically instrumental in instigating the conflicts, but thousands were killed and the country seriously damaged. It was interesting to us each time we crossed a border in the countries where we were to go. Jesse, Dick and I had no problem at all, but almost every time, Sally, D.J. and Josh had a problem. I finally asked one of the officials who spoke English why we could go straight through and they were always detained. He said, "Your government (the U.S.) has given us money, but their country has not helped us."

We were not on a sightseeing trip, but we did see many wonderful sights. Each country we visited had its own unique attractions. There were beautiful mountains that reminded us of Switzerland. We bought lovely handmade sweaters for gifts in picturesque shops. Some of the towns had buildings that were far older than the United States, and there were traditions that went with them. I loved the village greens with homes all around these park-like areas. It seems like Romania has always been known for their gypsies. I like their type of clothes (at least the way we picture them), and we weren't disappointed as we drove through a place where the street was lined with these colorful garments for sale. People may not have had much food, but they still made beautiful products.

Dick

We returned to Poland in time to take in the week of a giant tent crusade with Leighton Ford and Steve Hauss as evangelists. This tent crusade has been going each year for the past ten years, even under communism. It is under the direction of an organization led by Dr. Henry, a medical doctor. There were probably 2000 people attending, not counting about 900 children in another tent.

During the week we interviewed a number of key Christian leaders who were there from other parts of Eastern Europe for the crusade. Janina was a special lady who was trained from kindergarten to be a Communist leader. She even turned in her own Christian parents to the Communists. But God got hold of her life and she is now in charge of all the children's ministries for this Polish Christian organization.

Helen

In Poland, our teenage boys were thrilled with the little stands along the road that sold sausages. These greasy pieces of meat had no appeal to me, but the boys liked them. Living with three teenage boys was stimulating. They were there to help, and I don't know how we could have survived without them. They carried equipment, set up our tent, loaded the van and were always available for any job.

Paul gave this advice to Timothy in the Bible, and I believe David, Josh and Jesse tried to live this way: **"Don't let anyone think little of you because you are young. Be their ideal; let them follow you in the way you teach and live; be a pattern to them in your love, your faith, and your clean thoughts. . .Be sure to use the ability God has given you. . .Put those abilities to work; throw yourself into your tasks so that everyone may notice your improvement and progress. Keep a close watch on all you do and think. Stay**

true to what is right and God will bless you and use you to help others." (I Timothy 4:12-16)

Poland is a beautiful country, but all the surrounding countries seemed to want part of it. Poland had a large Jewish community, and the Jews living here were treated like animals under the Nazis during World War II. The horror stories were hard to comprehend, and their meeting places were destroyed or used for other purposes. However, the country itself was not damaged as much as some places, and the ancient buildings were their pride and joy. They even carried on some traditions that had begun hundreds of years ago.

Sally and her boys stayed on in Poland to help with other children's camps; but Dick, Jesse and I had commitments in the Philippines. We needed to return to England and then home to Manila.

Sally

This trip was one to remember all our lives. It brought blessings in countless ways, many of which we are still enjoying.

The privilege of making the videos was very great. It was wonderful to visit so many countries and hear, first-hand, of the conditions for their people in the Eastern Europe of today. Many of those were also a great blessing in and of themselves. Their testimonies amazed us such that we felt, at times, we were "sitting at their feet" rather than conducting interviews!

It was quite unforgettable to listen as NPP talked about being beaten by Securitate men until he lost consciousness and then hear him say he was grateful for this experience. The reason? Through it, he said, God healed him of fear. No challenge could frighten him after that experience. That was a principle we couldn't forget! God changed his attitude and the effects were miraculous.

It was also a time to learn as we listened to those who had suffered in Czechoslovakia. The pastors in big churches there were often removed from their posts by the Communists and placed in tiny villages to get them out of the way, so to speak. But the men we spoke to seized this opportunity to serve in a missionary capacity. And soon those tiny churches had turned into thriving ones with eager believers gathering in large numbers. What an example they proved, in the way they took miserable circumstances and used them for God's glory. There were, in fact, countless examples of moving testimonies in what we heard.

Psalms 62:5-7 seems to describe these heroes we were meeting. We felt like we could hear them saying: **"But I stand silently before the Lord, waiting for Him to rescue me. For salvation comes from Him alone. Yes, He alone is my Rock, my rescuer, defense and fortress—why then should I be tense with fears when troubles come? My protection and success come from God alone. He is my refuge, a Rock where no enemy can reach me."** Would we be this trusting and courageous?

Dick

This is only a very brief report. We are still sorting out our emotions to see how we can respond to what we have seen and heard. And we have nearly 20 hours of videotape that must be edited and made into documentaries. Our desire is to help these people who have suffered for so long and bring their stories and needs to Christians in other parts of the world. Perhaps you can get a better feeling for what we have learned when we put it all together in a video report.

CHAPTER 7

ADVENTURES IN FORGIVING – AND BEING FORGIVEN

We happened to be in town when Dick remembered that he had a very important meeting at Faith Academy, which was anywhere from 30 minutes to an hour and a half away, depending on traffic. Since we lived very near the school and far from town, I needed to go with Dick whenever he went there. I wasn't through shopping and Dick had a few things he needed to accomplish too so we made elaborate plans on an exact time and place to meet. He had the car, and I would have to take a taxi to the meeting place, so we could be on time for his meeting at Faith Academy.

Since I am usually late, I decided to be early and not keep him waiting. I actually did arrive at our agreed meeting place early, and then I waited — and waited — and waited. (This was before the invention of cell phones.) After waiting more than one and a half hours standing in the hot sun and humidity, and knowing there was no possibility now of getting to his meeting on time, I decided to phone the school, just in case they might know if something had happened to him.

When I finally got through, I was informed that Dick was in a meeting, but they would tell him I called. He couldn't call back because I was using the store phone. When I knew he was OK and that nothing bad had happened to him, and when I realized that he had gone off and left me when I had made such a big effort to be early, I was angry! Actually, I was furious! I had been exactly where we said we would meet. I knew I had to call him when the meeting was over, because he had to come back to town to pick me up and take me home. There was no other way for me to get home. At that point, I wasn't sure I wanted to go home with him, but I didn't have any alternative plan.

When we were eventually on the phone together I discovered he was as angry as I was. He informed me that he had waited over an hour for me at our designated meeting place and finally decided to just go on to his meeting without me. And of course, he was late! Dick and I were seldom that upset at the same time. Before I slammed the phone down, I managed to tell him I was still standing in front of Tropical Hut, where I had been for several hours by now. It's a good thing I told him where I was, or he might never have found me.

The air was thick with anger when I climbed into the car. When Dick finally spoke, he wanted to know why I wasn't where we had agreed to meet. I told him in no uncertain terms that I was exactly where I was supposed to be. To make a rather long, unhappy conversation bearable, I will just say that he had waited an hour in front of Uni-Mart while I was about a mile down the road standing outside Tropical Hut. Of course, we both claimed to be right, and I doubt if we ever came to an agreement on that score. After a long silence, we eventually tried to halfway apologize, but it was hard because both of us knew we were right. I eventually forgave Dick and he finally forgave me, but if we had obeyed God with a forgiving attitude, it would have saved hours of strained relationship and stress.

———

I remember hearing someone talk about all of our "instant" products— instant mashed potatoes, instant oatmeal, instant credit cards, instant cash—just about anything you can think of. We are a nation of wanting everything instantly. What we really need is instant forgiveness. Think of how much easier it would have been, if instead of getting more and more upset, I had instantly forgiven him, even if he did leave me.

In Matthew 6:12, The Lord's Prayer says, **"Forgive us our debts as we also have forgiven our debtors."** Mathew 6:14-15 declares: **"For if you forgive other people when they sin against you, your heavenly Father will also forgive you. But if you do not forgive others their sins, your Father will not forgive your sins."** (NIV)

Jesus was certainly our perfect example. He was not only totally innocent, but He spent His life here on earth doing good, helping and healing and loving people. Then He was accused, tortured, beaten and crucified, but His words were, "Father, forgive them. . ."

Actually, it's probably more for our benefit than it is for the one we are forgiving. I don't know where I first heard this, but it has really helped me:

"When we don't forgive, it's like taking poison and expecting the other person to die."

It seems like I have had to ask someone to forgive me more often than I have had to forgive. Like other instructions in the Bible, forgiving is not an option. It's a requirement, a command from God.

Once a shopkeeper in Manila changed my specific order on a nameplate to fit his taste saying, "because this one looks better." I hated the lettering and was furious; it was too late to reorder, and I told him off in no uncertain terms before I stalked out the door. And then God asked, "Helen, would you like to go back now and try to tell that clerk about Jesus and my love?" I knew what the Lord was getting at: I had destroyed any chance of witnessing for Him. My peace was gone and my stomach churned.

The next time we were in town I asked Dick to stop. "Wait just a minute. This won't take long!" If I don't know exactly what I need to say, I always end up ruining everything by adding "but. . ." making void my apology. The shopkeeper probably felt like hiding when I walked through the door, but instead he stood speechless as I calmly said, "I was disappointed when you changed my order and next time please honor my choice. However, I was wrong to react and get angry. I'm a Christian and my actions made Jesus unhappy. Will you please forgive me?"

Apologizing goes against every fiber of my nature and requires each ounce of will power I have at my disposal. Actually, my will power isn't strong enough. So once again, the Lord showed me: *It's not my will power, but God's power in my will.* Never have I seen anyone more shocked than that clerk. In the Philippines, Americans have the reputation of being arrogant, and he just stared in disbelief. But every time I passed by after that, he greeted me as a long-lost friend. Now I could tell him more of Jesus' love. Now he would listen. But it took a change of attitude on my part and became a different kind of adventure.

—*᠁*—

One time I thought that a friend had deliberately caused us to lose all of our meager savings. I became angry and bitter. I refused to forgive him. I'm sure he had no idea of my feeling toward him. Since I didn't have "instant forgiveness," I let my attitude fester toward him until it became a terrible sore. One day when I looked in the mirror I saw the effects it was having on my face. I had lost my joy and looked older and hard. It had begun to affect all of my actions and thoughts and change my personality. Finally it began harming our family and relationships. I was asking God to help me, and I'm sure he was working, but I guess I'm a slow learner.

One day while trying to have my devotions, I became desperate. I took my Bible and went into the bathroom, the only private room in our house. I pictured Jesus standing before me with His hands open. I said, "OK Lord, I am going to give you my anger and bitterness and unforgiving spirit. He doesn't deserve it, but I am going to place it all in Your hands right now." So I went through the motions of taking it from my heart and placing it into Jesus' open hands. Then I put my hands behind my back and said, "It's Yours now, God!" I wrote in my Bible what I had done, with the time and date. I really expected to feel new and different and elated and free.

However, I didn't really feel anything. But I knew I had given it to Jesus. So whenever I saw this man and the feelings began to return, Satan would tell me that I hadn't really forgiven him at all. If I was alone, I would say out loud, "Satan, get away from me and leave me alone. I gave that to Jesus, so just go and bug Him." If others were nearby, I still said it, but not out loud. I didn't want people to think I was crazy and I didn't want to have to explain things. My feelings toward the man did change, but it wasn't instantly. Satan doesn't give in easily and the adventure of a new attitude in forgiving is often a battle between our feelings and obedience to God's commands.

During this time, Corrie ten Boom's writings really helped me a lot. She talked about "cashing the check of God's love that has been poured into our hearts through the Holy Spirit which has been given to us." She also told about forcing her arm forward to shake the hand of a former Nazi guard who had been terribly mean to them as prisoners. With none of the right feelings, she did this as an act of obedience. When she did her part, God changed her heart. And then she told about the "ding dong" principle: when you keep pulling on the rope of a bell, it keeps ringing and even after you stop pulling on the rope, the bell will still ring for a while, but it gets weaker all the time until it stops. She said, "Forgiveness is not an emotion. Forgiveness is an act of the will, and the will can function regardless of the temperature of the heart."

There was a time when I wasn't sure I could forgive someone very close to our family. I had been seriously hurt, but since I didn't ever want to go through the agony of not forgiving again, I gave it to Jesus immediately. The most amazing thing happened as soon as I put it into His hands. It felt like Jesus put his hands on my head and love poured through my body and into the one I thought I couldn't forgive. All feelings of anger and disappointment left and since that time, I have had a wonderful and special relationship with that person.

We often get upset and angry by jumping to conclusions and then discover how wrong we were. One time when I was washing the dishes and my arms were covered with soapsuds, the phone rang. I thought Dick was in the other room and could easily answer. I called to him saying, "I can't get the phone. Will you please answer it?" But it kept ringing and by the time I wiped off all the soap and ran to answer, the person had hung up. This was before the days of answering machines and we were expecting an important call. Needless to say, I was very upset as I went to find out why my husband had not picked up the phone when I asked him to, only to discover that he was not anywhere in the house. He had gone out to the car to fix something and of course he hadn't heard the phone ring. Jumping to conclusions—and so often the wrong ones—is certainly an attitude issue and has always been a major problem with me. Here is a story that probably has helped me as much as anything:

> "It's hard enough to endure the midnight wails of an infant at home, but this baby had cried all the way from Chicago to Newark on the jet plane that left O'Hare Field at 11p.m. As the annoyed passengers deplaned, one of them spoke testily to the father: 'Next time you travel with a baby, take its mother along!'
>
> 'We're meeting her,' replied the father, in a taut voice. 'She came by herself—in a coffin!'
>
> The outspoken passenger's embarrassment is what many people would feel if their criticisms of others

were suddenly spotlighted by full information. It's so easy for us to supply a cocksure explanation of why Mrs. Clabber drove her car into a tree, or why Susie Black stopped coming to church, even if we know little or nothing about the real situation."

———

Sometimes I am so sure of what someone else is thinking that I don't even let them finish their sentence or thought. If I was a certified mind reader and had inside information about people, I might be justified in leaping to conclusions. But, since that's not the case, my attitude should always give the person the benefit of any doubt. When the Bible tells us how to love in I Corinthians 13, it clearly says, **"Love is very patient and kind, never jealous or envious, never boastful or proud, never haughty or selfish or rude. Love does not demand its own way. It is not irritable or touchy. It does not hold grudges and will hardly even notice when others do it wrong. It is never glad about injustice, but rejoices whenever truth wins out. . .Love never fails!"**

My experiences in forgiving are really nothing compared to stories I have read: rapes, murders, unfaithful mates, bodies permanently damaged by drunk drivers, lies. The list is endless.

How much does God require us to forgive? The Bible doesn't put any limit on what and how much we have to forgive. It does help to keep our eyes on *Jesus*, who by His example showed us how to forgive. There is never anything anyone can do to us that compares to what they did to Jesus. Jesus was perfect and never did anything to hurt people. He was kind and loving, but they beat Him and ridiculed Him, put horrible thorns on his Head and finally crucified Him. Not only that, He did something we could not do ourselves: He took all of our sins onto himself so we could not only be forgiven, but we could also forgive others.

We traveled to Eastern Europe several times. One of our trips was very soon after the "Iron Curtain" came down but before the terrible war there. We went again shortly after that awful conflict was over. The thousands of graves we saw were a result of an unforgiving spirit that had been passed down to each new generation. When the opportunity came, all of the hate that had been festering over the years exploded into unimaginable violence, death and destruction, affecting every family in that country. One of the saddest things we heard was a mother telling her young son to "never forget what they did to your brother and father! Someday you must repay them." Jesus is the only one who can change this kind of attitude and bring peace.

CHAPTER 8

ADVENTURES WITH HOSPITALITY AND GUESTS

O ver the years, Dick and I had become very anti-social. The quartet was gone so much of the time that when Dick was home, we wanted the time to be with each other and the children. We wanted our privacy! Just at the time when we were between jobs and struggling to keep afloat financially, we had a guest—an unexpected and uninvited guest! The quartet had met him during their travels, and he made our home his headquarters for several weeks. Even feeding our small children took real planning, but he was a big man and ate ravenously. He could be gone most of the day, but he managed to show up just as we sat down to eat. He never offered to pay for anything, and I resented him.

We were almost to the place of telling our "boarder" it was time for him to leave, when we began reading Hebrews 13. We got as far as the second verse, and it seemed that the Lord was right in the room talking to us. **"Do not neglect to extend hospitality to strangers in the brotherhood—being friendly, cordial and gracious, sharing the comforts of your home and doing your part generously. For through it, some have entertained angels without knowing it."** (AMP)

All the time that I had been disliking this man, the children had been loving him – his jovial personality and constant jokes. Dick and I decided that if this man was from the Lord, we'd better change our attitude toward him. So with God's help we began acting differently. We laughed at his jokes, and they were really funny. We welcomed him when he appeared at meal times, even when there wasn't enough food to go around. Before we realized what was happening, we actually began to enjoy him and he even drew our family closer together.

As so often happens, when our attitude is transformed, circumstances also change. I opened the refrigerator door one day and found it full of food—special things we hadn't had for weeks: roast beef, ground round, apples and even a box of candy. A few days later a note of thanks appeared on the kitchen table. Tucked inside was a $100 bill. While our attitude was wrong, we had an intruder who pulled us apart.

But with an attitude change, it became a beautiful experience for the whole family. And the Lord knew our attitude had to have a makeover before we could survive on the mission field.

To be a good influence on my children, here is something important I try to remember:

WORDS teach much; ACTIONS teach more;
ATTITUDES teach most!

—~~—

It would take an entire book to tell about our adventures with guests in the years that followed. We had the Billy Graham team in our home for lunch and enjoyed an afternoon of music around the piano. The quartet had been in some of their meetings in the U.S., so when they came to Manila, we were privileged to have them as guests at our house.

Often, our mission was host to various groups coming through the Philippines. To give you some idea of why our attitude had to change before we could survive there, here are some statistics: The first five years in Manila we averaged about 50 guest meals a month. One month we fed over 350 guests. We entertained Youth for Christ groups, college choirs, world famous speakers, authors, basketball teams, mission leaders and missionaries traveling through the country. We had people from Europe, Australia, Japan and other Asian countries.

Our lives were totally enriched by the guests we had in our home, and our children began asking, "When are more people coming?" This was in spite of the fact that Carolyn had to give up her bedroom and the other children had to share their rooms. When some of the Faith Academy kids from other countries couldn't go home for vacations, several stayed with us. When a typhoon almost destroyed Faith Academy, we had so many boarding students that you couldn't walk through our living room at night without stepping on someone. We didn't always have enough beds, but we had plenty of floor space.

We listened to all kinds of stories and adventures and customs of other countries. We heard about families, spiritual battles and God's amazing miracles. We sang together and prayed together and learned from each other. But we also played together. Several of the favorite games took place around our dinner table.

"Stinky Pinky" was probably the most popular, and it did require some thinking. Someone had to think of two words that rhymed and then describe them so the rest of us could guess the words they were thinking. As a simple example, someone might give the description "a naked horse." It didn't take long to guess they were thinking "a bare mare." "Stink Pinks" were one-syllable words and "Stinky Pinky" had two-syllables. "Stinkety Pinkety" needed three-syllables, and sometimes we even came up with a Sti-inkety Pi-inkety. One of the best ones was described as "soul-stirring meditation." It took a little longer to come up with the answer of "emotional devotional."

Sometimes we had contests with crazy prizes. Other times Dick would start a story and in the middle of a sentence, he rang a bell. The next person had to continue the story until the bell rang. By the time we got around the table, we had a colorful, crazy and unlikely tale. Guests continue to be a part of our lives, and I will always be thankful that God knows ahead of time what we need, and often the most important thing involves our attitude.

When I was growing up, we could always bring our friends home with us and our parents warmly welcomed them. Often they stayed for meals. Dick and I tried to have this "open house" policy for our children too. The results often brought us entirely new adventures and new friends.

As our children grew older, they wanted to see more of the Philippines. One year, Yvonne and LuAnne were traveling to new places. It was December, and they planned to be home for Christmas. By this time they had met several other young people from different countries. When they started to leave for home, they realized the others had no place to go, so they did the totally normal thing: they invited them to our home for the holidays. In the group that arrived, we welcomed an atheist and a Jew. We always tried to make Jesus the center of our Christmas celebrations. We also attempted to make out guests feel comfortable and join us as part of the family. That year was a new challenge, but we kept our traditions and everyone joined in.

Kathy (my brother's daughter), was teaching English in Japan. This seemed close enough to Manila for her to come and spend Christmas with us. She seldom came alone, but brought her new friends with her. Once again, we had unusual guests when she invited a Buddhist girl to join our family. Kathy was full of surprises, but she felt perfectly at ease in her invitations, and we felt honored that she was part of our family and trusted us. One of our most extraordinary experiences came through Kathy when she invited some fellow teachers to stay with us, even though she wasn't coming with them. A French girl accepted Kathy's invitation and came for five days, leaving us with hilarious stories and memories.

—⁓—

As years go by, it becomes more difficult to remember some of our life-changing experiences. However, I remember that one of the first things we were introduced to upon arrival in the Philippines was the "ministry" of volleyball. We lived on a compound with other missionaries, and most of them had come to Manila because of sports. Dick and I were certainly past our prime for most sports, but we tried to join in as much as possible. Volleyball was easier than most and was really fun. However, this was more than fun. It was a time to invite guests to dinner and then have a game of volleyball.

Most of the time our guests were people who had not met Jesus, and we wanted to get acquainted with them. An informal time of sharing food and games seemed to work perfectly. We got acquainted with each other, and they met other missionary couples in a relaxed different kind of setting. Since many people thought missionaries were "weird," we wanted them to know we were almost normal.

A young couple working for the U.S. Embassy became our special visitors. They enjoyed their time enough to come back almost every week when it only involved volleyball. When their baby died, we were there for them. And when there was danger from a political uprising, they were advocates for us. When she had to leave the country early, he came and stayed with us until he could go. Volleyball gave us opportunities for some extraordinary friendships.

Teaching school at Faith Academy gave us a two-month summer break. During this time, we had a chance to be involved in a different type of ministry. We helped in various camps and even cooked for a youth group. One of our favorite activities was getting acquainted with servicemen on the U.S. Bases. Our family began to be invited to perform and be in charge of banquets and programs on the bases. We often spent several weeks helping out at the Christian Servicemen's Centers. As we became friends with the young men, they began to come to Manila and stay with us when they had a break.

Many of the friendships we developed in the Philippines by inviting people into our home went on to give us some awesome and even astonishing adventures in future years. Several places in the Bible we are given specific instructions about hospitality. I Peter 4:9 tells us, **"Cheerfully share your home with those who need a meal or a place to stay for the night."** Again in Romans 12:13 we are told, **"Get into the habit of inviting guests home for dinner or, if they need lodging, for the night."** God knew how much joy we could have when we opened our hearts and learned to share with a positive and loving attitude.

CHAPTER 9

ADVENTURES WITH SCRIPTURE AND PRAYER

D ick and I learned how important prayer was in a relationship while we were still dating, and we often met
together with the Lord in the prayer room before going to
classes. So we actually learned to pray together as a couple
before we got married. When two redheads are put into close
contact with each other for very long, there is every ingredient
for an explosion. I'm convinced that learning to pray together
was the strong catalyst that kept us madly in love for 58 years,
without a totally destructive explosion. Yes, there were plenty
of small fireworks, but nothing devastating. However, we did
have some important lessons to learn.

We still had two years of college left after we were married.
Since there were so many veterans returning to school after
World War II ended, almost every college and university in
the country found they were totally lacking in proper housing.
Pacific College (now George Fox University) managed to
acquire several rows of "vet's houses." These were in units of
four small apartments attached to each other and were used
as temporary houses on the army bases throughout the U.S.
I'm guessing our college must have had 12–15 of these units
altogether and since Dick was a veteran, we had the privilege
of moving into one of these places. The walls were so thin

that one guy put his fist through the wall into another apartment. They were put together in such a way that the kitchen tables were right next to each other with only the thin wall in between. So if our neighbor hit their table just wrong, it could knock the dishes off in our house. It was hard to have a private conversation in your own home.

We made up a special little drama for our neighbors: Dick would hit his belt against a chair, and I would scream. However, if we were having a real fight, and we didn't want anyone else in on it, we simply didn't talk. At first, these silent periods didn't last long and we were soon back to normal. But each time something like this happened, the silent times grew longer, sometimes lasting more than a day.

One evening when everything was peaceful, Dick said, "Honey, do you realize what we are doing? Every time when we don't agree and don't talk about it, we're laying down a brick between us. We are actually building a wall. When we don't discuss our problems and ignore them, it is like cementing the bricks together. If the wall grows too tall, someday it will be impossible to break it down. And it can get so high, we won't be able to climb over it and reach each other. So let's get rid of it now!" We began talking and apologizing and crying and praying and reading the Bible, and the bricks came apart. The wall crumbled. As we hugged and loved, we decided we never again wanted even a tiny wall separating us. We took Ephesians 4:26-27 as our guide we wanted to follow: **"If you are angry, don't sin by nursing your grudge. Don't let the sun go down with you still angry — get over it quickly, for when you are angry you give a mighty foothold to the devil."**

There were times when we stayed up most of the night talking about our disagreements, hurts, etc. We finally had to come to the conclusion that we would never agree with each other in certain areas, so we just had to agree to disagree, and do it with love. We had to let go of a lot of little things, and keep in mind that we not only came from two different backgrounds, but he was male and I was female so our perspectives were different. We needed to be willing to compromise — to give and take. I believe that learning to pray together from the beginning of our relationship really helped us through the many adjustments of a difficult first year of marriage. We tried to keep the policy of never letting the sun go down on our wrath through most of our wonderful 58 years together. Once again, it took an attitude change to make it work, and we found that we couldn't have changed our attitudes without Jesus.

—∿—

When we moved to the Philippines, we found that one thing we had to get used to were the high walls that surrounded the compound where we lived with other missionary families. Around the top there was sharp broken glass to discourage anyone wanting to climb the wall. We also had big gates that had to be opened and closed again every time we went out or came in. In addition, we had dogs to discourage intruders. It always bothered me, and yet it was a comfort. That doesn't really make sense. But at home we were in our own safe little world, away from the runny-nosed "street urchins" who wanted to touch us and beg for money; away from the open sewers with their smells and mosquitoes; away from the tired and hungry adults; away from the pigs and cows and chickens that roamed the streets; away from the teenagers smoking pot; away from the heat and dirt and needs that surrounded us. Our children could play with the other missionary children inside the walls. They didn't have to be exposed to the dirt and disease and differences of the other world.

When we first arrived I didn't like this at all. I wanted to be part of the Filipino community. After all, this was why we were there. But after a while I began to be thankful for the walls and the separation. It would probably have been perfectly all right to have this haven, except that it wasn't long before I enjoyed the security and comfort of our compound too much.

It was easier to keep from becoming too involved—easier to shut out people and situations that bothered us!

And then one day I read Isaiah 58. The whole chapter is good. By "good," I mean it really spoke to me. But verses 7 through 11 said, **"I want you to share your food with the hungry and bring right into your own homes those who are helpless, poor and destitute. Clothe those who are cold and don't hide from relatives who need your help. If you do these things, God will shed His own glorious light upon you. He will heal you; your godliness will lead you forward, and goodness will be a shield before you, and the glory of the Lord will protect you from behind. Then, when you call, the Lord will answer. 'Yes, I am here,' He will quickly reply. All you need to do is to stop oppressing the weak, and to stop making false accusations and spreading vicious rumors! Feed the hungry! Help those in trouble! Then your light will shine out from the darkness, and the darkness around you shall be as bright as day. And the Lord will guide you continually, and satisfy you with all good things, and keep you healthy too; and you will be like a well-watered garden, like an ever-flowing spring."**

I thought, "This is excellent! I must share it with my family." And so after breakfast, we read it together. Now, I honestly thought it was important and a great idea! But at the same time, I didn't know how to begin to obey, and I didn't really think through what it could mean to my security. It got to me, but I discovered the penetration wasn't very deep.

Later in the week, I came home from town, hot, tired and exhausted. I stepped from the car, opened the gate and started to drive in. I couldn't believe what I was seeing! Little Filipino boys of assorted ages and sizes were running in and out of my house! Some were carrying glasses of juice and eating cookies. They were noisy, excited and dirty, but obviously having a wonderful time. I won't tell you about my first reaction. (It certainly wasn't that of a lovable, dedicated, Christ-like missionary who had just read Isaiah 58 and thought it was great!) However, I only had about 10 seconds to react because Jon appeared at my car door. My mouth was open, but before I had a chance to reveal my thoughts, my quiet teenage son was saying, "Remember the Scripture you read Mom? The one about bringing right into your home the hungry, poor, etc.? I just decided to try it! These are my new friends. Fellas, meet my mom. She's the greatest!"

Well, Jon's "great" Mom did a lot of thinking as she worked her way through the maze of boys and into her once clean kitchen. Luming (our wonderful house girl) was standing there somewhat dazed and bewildered by this strange turn of events. She moaned, "He fed them everything! There are no more cookies, crackers, cake, juice, fruit, pop! I couldn't stop him!" The small strangers kept running through the house, touching and admiring things they had obviously never seen before. By American standards we might fall into the category of low middle class, but by their standards we must have seemed like millionaires!

Jon finally gathered the boys outside and for a while played games with them. And then he told them about Jesus. Although they probably didn't understand very much of his English, they couldn't miss his language of love. While I thought the message of Isaiah sounded good, Jon was the one who really understood what it meant, and he did something about it!

Later, Jon came and thanked me for being such a "cool" mom! I wonder, does he really know how "uncool" I am? If he does know what I am really like and is trying to help me, he sure knows how to get through! People are more important than things or projects, or even privacy. Once again, the Lord had to show me my attitude that needed to change, and He used one of my children to be an example.

Another time, I was lying on the floor of our living room and began talking to the Lord. "Father, I'm nearly out of grocery money, and the month is only half gone. How can I get more? What shall I do?" I don't know what I expected the Lord to do or say, but He did talk to me. It was very clear, "Give 10% of your grocery money to help feed someone who is hungry." Now I certainly didn't expect to hear something like that. I'm not even sure I was expecting to hear anything. But my quick reply was, "Are You sure you heard me, Lord? What I said was that I didn't have enough grocery money for my family!" And I heard it again, "Give 10% of your grocery money to help feed someone who is hungry."

It just so happened that the next month was December – you know, the time when we needed extra money for special meals, guests, fudge and fun things! But I decided I had better at least try to follow the instructions I had heard when I was praying. I took out the 10% from my grocery allotment before I spent any money for our family. This was extra money. We had already taken tithes and offerings from our whole salary.

The most amazing thing happened. It was like blinders were taken from my eyes, and I began to see ways we were wasting foods. At the same time, I suddenly had brilliant ideas of how to use things I had been throwing away. It was like the Lord just gave me some incredible new recipes: simple, delicious things that I still get requests for whenever I serve them. We seemed to be eating better, and at the end of the month I still had money left over, even with all the Christmas celebrations. I really can't explain it all, but it certainly paid off to follow the instructions I heard while talking to God.

———

The Lord has shown me how to act in love, even when I don't feel like it. But sometimes I forget and God has to remind me again. Shortly before we were to leave Manila for the U.S. with our Madri-Gals & Guys group, we began getting phone calls from a pastor in the U.S. We were scheduled to sing in his church on a Sunday morning. However, we were also scheduled to sing at another church for an earlier service the same morning. The pastor of the early church said he would do everything he could to get us to the next service on time. But the pastor of the later service wanted us to cancel the first church. He was afraid we might be late, or we might make a disturbance when we came in, or we might not be as "fresh" for his service. Clearly, this man could think of no one but himself.

I began to totally dislike this man long before we even reached the U.S. After much consultation with the adults in our group, our business manager called the pastor and told him that it seemed we had too many problems for his church, so we would just cancel his service. At that point, the pastor panicked and said we couldn't do that because he had advertised we were coming. He finally reluctantly agreed to the original agreement that we would take the other church as planned. But he still kept calling and giving suggestions and instructions. Our choir kids had no idea what was going on, but I really resented him. He was selfish, obnoxious, over-bearing and demanding.

We always had prayer together before every service and our choir was having a tremendous impact wherever they went. If anyone from the church wanted to join us in our prayer time, they were very welcome. It was a time of bonding, first with the Lord and also with each other. As I was getting my music ready, I began asking the Lord to give us a good service in spite of the pastor. I'm sure it was from God when I suddenly realized that my attitude could ruin the service. It might even keep someone from finding Jesus. So I said, "Lord, please help me to love this man." And I clearly heard, "I have already shown you how to love. Now it's up to you!" I knew what He meant. God had already taught me that love is an action, not a feeling. And He has shown us how to love in His word, especially in I Cor. 13. So when the man I disliked came to our prayer time, I knew what I had to do. But I didn't want to lie, so I had to really think about what I wanted to say. With every ounce of willpower, I went to him, introduced myself, put my hand out to shake his and said, "Thank you for joining us today. We want to honor the Lord in your service." The very moment that I took the first step, God changed my attitude from anger to love—His love—and we had a wonderful service and fellowship in that church.

Another experience that happened on one of our choir trips to the U.S. is something I would just as soon forget, but it's probably important to remember. This world is not our permanent home, and it is a battlefield. Satan will never leave us alone. I Peter 5:8 warns, **"Be careful — watch out for attacks from Satan, your great enemy. He prowls around like a hungry, roaring lion, looking for some victim to tear apart. Stand firm when he attacks. Trust the Lord."**

Our Madri-Gals and Guys were constantly winning other young people to the Lord, but the two adult couples (Arvans and Cadds) were constantly hearing all the problems of the churches. One church was in mourning over a pastor who had run off with his secretary. In another church, it was the head deacon who left his wife for a teenage girl. Depression over some of these circumstances, tired bodies and pressure from constant meetings began to affect our dispositions.

I think Dick and I had the most beautiful relationship possible, and yet one day, we became angry at each other. For the first time on the whole tour, a church we sang for put Dick and me in a deluxe motel all by ourselves. This should have been a wonderful, relaxing time together, and yet by the time we reached our room we were hardly speaking. When we did speak, it wasn't with love or in an effort to understand each other. Every word seemed to be angry and hateful. I can't ever remember being that angry. Dick obviously felt exactly the same way. As I clung to a dresser for support, he remained across the room. The air was charged with our hostility! My feelings urged me to walk out of that motel and never come back. Always before when Dick and I were at odds with each other, I desperately wanted to make up, but not this night. We both felt like we were bound and couldn't possibly move toward each other. Even breathing was difficult.

Once again, Jesus somehow broke through the barrier and revealed the problem to Dick. My husband said flatly, "I think this is Satan." Unemotionally, I agreed. Again Dick spoke, "Then we need to get rid of him." Again I agreed, yet neither of us could move one step closer to each other, even to pray.

After a few moments of silence, having no feelings or desire to pray, and with only a knowledge in our heads that Christ alone could take care of this ugly situation, we deliberately and by a forcing of our wills, moved contrary to our feelings and called upon Jesus to help us. Then Dick commanded, "Satan, in the name of Jesus Christ and because He defeated you at Calvary, I demand that you get out of this room and leave us alone."

There is no adequate description for what happened next. It was like turning night into day, or winter into summer. We both felt as though chains fell off, and we were so weak we could hardly stand. Instead of heaviness and hate, the room was filled with light and love. Dick and I fell into each other's arms, completely exhausted physically from this spiritual battle. This was a new and very unwelcome experience for us.

We had no intention of relating this event to anyone. After all, everyone knew we had a special love for each other, and our pride did not want to reveal this crisis. Yet as we talked together the next day, we realized that if Satan was so determined to destroy our ministry, maybe we should recognize him and be alert for his battle tactics. The next night during our prayer and share time before the service, we related our struggle to the kids and warned of Satan's desire to ruin everything. We were truly on a battlefield. Every time a young person turned from drugs to Jesus, it meant we had invaded Satan's territory and Christ had gained a victory.

The young people began to express their battles too, and suddenly one girl joyfully declared, "This is fantastic! If Satan is working so hard against us, it must mean that Jesus wants to use us even more." We began to praise God. And our ministry became even more effective.

We remembered a story told to us by a veteran missionary from China several years earlier, and it seemed appropriate now for our choir kids:

After World War II an unscrupulous Chinese man got possession of a German Luger and several rounds of ammunition, one of a kind in that part of China. He went into the interior of China and began holding up buses and terrorizing the people. He became such a menace, the government sent out men to capture him and after a struggle they did succeed in arresting the bandit. They emptied his gun and put the ammunition in their pockets. The law officers tied up their captive and headed him off toward prison.

While stopping to eat along the way, somehow the outlaw broke loose and even managed to find the gun. It wasn't long before he was out stealing and terrorizing as he had done before. Once again more government men were sent out to find him by riding the busses. Before long the bus they were riding was held up and everyone was told to form a line outside with their hands up. And once again the bandit began stealing from each person. But when he came to the government men, they said, "You don't frighten us!" This infuriated the thief and he was threatening to kill them when they calmly announced, "Your gun is empty because we have your ammunition." When confronted with this fact, he gave up.

Jesus took Satan's ammunition when he died and rose again. Satan is still around stealing and terrorizing, and we allow him to scare us into submission unless we remember that Jesus defeated Satan at Calvary. We have nothing to fear when we have Jesus. PRAISE THE LORD!

Satan has all kinds of tactics, and the Bible tells us that he can even change himself to appear as an angel of light. But it's great to read I Corinthians 15:57-58: **"How we thank God for all of this! It is he who makes us victorious through Jesus Christ our Lord! So, my dear brothers, since future victory is sure, be strong and steady, always abounding in the Lord's work, for you know that nothing you do for the Lord is ever wasted as it would be if there were no resurrection."**

Ephesians 6:13-18 also tells us how to put on God's armor in order to defeat the devil: **"So use every piece of God's armor to resist the enemy whenever he attacks, and when it is all over, you will still be standing up. But to do this, you will need the strong belt of truth and the breastplate of God's approval. Wear shoes that are able to speed you on as you preach the Good News of peace with God. In every battle you will need faith as your shield to stop the fiery arrows aimed at you by Satan. And you will need the helmet of salvation and the sword of the Spirit — which is the Word of God. Pray all the time. Ask God for anything in line with the Holy Spirit's wishes."**

One of my sons was praying over a friend that was unconscious and appeared to be in a life and death battle with Satan. The only thing he felt he could do was to visualize putting on God's armor, and at this point Satan began to retreat and the battle was won.

———⁓⁓———

I read something the other day that I totally agree with:

"Prayer is the key to making life an adventure."

And prayer is also the key to changing our attitude from negative to positive.

There are numerous books written about prayer, but I don't think we will ever understand how or when or why God answers our prayers, or answers them in ways we don't expect or even like. I do know He has told us to **"pray without ceasing"** (I Thessalonians 5:17). I have seen and experienced real miracles in answer to prayer, but I have also felt the disappointment when my prayers were not answered, at least in the way I wanted them answered. One explanation I have heard is that God always answers, but His answers are "Yes!" or "No!" or "Not yet!" One thing I do know: the Lord loves us, and His love is perfect, and He knows what is best for us.

He doesn't make mistakes, and I trust Him. This is not easy when someone we love isn't healed, and they suffer and die. It is easier and exciting to see God heal someone instantly. I've experienced both kinds of answers to prayer.

One time, in the Philippines, I had a skin problem. It began when I discovered a reddish spot about the size of a quarter on one of my legs. It never actually hurt or gave me any trouble, but I dabbed medicine on it when I remembered. The spot was there for more than a year and remained the same. I seldom even thought about it. Only once did I have any apprehension about it. That was when Dick teasingly remarked that it might be leprosy.

One morning, I realized I was scratching. It was almost an unconscious act, but looking at the spot on my leg, I noticed it was larger and no longer alone. Several other smaller spots had appeared nearby. Now I remembered the medicine in earnest, but the spots kept spreading and nothing was able to stop the growth. I consulted doctors and tried different medications that they recommended. I began to itch constantly and no longer was it a small reddish spot on one leg, but both legs were infected with horrible-looking, runny, open sores.

One week while I was sitting in Sunday School class, I realized the woman across from me was looking at my legs. I didn't appreciate it, yet I couldn't blame her for staring. My kind of sores were only seen on dirty beggars, not on clean, educated Americans! I came to the conclusion that perhaps I shouldn't attend any more public meetings.

The next day my neighbor, Lyn Montgomery, and I were talking together in the driveway between our two houses. She began to question me, "Helen, did you see a skin specialist?" I could answer that one, "Yes!" "But hasn't the medicine helped at all?" To this I replied, "No! And I'm going into seclusion; I can't stand the way people look at me." Then Lyn simply inquired, "Have you prayed about it?" What a question to ask a missionary! Don't we always pray about everything?

Yes, I guess you might say I prayed, but only a very nebulous, un-expectant kind of prayer, such as, "Lord, take care of my leg." Actually, I hadn't thought about praying for myself in this area. Lyn and I had been interested in healing for this day and age. We wondered if Jesus really meant it when He said in John 14:11-14, **"Just believe it—that I am in the Father and the Father is in me. Or else believe it because of the mighty miracles you have seen me do. In solemn truth I tell you, anyone believing in me shall do the same miracles I have done, and even greater ones, because I am going to be with the Father. You can ask Him for anything, using My name, and I will do it, for this will bring praise to the Father because of what I, the Son, will do for you. Yes, ask anything, using my name, and I will do it!"** Even if Jesus meant this for *today*, it must be for someone else—not me!

In all honesty, I had to answer Lyn's question, "Well, sort of, maybe—but not really! I don't have much faith along that line." She calmly announced, "I'm going in my house and pray for you right now!" She turned around and left me standing alone. I shrugged and withdrew into my house to feel sorry for myself.

Itching had become so routine for me that I had to concentrate in order to keep from scratching. I sat down at my desk and tried to write letters. I suppose an hour went by when I was startled to realize that I didn't itch. I glanced at my legs to see what was wrong and could hardly believe my eyes! The ugly running sores of an hour ago were drying up.

I couldn't find Lyn fast enough to exclaim, "You've been praying for me!" In her calm, matter of fact way, she responded, "Sure! And your legs are better, aren't they!" She was making a statement rather than questioning, She had complete confidence God would answer her prayer and heal my legs.

By afternoon the sores were all dried up, and within two days there wasn't a sign of them. Even my little "quarter size" sore was gone, after having it for about a year and a half. Maybe God would do more miracles if we would just ask Him.

—*m*—

Periodically, Dick and I would speak at Union Church in Manila. I don't know what our topic was one morning when we spoke, but I evidently said something about talking to the Lord and mentioned that He told me what to do. There was a stranger in the audience that day, a professional gambler who didn't make a habit of going to church. But a few weeks later at the same church, he came to me and said, "I couldn't believe it when you said that God talked to you. I thought you were crazy. But I was interested enough to come back and learn more and I have accepted Jesus as my Savior. Did you actually hear God's voice?"

That's not an easy question to answer. I can't say I heard a voice. But there have been times when I knew exactly what God was saying to me. There was no mistake. I heard it! He has told me things to do. God does talk to us through His Word the Bible, but to me, prayer is a conversation with the Lord. We not only talk, but we need to listen, too.

One evening, we were invited to a beautiful restaurant as guests of a wealthy businessman and his wife. We should have had a wonderful time, but it turned out to be a miserable evening. For several hours, I listened to a monologue from this wealthy woman. When I tried to respond, it didn't work! I don't think I had the opportunity to finish even one sentence the whole night. I came away disliking this lady and had no desire to spend more time with her. (Later, when we finally got acquainted, we became very good friends and had lots of experiences together.)

It made me wonder if God might get weary of a one-sided conversation. Think of the terrific wisdom and joy we are missing when we do all of the talking. Prayer is communicating with our Creator, the King of all Kings. The greatest privilege in the world is to be able to come directly into His presence and worship and share with Him, but with a listening ear. Sometimes I'm not sure if it's God speaking to me, or if it's just my own mind, my desires, or my emotions. But other times, there is no question about what God is saying. I know He's talking to me and giving me instructions.

—⚡—

Our youngest daughter, LuAnne, was on her way to South Africa to be an apprentice photographer for a newspaper there. She was coming through Hong Kong and we were in Manila — only a little over an hour away by plane. It was her birthday and we hadn't seen her for ages. She would be in Hong Kong for about three hours. Was it worth the expense to fly over and *maybe* get to see her if connections were perfect? There were so many questions and problems that, after debating every angle, Dick and I finally decided it was an expensive gamble, and we couldn't do it. Too many things had to be timed perfectly and airline officials had to cooperate.

However, two days before Lu was to arrive in Hong Kong, Dick and I were having our personal devotions in separate rooms. I can't explain it, but suddenly I knew we must go to Hong Kong. I went to Dick and said, "Honey, we have to go to Hong Kong." He instantly replied, "I know!" We both knew God had spoken to us. Complications of time, travel and meeting are too numerous to mention and dealing with immigration, plane tickets and reservations at that late date would be considered impossible. But when God is in charge, *nothing* is *impossible!* He worked out every detail. We not only got on a plane, but they put us in business class and we arrived in Hong Kong about an hour before LuAnne arrived. This meant that we were in the same area as Lu's arrival, so we didn't even have to talk to any officials or ask for special privileges.

LuAnne came at the right time, and as we were talking, Lu suddenly said, "My money belt! It's missing!" The neck pouch contained everything of importance: her passport, tickets, visas, identification, traveler's checks, credit cards, etc.! Panic set in when LuAnne realized she had probably been robbed when she was asleep and that she couldn't continue her flight. She really was helpless and couldn't do anything. They wouldn't even let her leave the airport, and yet the airport closed down for the night, and she couldn't stay there either.

At this point, we were probably the only people in the world who could help her. We signed papers, swore she was our daughter, cancelled credit cards, paid bills, etc. We were the last people out of the airport, and they let her go with us to our hotel, with firm instructions to get a new passport in the morning and return to the airport to prove she was an American citizen. The next plane to South Africa didn't leave for a week, but it took us most of that time to get the visa and everything else in place. However, we had a wonderful seven days with our daughter, and she really needed us to help get important papers and documents since she had no identification.

Later, we heard on the news that a prominent black leader had been killed and South Africa had some of their very worst riots. Many people were killed, including photographers for newspapers. This is the job Lu would have been doing. Although LuAnne was lamenting the fact that she missed out on the action, Dick and I were convinced that God had intervened and protected and possibly saved her life. We knew God had spoken to us, and we had obeyed. I wish it were always that clear. Perhaps it's because we usually do all the talking or are too busy to listen when God wants to have a conversation with us.

The last day before we went back to Manila and LuAnne continued her trip to Africa, we had an interesting experience. We were staying on Lantau Island, about an hour by ferry from the city. Our special friends, the Begbies, had as many guests as they could possibly accommodate. We couldn't stay with them, but they found us an empty Christian campground that would let us sleep in a cabin there. It was about a 20-minute walk from the ferry. The weather had been lovely the past week, but as we were walking to the camp, there was a sudden cloudburst. We didn't have any coats or sweaters or umbrellas or even a newspaper to cover us. We passed a small hotel, so stopped on their front porch in hopes of the rain stopping. We looked and felt like we had been swimming. One of the hotel helpers saw us and felt sorry for us. He soon came out with some huge plastic bags to partially cover us. We finally made it to our cabin, and we were totally drenched!

This created a problem. We had no way to dry our clothes, and we had to leave very early in the morning to catch our plane. We would have a 20-minute walk to the ferry with our suitcases; an hour on the ferry, a long taxi ride to the airport (if we could get a taxi that time of day), and we needed to be there an hour early. Since we only had one fan and no heat, we tried hanging our clothes so the fan would blow on them. We really didn't want to pack wet clothes in our suitcases. We got up extra early because LuAnne wanted to shower and wash her hair since she had a long trip ahead of her. Dick and I were trying to get ready to go when Lu began yelling for help. Her body was covered with soap and her hair full of shampoo when suddenly there was no more water. No one had told us they turned the water off at a certain time.

Dick grabbed a kettle and ran around to every faucet he could find on the campground and drained the tiny bit of water left in each of them. I then, very carefully so as not to waste even one drop, poured the precious water over LuAnne's head and body. We did the best we could, but now our time was running out. If we missed the early ferry, we would miss our plane. We wrapped our still damp clothes in the plastic and raced to the docks. We barely made it on time, but we did manage to catch our planes.

It was hard to tell Lu goodbye, especially knowing where she was going and the dangers she would probably encounter. But remembering how the Lord had protected her earlier, we knew He was in control and could take care of her far better than we could. And He had given us the special gift of being together for a full week.

—*m*—

I am often reminded of another story because I have hanging in my hallway a lovely gold-framed cross-stitch picture of a butterfly. This is one of my prized possessions as Yvonne made it especially for me to go in our section of the big house where we lived together. Whenever I stop to admire this special picture, I usually end up crying and thanking God for loving us enough to be concerned about "little things" in our lives.

Steve's wife, Shelley, and Yvonne were both pregnant, and they had just learned how to cross-stitch. Both of them were working on a project, and it seemed to be relaxing for them, though it would have driven me crazy. They took their projects with them wherever they went, and Yvonne was especially intent on finishing hers. Since Yvonne was sick most of the nine months of pregnancy, it helped take her mind off her stomach.

Our family kept singing together, and we just adjusted the parts to accommodate whoever was available. At this point in time, there were three couples: Dick and me, Steve and Shelley, and Walt and Yvonne. All of us sang and we used recorded accompaniment, which required a certain amount of equipment. One Sunday evening we had a meeting at a small church on the other side of the city from where we lived. It was also in a poor area of Manila that was notorious for crime. We had a long hot ride, and we went early enough for the guys to set up the equipment before the service began. This was an ideal time for the girls to work on their new hobby. Yvonne was almost finished with her project, and was very excited about what she had done. I really didn't pay much attention to what they were working on. I took a book to read instead.

We had a good service and fellowship with people afterward, but we were hot and tired. Someone remembered something we really needed at the grocery store, so we stopped there for just a few minutes. And then we did the only natural thing to do: we stopped at our favorite ice cream parlor. By the time we got home, it was dark and late and we were tired. As we unloaded the car, the girls reached under the seat to get their cross-stitch materials. Shelley found hers, but Yvonne's was not there. We all searched our large van, but we couldn't find it. We decided that maybe she left it under a bench at the church, or it could have fallen out of the car when we kept getting out at the places where we stopped on the way home. At any rate, it was gone!

Walt and Yvonne went into their room and as Dick and I were heading for ours, we heard the most heart-wrenching sobs. We knew Yvonne had been putting every spare minute into this endeavor for weeks, and it was almost finished. She didn't feel good, was terribly tired, and now it sounded like her heart was breaking. It was more than Dick and I could bear. We talked it over, and decided that we would go back to every place where we had been, even as far as the church. We didn't tell Walt and Yvonne what we were doing. We just went.

On our way back to town, we did a lot of praying. We told the Lord that we knew it wasn't the most important thing in the world, but it did mean a lot to Yvonne. We asked if He would please show us where it was. The first place we stopped was the parking lot of the grocery store. We went to where we had parked and with flashlights, began searching the area and looking under cars. Since every place in the Philippines has guards and there are so many robberies, it's a wonder we didn't get shot. We did not find a sign of the lost cloth.

We really thought we would have to go back to the church and find the pastor, but we went to the ice cream place, just in case. We were once again searching under cars, around bushes, and the whole area with our flashlights. I was just getting ready to go inside and ask if anyone had turned it in, when a guard came and asked us what we were doing. I told him all about Yvonne, that she was pregnant and sick and that she had been working on the thing for many days. I tried to describe what it looked like when he suddenly said, "Wait." He went over to another set of bushes, reached into his bag he kept there and pulled out Yvonne's butterfly cross-stitch. "Is this what you're talking about? I found it on the ground, and since I had no idea where it came from, I was going to take it home with me." I think I threw my arms around him and hugged him. We couldn't thank him enough. Dick tried to give him some money, but he wouldn't take it.

I think we thanked the Lord all the way home, and we couldn't get over how much He cares for every thing that concerns us, no matter how small it might be. There were so many things that seemed almost impossible, but God took care of all the details. When we knocked on Yvonne's bedroom door and handed her the cross-stitch, she cried again, but this time it was for joy. She hadn't even known that we left. And now she told me that she had been working on this as my Christmas present. It was going to be a surprise, but she couldn't keep from telling me. However, it was a surprise, because she had it framed in a beautiful gold frame, and it has been hanging in a prominent place in every house we have lived in since that time at least 31 years ago. Every time I look at it, I still thank the Lord. He does care about us. He loves us and likes to show it in so many ways, even "little things!"

—⁓—

A more recent experience was when I misplaced a special red-covered book that had all of the information I needed about each of the television shows we did for six years. Before we left the Philippines, Dick had made me videos of most of the shows, but the forms that told what was on each program were lost. I had seen this red book in the house where I am living, but that had been several years ago, and I had been searching the house from top to bottom for about four years. I often forgot about it for a while, but then something would remind me and I began the search again. I decided I wanted to make a DVD of family members doing something special, as a memory for my grandchildren so they would know and remember Dick and others. I knew some of the things I wanted to use were in the big box of videos, but the information on how to find things was in the red book.

As I lay in bed trying to convince myself it was time to get up, I thought, "I really want that book!!" So I did as I had often done over the years, I prayed, "Lord, please show me where the book is." Then suddenly it was more than the half-hearted unthinking words I had repeated so often before. I think I even said it loud and clear, "Father God, if that book is in this house somewhere, please show me where it is today. I really need it now. I don't think it's here, and I have no faith at all, but if it is here, I want it now. Please let me know somehow so I can stop thinking and looking for it."

After my very clear request to God, I got up and started my usual morning routine. I had put a lot of papers and things on my bed that needed sorting, so that was my first job. I stood up and leaned over the bed, but my back began to hurt. I needed to sit down. LuAnne had bought my dogs some dog stairs so they could get up on the bed since they were getting too old to jump up. It was conveniently right where I needed it, so I did the natural thing to do: I sat on it. However, this unit was made for small dogs, not for big people and it collapsed. I fell backward pretty hard and hit my head on the floor. Old people really shouldn't fall, because they often break bones and do other serious things to their bodies. I waited a few minutes to see where I hurt.

Amazingly, I didn't hurt anywhere and seemed fine. But because I was on the floor and next to the curtain covering my closet, I decided to turn over and look to see if I might have left some dirty socks in any shoes since I planned to do laundry that day. I pulled out a pair of nice shoes and noticed that there was something on the floor behind the shoes: an old box full of my special "How to Organize" magazines. (Obviously, they hadn't been used!) I thought I might as well throw out the whole box, but decided to take a quick look at these special magazines I had saved. I picked up a few and right in the middle of them was my long lost red book. I would never have looked on the floor at the back of my closet behind the shoe rack if I hadn't fallen in that exact place.

When I was telling someone about how God answered my very specific prayer, they began to laugh and remarked that they could just picture the Lord and some angels enjoying watching me and discussing about how long it would take me to find the book. I spent the rest of the day thanking God and thinking how creative He is and how much fun He must have at times like that.

Sometimes we think God doesn't care, but Scripture tells us the opposite. **"Don't worry about anything; instead, pray about everything; tell God your needs and don't forget to thank Him for His answers. If you do this you will experience God's peace, which is far more wonderful than the human mind can understand. His peace will keep your thoughts and your hearts quiet and at rest as you trust in Christ Jesus."** (Philippians 4:6-7) It does involve an attitude of trust, obedience and gratitude.

CHAPTER 10

ADVENTURES WITH BILLIE AND TELEVISION

I mentioned in another section that we were invited to dinner with important people to a lovely restaurant with great food, but I had a miserable evening. I had a bad attitude, but it was for "a good reason." I was sitting next to someone who blew in like a tornado and took over every conversation. I really didn't like her. Her name was Billie and with her husband, Ciso Padilla, they owned the beautiful building we were sitting in. They had come to know Jesus through watching the *700 Club* on TV. Ciso's life was changed and he was so excited about Jesus that he wanted everyone else to know Jesus too. To him, television was the answer! Since they owned a big factory and had the money, he went to Germany and bought a million dollars worth of top quality television equipment. Dick was asked to help them start a Christian TV station.

Billie liked Dick. Every time she came into the television office, she looked around to see who was there and inevitably spotted Dick. Her habit was to walk to his desk and begin to tell him all of her problems. Each evening when Dick came home, he would say to me, "Honey, Billie really needs a woman to talk to. She needs a friend." My firm answer was always the same: "She doesn't need me! She doesn't even know who I am!"

Because of his work at the television station, Dick was involved in a Bible study with a group of professionals and businessmen. Most of them were new Christians, and they met for breakfast each Saturday morning. They had become close enough to trust each other with their personal problems, and many of their problems involved relationship issues with their wives. Dick thought the wives should have a time together, too. I was still in my pajamas when Dick was getting ready to go to his Saturday group. He came to me and said, "Honey, why don't you give Billie a call and see if she might like to start meeting with the wives of these men? I think you could really help them." My instant answer was, "I can't. She still doesn't know my name, or that I am your wife. And besides, she has so many servants I could never get through to her. She wouldn't know who I am, and she's probably still in bed." As far as I was concerned, that was the end of the conversation — permanently!

My husband did not consider it the end at all. Just before going out the door he handed me a slip of paper and said, "Here's Billie's phone number. Do try to call her." I had no intention of ever trying to call her. I got my Bible and planned to have a nice quiet time with the Lord. But the strangest thing happened. No matter where I tried to read in the Bible, all I could see was, "Call Billie!" I tried to pray, but couldn't get past, "Call Billie!" I finally decided the Lord wanted me to call Billie! My response was, "OK Lord, I will try to call Billie. But I know she won't answer the phone. It's impossible to get through to her. And even if I do get to talk to her, I don't have a clue what to say and she won't have any idea who I am. You will have to totally take over."

I picked up the phone and dialed. Amazingly, Billie answered the phone herself. I introduced myself as Dick's wife and mumbled something about our husbands having this wonderful Bible Study and fellowship time and I wondered if maybe she might like to start a group with their wives. She shot back instantly with, "No!! I hate women's groups. All they do is talk about other people and their problems, and if you share anything, they immediately spread it all over the country." I thought, "Great! That's the end of a crazy idea. I don't have to worry about it any more." But instead, I heard myself saying, "OK I will never invite anyone. You can be the one to invite whoever you want, or you don't have to invite anyone. I thought you might like to have someone to talk to." I couldn't believe I said that. It didn't come from me. I guess the Lord took me at my word when I told Him that He would have to totally take over.

There was dead silence on the other end of the line, and I figured she had hung up on me, which wouldn't have surprised me at all. But suddenly she said, "My driver will pick you up in 10 minutes." Remember, I was still in my pajamas, and she didn't live that far away. I am not fast at getting ready in the morning, but I hurried to get dressed because I figured that if she said "10 minutes," it probably meant exactly 10 minutes. I'm sure it is very obvious that I did not have the right attitude. It was definitely not good! Sometimes we have to go against our feelings and our wrong attitudes and just obey God!

So we met, just the two of us. I mostly listened, but I learned a lot that day. I learned that no matter how much money you have, it can't solve all of your problems. It can't make your children obey or love you. It can't keep your kids off drugs. It can't choose your children's friends. I found that I could learn to like Billie if I got acquainted with her. I learned that although first impressions are important, they are not always correct. I learned that we need to give people a chance, and best of all, I found a new friend.

For the next few years we met together every Saturday morning when both of us were in town. Billie did invite her choice of friends, mostly older Spanish ladies. My special friend and also a friend of Billie, Ruth Thomas, soon joined us. Ruth and I were in charge of the Bible study part, although it was almost impossible to do much teaching, because some of Billie's friends liked to talk as much as she did. Most of the time the sharing and talking were vitally important, and a few appropriate Scriptures and a little discussion were all that was needed.

I often wondered if any of them heard anything we said, and yet I often heard Billie quoting Ruth or me to someone else. Actually, I was the one who needed a total makeover—a new attitude. And with that change, there were startling results. It's amazing what God can and does do when attitudes are right.

Because of martial law, the TV station never got permission to go on the air, but Billie and her husband wanted their studio to be used to make Christian programs. Then the programs could be aired on the most powerful station in the Philippines. Billie decided she wanted a show for women and she asked Dick and me to produce and direct it. She had no idea what she wanted, and so we had total freedom to do whatever we wanted. This was exciting, because. . .well, let me backtrack.

When Dick and I first saw television sets appear in stores for home use, I remember asking Dick if maybe someday we could afford to buy one. "Who wants black and white?" he replied. "I'll wait until it comes out in full color!" He laughed sarcastically, because he actually thought he was making a big joke and that it would never be in color. And we did eventually buy a black and white TV.

When we arrived in the Philippines in 1962, we were surprised to find that they had more TV stations than New York City. At first, only the rich had sets, but before long television became a top priority, often before food and clothes!

There were no local Christian programs on television until Greg Tingson, a dynamic Filipino evangelist, had a vision and the financial backing for a live Gospel TV broadcast in Manila. When he first approached Dick for help in 1965, we thought he simply meant as an outside advisor, but in reality he was asking Dick to be the producer and director. Dick tried to decline since he had never done anything like this, but because he had been on television with the quartet, he was considered an expert. I was concerned about Dick's already overloaded schedule, and the thought of adding this colossal responsibility didn't make me the slightest bit happy. In fact, I was angry! I wanted to protect my husband and have a little of him left for me.

Dick prayed for God's direction, while I had a terrible spiritual struggle. I knew without any question it was a full-time job, and Dick already had several other full-time jobs; so I fought it with all my energy. But since my fight turned out to be against God, I lost! Dick followed God's leading instead of mine, for which I am truly thankful! My selfish motives completely blinded me to the tremendous opportunity of telling millions about Jesus and His love. God reminded me through His Word in Matthew 10:39: **"If you cling to your life** (or Dick's life), **you will lose it; but if you give it up for me, you will save it."** My attitude almost ruined Dick's ministry, health and our relationship, but God stepped in and rescued me from myself. When I gave not only my life but also Dick back to Jesus, He turned around and let the whole family be a part of the television ministry: a stimulating, exciting, fascinating and educational privilege and opportunity. This experience took place in 1965.

God had some other lessons to teach me about television. One day, my American neighbor and I decided we wanted to get acquainted with the women in our block. We planned a beautiful Valentine luncheon. When we went to deliver our special invitations, we found that it wasn't nearly as easy as we had anticipated. Although our neighborhood was not considered a wealthy area, we found walls around every house. Then there were guards, first house girl and a second house girl. But because we were foreigners, we sometimes got in to see the woman who lived there. There were questions, excuses and suspicions. We did end up with fourteen women (probably more out of curiosity than anything else), but they did not know each other. Some had lived in the neighborhood for twenty years. We began to realize how hard it was to meet even our closest neighbors.

—*᠁*—

When Dick began working to help start Padilla's new television station, I had the bright idea of a show just for women. Since I barely knew how to turn on the TV set, I asked Dick to show me where to begin. He taught me how to put together a format and script and presented my idea to the others involved in the station. Suddenly, I was really scared.

I was scheduled to meet with the officers and present my ideas, but what if they accepted my proposals and expected me to prepare programs? That's when I told the Lord to please forget all my bright ideas. I had been acting in total ignorance and was happy to stay that way! But as I was praying in my upstairs bedroom, the Lord pointed out to me the dozens of rooftops just outside my window: my neighbors! Probably every home I could see had a TV. Through TV, I could share Jesus with hurting women in those homes! So we proceeded to plan for one hour a day, five days a week: a TV show just for women. That tells you how little I knew about television. I found it takes a number of fulltime staff workers to produce even one 30-minute show a week. Daily programs are only for big networks with loads of money and people!

Then everything fell apart. President Marcos refused to let the Christian station go on the air. All media came under his control. There was nothing anyone could do. So Dick took over the job of being personnel director for our mission, and I began teaching a Bible study, with mostly Chinese women. And it was about this time that I began to meet with Billie and her special friends. Between the Chinese women and Billie's group, I learned that money does not solve the problems of hurt and pain and agony. I'm sure the Lord knew I needed compassion before I ever attempted to go into women's homes via television.

Billie now asked Dick and me to produce and direct a half-hour show once a week. She would furnish everything we needed, including the airtime on the most powerful, nationwide, popular TV station in the Philippines. Our opportunity jumped from just Manila to nationwide! That was in December 1984. Billie and her husband also presented us with a lovely place for a follow-up counseling center, right in the heart of one of Manila's largest and nicest shopping centers. Women could come for Bible studies, seminars and fellowship, as well as counseling. There were Christian books, audiotapes, magazines and coffee available in a beautiful "tea room" setting. This was just the beginning of wonderful experiences with Billie and her husband, and they only happened when I finally obeyed God (and my husband). It did take an attitude makeover.

Since I was ignorant about television production and Dick knew how to put it together, he was a good teacher for me. With his help, I planned and produced the show. This involved a theme, with different sections, including drama, discussions, music, cooking, fashion, helpful hints, and most important of all, a testimony interview. I needed hosts and someone to do each section. Everything had to be perfectly timed. We pre-recorded the show each week, and Dick was in charge here. We had a beautiful studio with some of the best equipment available at that time. Pre-recording made it possible to edit our mistakes and adjust the timing, which was another part of Dick's job.

We had an amazing staff that worked with us. Gina Fernandez, a beautiful Filipina, was our lead host. Kris Nelson presented the cooking section. She only had a hot plate and counter to work with, and I gave her just five minutes. She demonstrated how to create delicious recipes: desserts, main dishes and even breads. Her method was to make the finished dish at home and bring every measured ingredient to show how to put it together. Kris had a large copy of the recipe hanging behind her where it could easily be seen and copied. Wil and Jacquie Chevalier were also an integral part of our team. Jacquie hosted and gave fashion tips, while Wil led discussions about the drama topic. He also helped set up the World of Women Center. They were available for any assistance we needed. They also became our bowling partners, which was a great stress-reliever for all of us. We had a delightful and talented international staff of excellent people.

If possible, our interviewed guest would spend specified times at the World of Women Center the following week. Meeting with this person was often vital. As one example: Kris shared her testimony about being alone when her 7-month-old baby girl died in the night. This was a traumatic experience, and Kris cried while telling how Jesus was there ministering to her. As Kris spent time in the World of Women Center the following week, she had the opportunity to help people who were also grieving. She understood their agony and knew how to lead them to Jesus.

We had a remarkable staff of volunteers who worked at the WOW center. Jean Rus was the manager and she also led seminars and planned retreats.

We also had outstanding assistance from several groups: Campus Crusade, YWAM, Youth for Christ, Operation Mobilization, World Vision and others missions who volunteered to counsel, present seminars, Bible Studies, etc.

Television is an expensive ministry, and we often wondered if it was worth the time, money and effort. But it was the most effective way to get into homes. Then we had personal contact through telephone, letters and the World of Women Center.

In a third world country where poverty is a way of life, where more than a million children live on the streets, many of them prostitutes before the age of seven — a country notorious for its garbage dump with a village of about 10,000 people at its base and millions of squatters — the question often came up: "Is television effective or useful or appropriate in the Philippines?" In a way, I have already answered that, but let me stress this point: television is a top priority to most Filipinos.

In one squatter area where the tin roofs are held down with old tires or big rocks and where the houses are so close together it is difficult to walk between them, the TV antennas are so thick they look like a metal forest. And when someone has a television set in the poor areas, they always share with the neighborhood, so the places are saturated with viewers.

There did come a time of discouragement and the over-whelming feeling we couldn't go on. My main helper in charge of the World of Women Center was asked to do a different job for our mission organization, so she could no longer work with me. Ciso and Billie had personally been paying for the show to go on the air, and now they asked us if we could get a sponsor to help with the increasing expenses.

There were so many needs. We seriously began to wonder if it was worthwhile and if it was what the Lord wanted us to continue doing. Should we be working with the poor, especially since this was the basic thrust of Action International Ministries, the mission we were now connected with? I was having my devotions and praying earnestly for God to show me what to do.

One morning, I was reading the book of Esther, and as I read, the Lord began to talk to me. Esther was a woman — just one woman — but God used her to save the Jewish nation. We were dealing with some very influential women, but God can use anyone He chooses. I was also learning that there is more than one kind of poverty, and spiritual poverty is the most dev-astating. Billie told me once, "The only difference between the rich and the poor is that the rich are more comfortable in their misery." The important message God wanted to get across to me was that what we were doing was very important and it wasn't time to quit. But we still needed help and sponsors.

As I was describing to the Lord the kind of person we needed, I finally said, "We need someone like Sandra!" Sandra Sagun had been a host on the show, an actress in some of the dramas, a great secretary at our World of Women Center and was wonderful in dealing with people. But Sandra had married and moved to another island where she worked with her husband, Carlo Ratilla and YWAM (Youth With A Mission). I knew she was out of the question, but I wanted someone just like her. And as far as a sponsor was concerned, I didn't even have any suggestions for the Lord. He would just have to be in charge if He wanted us to continue with the show. I really wanted an unmistakable sign from the Lord that it was His idea and desire for our television program to continue, not mine.

When we arrived at the World of Women Center that morning, everyone was so excited they could hardly talk. Sandra and her husband were back in Manila, and she wanted to come back and work with World of Women in any place we needed her. She wanted me to phone her as soon as possible.

That was the most exciting news, but then someone remembered I was supposed to call another number, too. When I finally got around to returning this other phone call, I could hardly believe what I was hearing. A Chinese company that was selling a new toothpaste in the Philippines wanted to advertise their product on our television program. They wanted to be one of our sponsors. A milk company from Holland was also interested in advertising, and a big business based on the idea of Costco in the U.S. became one of our sponsors. Amazingly, we didn't have to go after sponsors. They came to us. Every major problem was suddenly solved without our help!

While electronic media has its problems, it has made it possible to go into almost every corner of the world by either radio or TV. We have been able to cross all boundaries and go through any kind of "iron or bamboo curtain." Thousands of people can be reached at one time, and we can even go into the privacy of their homes. Jesus said, **"If I be lifted up, I will draw all men to me."** Our job is to lift Him up by all means and to as many people as possible. It is His job to work in their lives.

—∞—

Once again, an attitude change gave Dick and me some unusual and exciting experiences that I'm sure we could never have had without our friendship with Ciso and Billie Padilla. I have mentioned playing and singing at a Presidential Prayer Breakfast in Manila, but even more memorable is our experience at a Presidential Prayer Breakfast in Washington, D.C. The Padillas were asked to represent the Philippines at this breakfast, but they didn't want to go alone, so they invited Dick and me to go with them. We were also to represent the Philippines.

The week before the Prayer Breakfast, we were scheduled to attend the National Broadcaster's Convention and this was also held in Washington D.C. I think the two events were scheduled back-to-back intentionally. The Padillas came to some of the Broadcaster's Convention, but we were not able to stay at the same hotel as Ciso and Billie. We stayed at the Sheraton where the National Broadcaster's Convention was held, and they were in the Hilton where the Prayer Breakfast would be served. We thoroughly enjoyed all of the speakers, classes, musicians, etc. On the last day, Billie contacted us and said, "You missed out on the breakfast at the Hilton Hotel. You were supposed to be there today. You must go to the Hilton right away and find out where you are to be and what you should be doing."

We had no idea what was involved, so we were surprised to find that it was a lot more than just attending the Presidential Prayer Breakfast. Because we were representing the Philippines, we were considered international guests and were given "red carpet" treatment and privileges. It was wonderful, but also frustrating that first day because the two events overlapped. We were running from one hotel to the other one. Instead of one Prayer Breakfast, we had three days of breakfasts, lunches, dinners, seminars and meetings. We sat with top officials from other countries: a senator from Korea, the Social Welfare Minister of Taiwan, the U.S. Minister of Agriculture, etc. We had several special meals with various top officials in the government, including congressmen and senators. I wish I could remember names, because some of the leaders from other countries invited us to visit them personally. Ciso and Dick had breakfast with a group of senators, and they were privileged to ride in a part of the private underground system.

While our husbands were being shown around and having breakfast with the senators, Billie and I met with the Christian Congressional wives for an unforgettable luncheon. This was a special time for Internationals, and we were invited. There were women present from many countries around the world. I'm sure the lunch was great, but the best part was the sharing and prayer time for each country. To see these beautiful, talented women weep openly before the Lord as they prayed for the different countries represented, and to hear them pray for each of us, was meaningful and powerful. At that time we were very encouraged with the number of concerned Christians in our government.

During this time I became aware of all Ciso and Billie have done for their fellow countrymen. They helped build a hospital for the poor and challenged some of the best doctors in the Philippines to donate time to serve others. They started a Bible Study in their factory and built apartments for their workers. Because of martial law, when their station did not get permission to operate, they offered the use of their studio to several Christian groups and then paid to have the programs aired on the existing stations. Dick and I were recipients of their generosity over and over again, and Billie and I became special friends. It's amazing what a change in attitude and a little obedience can accomplish.

As far back as 1965, Dick produced a Christian television show in the Philippines and involved the whole family.

Although I don't see Billie Padilla now, she was able to meet up with my son Steve, and his wife Mayen in the Philippines.

During the years that we produced the Christian women's television show "World of Women," my daughters appeared on the show during visits to the Philippines.

Beginning in 1984, Dick and I produced and directed the weekly half-hour show that aired on the most popular nationwide TV station in the Philippines.

The "World of Women" show included Jacquie Chevalier who hosted and gave fashion tips, a cooking segment, musical entertainment, and guest interviews. Women watching the show were invited to the World of Women Center where they could receive counseling.

CHAPTER 11

ADVENTURES WITH MOVING

I suspect Dick and I would win an award if there were a contest for the most moves during our married years. At the moment, the thought of moving brings on a form of paralysis to my mind and body, but fortunately that wasn't always the case or I would never have survived this long. I have no recollection of moving from the time I was born until I left to go to college in Oregon, although I was about four years old when my family made the transition from the tiny community of Greenleaf, Idaho to the "big" town of Nampa, 20 miles away.

The house on Holly Street was where my adventures of growing up took place. Our home in Nampa was my area of security. It wasn't until I went away to attend Pacific College in Newberg, Oregon that I began to experience the world of packing up and leaving the familiar to unpack and start over again. Perhaps our attitude makes more difference at this time than almost any other area in our lives. Moving can be exciting and energizing, or it can be devastating and depressing. There is so much more to moving than just the sorting, decisions, packing and going to a new location, although that part can be confusing as well as extremely tiring. I'm convinced that the hardest part of moving is leaving people we love.

I was content in Nampa. It probably wouldn't be considered an exciting, unusual life, but it was a good life. My Dad owned an ice cream factory, so that helped my popularity when acquaintances discovered they could get a pint of soft ice cream by walking home with me if we went by way of Dad's creamery. Later, I thought maybe Dick fell in love with my Dad's ice cream before he fell in love with me, and it didn't hurt to have a freezer full of all kinds of ice cream at our home.

Childhood friends are often forgotten as we move on in life. But my best friend from grade school days remained my best friend forever. Mary lived out in the country and she often stayed with my family during the week when we were in high school. We both skipped our senior year in high school and moved together to Pacific College in Newberg, Oregon. We both married guys in the Four Flats Quartet and spent several years living either together or across the street from each other. We moved from Oregon to California together, had babies about the same time and were never really separated very far apart until the quartet disbanded and our family moved to the Philippines.

Our children thought they were all related. Mary's son David and my son Jonathan were best friends forever. Mary's daughter Marilyn came to live with us for a year in Manila to attend college with my daughter Yvonne and her other daughter Marcia traveled around the world with our youngest child LuAnne. Even though oceans came between us, we remained best friends until Mary went to be with Jesus in 2010.

Dick and I were married in 1947 and lived in a vet's housing unit on Pacific College campus until we graduated in 1949. We had very few possessions or collections at that time, so after graduation, moving from Newberg to the Portland area was quite simple. Norval and Mary moved with us to a large home where we lived together while the quartet traveled for Youth for Christ and World Vision. The home we lived in was furnished, and once again we had only a few things when it came time to move to another location. So up to this time, moving had not been a big, stressful event. During the years when the quartet was singing together, we seemed to constantly be on the move, but not necessarily to different houses. We were all over the United Stages, traveling in cars, staying with other people and having meetings.

When the quartet felt it was time for something different, they began to take jobs in different locations away from each other. Dick was invited to teach school back in Idaho, in the small community of Greenleaf where I was born. Once again, we were with family and friends and the quartet was in such demand that we made numerous trips to Oregon. We lived in at least four different houses during the few years we were in Idaho. We finally decided it was time to be closer to the other quartet families since we were making long trips to Oregon.

Moving is considered one of the most stressful events in people's lives. By now, I couldn't tell you how many different houses we had lived in, although none of the moves were traumatic. However, when Bob Pierce and World Vision asked us to move to California, it involved a monumental decision for each quartet family. By now we had 11 children among us and three on the way. When each family agreed that we felt this was the Lord's will for us at that time, World Vision said they would pay for the move.

But first we needed to make an exploratory trip to find housing for each family. This involved a plane trip together, which was pretty exciting for the four wives. Our husbands had traveled by air many times, but none of the wives had ever been on an airplane. We were a little apprehensive, since we were all leaving small children behind. Then as the plane was taxiing down the runway to take off, someone across the aisle opened a newspaper to one of the biggest headlines I had ever seen. "Two Passenger Planes Collide in Midair. Worst Plane Disaster in History." This happened over the Grand Canyon. Both planes went down and everyone was killed. That certainly didn't help our nerves, but it was too late to get out!

Before we left, the guys were warned, "It would probably be a good idea if you didn't live close to each other, maybe even in different towns. You fellas might be able to get along with each other, but your wives will never make it." I don't know how anyone could be so wrong. Our friendship and living near each other was our survival. I still consider Mary, Gertie and Divonna my closest friends. We found tract homes that were very close together, and three of us lived just across a narrow street while the other family lived a block away. These houses were considered a great bargain. They had never been lived in, but had been built more than a year before and because of some trouble with the contractor, hadn't been sold, so they were vacant. Now they needed to be sold fast, and we were there at the right time. This was in the town of Glendora and a great location, except for one small problem.

A railroad track ran directly behind Hadley's and Ankeny's houses. Our house was just across the street. At first it seemed as though the train went right through our kitchen, and all conversation stopped. But in a few days, we didn't even notice the train was going past. We often argued about who had the loudest noise from the train. Harlow and Norval declared that the sound sort of jumped over their houses and hit ours full force. However, one night years later when we were selling our home to go to the Philippines, we stayed at Hadley's house a few days while they were gone. Dick and I slept in their bed, and in the middle of the night the train went by and the whole house shook. Dick stood up in the middle of the bed and shouted, "What was that?" It was much louder than in our house, but I guess you can get used to almost anything.

Living in Glendora near the other quartet families was ideal for all of us. The guys were close enough to rehearse, plan trips and ride together. During times when the quartet was traveling, the women had each other to lean on. We babysat for each other, shopped together, shared rides, and in every way were a family. As for our children, they always had someone in the other families as special friends and play-mates, and the boys had someone to get into trouble with. Steve and Rodney loved playing together, and we could never anticipate what they might think of next. One day they found some pitch on a tree and decided to put it in their hair. As if that wasn't enough, they twisted the hair with the sticky pitch all through it. I'm not sure what they were thinking. Maybe they were trying to get it out before their mothers saw it, but both boys ended with a big bald spot that we were convinced would never recover. Fortunately, the hair finally grew back, but it was embarrassing to take them anywhere.

It wasn't always easy being a quartet wife, especially having our husbands gone so much of the time. I think we learned to appreciate and cherish every minute we had together, and it's something we never forgot. I wouldn't trade those years and experiences for anything, and there were also a lot of fun advantages. We never got tired of hearing them sing and watching them perform, and we had the privilege of meeting many interesting and famous people.

Of course, we often sat at home or in a hotel lobby eating our peanut butter sandwiches while the guys were singing (and eating) at the exclusive banquet in the private ballroom. We enjoyed going with the quartet when they were singing in our area, but it wasn't easy for all eight of us to go at the same time because of the children. Babysitting was a problem and was expensive, so we often took turns. Two of us would go and the other two would stay with the kids. Once in a while, the wives were actually invited to the special meetings or banquets, but not often!

One time, the guys were on the same program with Ronald Reagan, Pat Boone, Roy Rogers and Dale Evans and other well-known celebrities. Dick happened to be sitting by Ronald Reagan when people began coming by and wanting Ronald's autograph. My husband placed his packet of music on Ronald's knee to give him a support base for writing his name. Occasionally we attended the Hollywood Christian Fellowship group where we met other Christian celebrities. I began to learn that even famous people have problems, insecurities, fears and hang-ups. Everyone needs Jesus!

I admit it was a different kind of life when my husband couldn't get dressed until he found out what three other guys were wearing that day. It was a good life, but we knew it couldn't last forever. The quartet had been singing together, on and off, since college days. They were with World Vision for five years. Our children were getting older and really needed their dads home. By this time we had 18 children between us! So after much prayer, numerous discussions among ourselves and with World Vision people and more prayer, the day came when we decided it was time for the quartet to disband and go our separate ways.

Although we were convinced this was the right move to make, it wasn't easy. Our lives had become so integrated with all of the others that it was like a family separating. The children probably felt it as much as anyone. They were known as "The Quartet Kids" and they felt it was an honor and maybe made them a little famous. But it was the loss of each other that hurt the most.

When someone says, "I'm moving!" it can sound like a curse or a declaration of freedom. Once again, attitude makes all the difference. It can bring fear and dread, or joy and excitement. However, whatever else it brings, there are always decisions involved and then work, work and more work. Each of our families had to go through this agonizing time, and each of the guys needed to have another job lined up before leaving World Vision. We all wanted to do what God wanted us to do, but sometimes we really didn't know what that was. I remember Norval saying to us, "God wants us to do His will even more than we want to do it. If we are really willing for anything, then we can rest assured that He won't let us make a mistake. He opens and closes doors and keeps us in His will when we are willing."

———

Chris took a job as youth director at Lake Avenue Congregational Church, but later became Chaplain of the Brown Military Academy. He stayed in California for a few years before returning to Newberg, Oregon to become

Chaplain of George Fox College (formerly Pacific College), our old alma mater. After a couple of years, Harlow brought his family back to Newberg, so he could lead Barclay Press, the printing arm of the Friends church in the Northwest. He later moved to the Oregon coast to become the director of Twin Rocks Friends Campground. Norval stayed with World Vision for 28 more years and became Assistant to Bob Pierce for as long as Bob lived. In 1972, the Hadley family moved back to Newberg where Norval was the Superintendent of Northwest Yearly Meeting of Friends churches. He has also been Director of Evangelical Friends Mission and chaplain at Quaker Gardens Retirement Center in California. For several years, the other three men in the Four Flats Quartet were together in Newberg.

Dick and I were having a harder time finding what we ought to do. We both did substitute teaching and Dick directed the choir at San Gabriel Church in California, but we knew this was very temporary. One day when we were discussing our situation, I asked the question, "What about the mission field?" We had always said we were willing to go if that's what God wanted. Dick had written home from the Philippines saying that if the children and I weren't in the U.S., he wouldn't come back. He had fallen in love with the Filipinos. However, he now shot back, "Yes, but now we're too old. No one would accept us, especially with five kids. And what would we do? We aren't trained for mission work." For some reason I responded, "But we've never made ourselves available!"

We had to find out what God wanted. So we asked the other quartet families to take care of our five children while we got a motel at the beach to spend a few days fasting, praying and reading the Bible. We were especially concerned about our children. We finally told the Lord we were willing for anything and anywhere, even as missionaries, if any mission would have us. As soon as we committed ourselves to God, He committed Himself to us. He presented us with this challenge and guarantee from Hebrews 13:5 (AMP):

"Let your character or moral disposition be free from love of money—including greed, avarice, lust and craving for earthly possessions—and be satisfied with your present circumstances and with what you have, for He (God) Himself has said, 'I will not in any way fail you nor give you up nor leave you without support. I will not, I will not, I will not in any degree leave you helpless, nor forsake, nor let you down or relax My hold on you, assuredly not.'"

Now we both knew beyond a shadow of a doubt that we had to make ourselves available for mission work. Although we were sure no mission would have us and that would settle everything, we were committed to one thing. We would be available. Our position now gave us no alternative but to watch God work! We had nothing except His promise, His peace, His joy! We headed home and immediately saw God's perfect timing. When we arrived in Glendora, there on Dick's desk were five letters offering him wonderful jobs: teach in a college and work with Youth for Christ in Hawaii; television director for Youth for Christ in Portland; youth director in a large church, etc. If he had received any one of these offers before we went to the beach, he probably would have jumped on it. But God knew He wanted us to be alone where He could get our attention, and we were now committed to making ourselves available.

—*w*—

And so we moved to the Philippines! Well, not exactly! First of all we had to apply to a mission organization. Dick immediately thought of applying to Overseas Crusades because the quartet had worked with this group in the Philippines and Taiwan, and they were totally impressed with everyone they met. He knew they talked about needing teachers at Faith Academy in the Philippines and he was a teacher, so that might be a possibility. And we had heard Dick Hillis, the director of Overseas Crusades say, "God doesn't want your ability, but He does want your availability."

Once we turned in our application to Overseas Crusades, it wasn't too long before we got word that the O.C. board wanted to meet with us. They had a lot of questions and then told us they would make a decision and let us know within a few days. It has always been hard for me to wait for anything, and it wasn't easy waiting to find out what we were going to do. I had been thoroughly convinced we would be turned down as missionaries, but now with the possibility of acceptance, I really became afraid of everything! I thought of the bugs and snakes and leaving family and friends. What if we were making a mistake in finding God's will? This would be the mistake of all mistakes! We wanted God to write it in the sky, or hit us over the head, or speak out loud and clear. Then we were reminded of Norval's assurance that God wouldn't let us make a mistake when we really wanted what He wanted. The Lord could close the door as easily as He could open it. His choice! I just needed the right attitude.

We really were surprised and found it hard to believe when we received word that we had been appointed as missionaries to the Philippines and Overseas Crusades wanted us to start deputation travels immediately. Since we weren't committed to any other full time job, we could do this, except for a few not-so-simple details like selling our house and everything in it. The Lord continually performed miracle after miracle (which I wrote about in my first book), and He kept His promise to **"never fail us or give us up or leave us without support or leave us helpless or forsake us or let us down or relax His hold on us."** Hebrews 13:5 (AMP)

After an unusual, exciting, sometimes anxious, busy year of travel, speaking, new experiences, many lessons, meeting with people and learning to trust God more each day, we were finally ready to leave for the Philippines. However, there were a few snags along the way. For one thing, without a round trip ticket, it was not possible to leave the United States without a visa for the country we were going to. Since we were traveling by ship and didn't plan to stay in any country along the way, all we really needed was a visa for the Philippines, but without that vital document, the ship would leave without us. A cable came from our Manila office saying that our "Pre-Arranged Employment Visa" had been granted. It now had to be sent to the Philippine Consulate in the United States and the number stamped in our passports before we could get on any ship or plane.

It was not easy to schedule seven people for rooms aboard a ship. Reservations had to be made several months in advance, and ours were for October 11. But it is easier to leave Siberia than it is to cancel that many tickets at the last minute without forfeiting ticket money; and the closer the sailing date, the more percentage lost by cancelling! Our type of visa information came only once a week by "diplomatic pouch." We checked constantly at the Philippine Consulate. When the last pouch had arrived before our departure date and there was still no visa, we became desperate. We explained our plight to the Philippine Consul, and he was incredibly sympathetic and understanding. He closed the door to his office and when he appeared a few minutes later he happily announced. "It's all set. As a personal favor to me you will be issued a visa for Hong Kong. I'll arrange for your Philippine visa to be sent to our Hong Kong office."

That crucial phone call took place on the afternoon before we were to depart the next day. Our problems still weren't over because the Hong Kong office was located across town and would be closed in two hours. Unless we secured that visa, we couldn't leave and would lose 75% of our fare for seven people. After racing across town, we arrived at the Hong Kong office only to be told by the secretary that it was too late to see the Consul. Obviously she hadn't been informed that we were coming. As I was preparing to make a mad dash into his office, he appeared and was looking for us. He gave us the visa we needed and now we were ready to leave the U.S.

This was probably one of the biggest, most traumatic moves we ever had to make, and we began learning the most difficult experience in the life of a missionary: saying "goodbye!"

—␣—

We were finally on the ship and on our way. I wish I could say that was the end of our visa problems. The day before we were to arrive in Hawaii, the ship's purser called Dick into his office and told him we would have to get off the ship unless we could pick up our visas in Hawaii. Inexperienced at traveling, we believed him. We spent all morning and part of the afternoon at the Philippine Consulate instead of having fun on the beach and shopping.

Because of the time difference, it was a different day in Manila and all the offices were closed. They couldn't even make a phone call, but they did do one big favor for us. They assured us the ship could not put us off in Hawaii because we had visas to Hong Kong. They could put us off in Hong Kong if our visas weren't there yet, but Hong Kong was several weeks away and much closer to Manila! We went back to the ship and told the purser we were staying on until Hong Kong where we would be getting our visas to Manila. He assured us we would have to get off in Hong Kong. We assured him our visas would be waiting for us there. And so our children had about one hour on Waikiki Beach before heading back to our tiny room in the hold of the ship.

My mom had given me some special scriptures before we left Idaho. Job 19:25 was an affirmation: **"For I know that my redeemer lives, and that He shall stand at the latter day upon the earth."** The verse from II Timothy 1:12 agrees with Job: **"I know whom I have believed, and am persuaded that He is able to keep that which I have committed unto Him against that day."** (KJV) My desire was to have the right attitude, but I found it hard at times when I was so disappointed with our tiny cabin on the ship, our lost holiday in Hawaii and the storms and seasickness most of the trip. However, these discomforts didn't change the fact that Jesus is alive, and He is the answer to life! That's why we were on our way to the Philippines. And yet the Lord had to teach us many lessons before we arrived there to serve. Fortunately, in Psalms 86:15, the Bible declares, **"But thou, O Lord, art a God full of compassion, and gracious, longsuffering, and plenteous in mercy and truth."** (KJV) I might add, and patient with slow learners.

After an interesting, but short day in Japan, we were finally on our way to Hong Kong. It was a beautiful day when the ship pulled into the harbor, and everything was exactly as we had always pictured it would be. But one thought occupied our minds—visas!! Arrangements had been made for a certain missionary to meet us at the dock and take us directly to the Philippine Consulate. After this most important business was over, we looked forward to a wonderful day shopping in what was known at that time as "the world's greatest bargain center." We arrived a little early and began looking expectantly for someone who seemed to be looking for us expectantly. We had never met the person who was to meet us, but figured they had a better chance of recognizing seven red heads than we had of finding one unknown man.

We waited and watched, watched and waited. I can't say we waited patiently. How does one wait patiently with five children on a busy dock? I didn't want to waste another whole day again, and no one even acted like they were looking for us. Dick finally decided we couldn't stand around any longer, so he flagged a taxi and asked for the Philippine Embassy. Fortunately, most taxi drivers spoke English, because we didn't even have an address. When we arrived at the Embassy, we waited again! Dick and I had a brilliant idea: let the kids go free and don't even try to keep them under control. It worked! While the little girls were peeking under desks and dumping out wastebaskets, the boys headed for the fire escape. Since we were quite high up in the building, this got us plenty of attention! Dick explained that all we wanted was to have our visa numbers stamped into our passports and we would leave with all of the children.

Someone immediately began looking in his files. Before long someone else joined in the search. Soon everyone in the office was involved, but they didn't find anything for us, or even any information *about* us. This was truly a cause for panic. The officials told Dick he could use their phone to call our Manila office. Although our missionaries were surprised to hear from Dick, they knew all about the visas not being sent yet. They had made arrangements for a Hong Kong missionary to find us a place to stay, meet us, help us evacuate the ship with our entire luggage and get us settled. It would be more than a week before the next diplomatic pouch arrived and they thought we were being taken care of. Dick hung up the phone and we just stood there staring at each other in a stunned stupor. We didn't even know the name of anyone in Hong Kong.

For a few minutes we completely forgot the wonderful promises God had given us — the foundation we were counting on. I don't think we even prayed. We didn't remember that God had said He would never fail us or leave us helpless or forsake us or relax His hold on us. By now the children were not only tired, but also hungry and out of control. Jon and Steve began testing the elevators, Yvonne and LuAnne cried, Carolyn was getting grouchy, I was in shock, and Dick was upset! Suddenly in this confused condition, we heard our name being paged. We had a phone call!

The caller was Mrs. Florence Raetz, a missionary working with World Vision in Hong Kong. After our ship was already docked, the man scheduled to meet us had called her to ask if she could take care of us, meet us, find a place to stay and get us settled. She agreed, but by the time she got to the dock, we had been long gone. She figured the only logical place for us to go was to the Philippine Embassy, so that's where she called. By that time, everyone in the Philippine office was thoroughly acquainted with our names. Mrs. Raetz told us when and where to meet her, but before we were ready to meet anyone, we had a major job to do.

Back at the ship, the children and I began packing while Dick swallowed his pride and went to inform the purser we would be leaving the ship. This wasn't easy, because even

144

though we were taking all of our cabin baggage, there were still crates and barrels in the hold, which involved signing dozens of papers. When everything was finally settled, we began the backbreaking trek with our 33 pieces of heavy baggage. First we had to climb up four decks to the gang-plank, then down the gangplank to the dock, and then hike four long blocks to get any transportation. This was reversed and repeated four times. We were a pathetic procession as the two little girls pushed and pulled their big suitcases and the rest of us struggled with our loaded pieces of luggage. Since we were moving to another country, we were taking almost everything we owned.

Mrs. Raetz met us with transportation, but she was dis-couraged. She had tried almost every hotel in the city and found them completely filled because of a big convention. She finally found us two "boarding homes" in the same building. Hong Kong is a huge city, very crowded, and land is very valuable. Hardly anyone has a house and yard and most people live in apartments. In the business district there are usually shops on the first few floors, and then people live above them. Some buildings were 14-15 stories high. People often rented out one of their rooms in order to make a little extra money.

Obviously, no one family could take in another family of seven, so we couldn't all stay in one home. It was good that we could be in the same building. I went to the 12th floor with the girls, and Dick stayed on the 9th floor with the boys. Since we were only going to be in these Chinese homes one night, Mrs. Raetz took most of our luggage home with her. She didn't know us, and yet she had spent all day working tirelessly for us.

Even though the bed was only a board with four legs and a sheet spread over it, we were probably asleep the minute we crashed on it. I think every adult Chinese in the city must have stayed up all night playing the noisy, clacking game of Mahjong. I even met my first Asian cockroach, which bore no resemblance to the ones I had seen in California. This gigantic monster, with its constantly wiggling antennas, looked about the size of a small mouse. But I was too groggy to care. We were tired enough to sleep most of the night, although somewhat aware of our surroundings. Circumstances were not working out the way we had planned, but we would think about that in the morning.

Morning did come, and Mrs. Raetz was right there to pay for our rooms and take us to her home for a wonderful breakfast. By now she had made different arrangements for our stay in Hong Kong. Dick and I, with Yvonne and LuAnne, were given a lovely hotel room (with real beds) almost next door to the Raetz home, where Carolyn, Jon and Steve would be staying.

Now we had a choice. We had been put off our ship unexpectedly and landed in a large, unusual, frightening, foreign city with five young children. We were fearful for their health and safety, had no extra money, no plans, thrown in with total strangers, different foods and no idea of what to expect or how long we might be here. Our situation had all of the ingredients for fear, apprehension, worry, depression and stress.

On the other hand, with no scheduled meetings or obligations, a terrific place to stay and World Vision paying the bills for us until our mission could send money, our family was in a position to have one of the most exciting vacations of a lifetime. Hong Kong was the kind of place most people only saw in intriguing and adventurous movies. We were given the opportunity to learn about a new culture, see new things we had never even dreamed of seeing and have experiences beyond our wildest imaginations. We couldn't begin to anticipate what this might do for our children.

—*m*—

What happened in the next 10 days was totally dependent on our attitude! Since parents' attitudes seem to be contagious for their children, Dick and I needed to make the right choices. And we did have a choice. I had always been very protective of our children. I tried to feed them healthy foods and make sure they had their vitamins. They were required to wash hands before eating, and although it wasn't really possible, I did try to keep them reasonably clean. This was a different environment, and we weren't sure what our kids might be exposed to. However, after praying for wisdom and with God's help, we made the choice to turn this experience into a fun adventure.

Mr. and Mrs. Raetz had been in Hong Kong for many years and were better than the most qualified tour guides available anywhere. World Vision supported a number of unusual ministries around Hong Kong. Mrs. Raetz had numerous responsibilities, but she included us as she went about her work.

One of the first places we visited was a boat ministry World Vision was helping. The mission operated a boat with schoolrooms, a clinic and a chapel on board. This boat was huge compared to the small boats that thousands of people lived on. My dad had a small speedboat, but these boat homes were even smaller. We were told that many of these people spent their entire lives living in these tiny boats. You could probably walk for miles in that crowded cove by stepping from one boat to the next. And to think that I complained about the small room we had on the large ship. I remembered the saying, "I complained because I had no shoes, until I met a man who had no feet."

Hong Kong was notorious for their H-Buildings. These were shaped like an H, about 10 stories high, had hundreds of 10` by 10` rooms and were built to give the refugees from Communist China a place to live. The rooms had no plumbing, but each floor had a central area for water and bathrooms. In many cases, whole families lived in one little room. I don't think there was electricity in any of the buildings, so of course that meant no elevators. The roofs were flat and used for services on Sunday and school during the week.

We walked up the 10 flights of stairs for one of the rooftop meetings. That was no easy task, and I couldn't help but think of the older people, the small children, pregnant women, the sick and lame, especially if they lived on one of the upper floors. It was hard to comprehend that many of the people living in these places had been educated, well-to-do businessmen, doctors, engineers, teachers, etc. but had given up everything they had in order to be free. The Bible talks so much about being thankful and grateful, especially thanking and praising God, but it's so easy to forget and take everything for granted.

—*m*—

Probably one of our most memorable experiences is one that we could never have again, because the place has been destroyed. An older missionary couple took us to the "Old Walled City," a place of intrigue, murder, opium dens, prostitutes and mystery just like we used to see in movies and on TV. This "city within a city" had no government jurisdiction over it at all. It was independent of Hong Kong, and the police wouldn't think of entering in this place.

After parking the car, we walked along the wall until we came to a small opening. We stooped down to enter, and it took a few minutes for our eyes to adjust to the darkness. We had to be very careful where we stepped because the edges of the pathway were also the "toilet." It was so narrow we walked single file, continually passing forms lying on cots. We detected a really different smell, even distinguishable from the open sewers along the way. The odor came from the famous Hong Kong "opium dens" we were passing. A shaft of light occasionally filtered through, but mostly it was dark, damp and smelly. All the mystery stories ever written about Hong Kong didn't compare to what we actually saw.

Suddenly we came to one "bright spot" which seemed to be in the center of the city. This was a school run by the older missionary couple we were accompanying. It had some light and color. It wasn't much, but it was definitely a contrast to everything else around it! The school building had several stories, with terribly narrow, winding and dark stairs. While there, we were allowed to help give out milk and cookies supplied by World Vision, but it was all I could do to keep from crying. Little children carried smaller children, and in order that all could have at least something, they had cards to be punched. So many children kept coming out of the darkness surrounding us. Our animals in the U.S. have more to eat and live in more sanitary conditions than these children did. I never want to forget the things I saw in Hong Kong. I want to have compassion and love. I want to share Jesus, the only hope for the world. I want to the light in the darkness.

I don't want to leave the impression that these were the only kinds of things we experienced. We also saw the beautiful side of Hong Kong. We probably had the greatest vacation anyone could ever have. We had the best guides possible, wonderful accommodations, delicious meals, unforgettable experiences, new friends, unusual activities and fun shopping in the world's greatest bargain center.

—*m*—

When our visas finally arrived, we were ready to move on. There was no way we could get on a ship again. We had to fly. Even in those days, baggage had a limit, and we had 33 heavy pieces of luggage. There was no limit on the ship, so we had suitcases filled with books so the kids could study. We also had instruments and numerous bags for other people. Every one of us, including Yvonne and LuAnne (who were only six and four years old), were so loaded with "carry-on" baggage that we could hardly walk. The things we couldn't carry with us were taken to be weighed.

We were almost 300 pounds overweight. The girl at the counter was totally bewildered, especially when we began trying to decide what we had to leave behind. We kept taking things off and then putting them back again. The plane was about ready to leave and we were still confused. We certainly couldn't afford the $1.00 a pound overweight. In the midst of our dilemma, the girl at the counter who had filled out papers for our overweight baggage motioned Dick over and said very quietly, "The plane is not very full today." Dick watched in wonder as she tore up all the papers and threw them in the wastebasket. She then sent all of our things to go on the plane, free of charge!

Although at times we wondered what God had in mind for this move, we constantly saw Him at work in the smallest and the biggest details. In our minds, He sometimes seemed a little later than we wanted, but He never failed, and He was never late! Philippians 4:6-7 tells us, **"Don't worry about anything; instead, pray about everything: tell God your needs and don't forget to thank Him for His answers. If you do this you will experience God's peace, which is far more wonderful than the human mind can understand."** God does want us to have an attitude of gratitude, to be thankful and to praise Him.

———

We have moved so often in our married lives that I have completely forgotten just how many times and different places. At first it didn't seem so hard, but each move seemed to be more difficult. I remember one of the final moves in the Philippines. It wasn't so far from where we were living and the move was into a lovely condominium. Possibly because I was older, tired and we had accumulated too many things, I fell apart! After others had helped us pack and move all of our possessions, I simply sat down in the middle of the floor, surrounded by dozens of boxes and cried. Dick was working in the other room, but he came in and put his arms around me and asked what was wrong. "It's such a mess. I don't know where to begin!" I sobbed.

We'd probably had this conversation on other occasions, but my wise husband quietly asked, "Honey, how do you eat an elephant?" I knew the answer, but it didn't want to come out. Finally I managed to whisper, "One bite at a time, but I still don't know where to begin!" Dick responded, "All you have to do is find one tiny thing you think you can handle.

That's the first bite. After that it's still one bite at a time, not the whole thing all at once. Let's take a bite together."

I still firmly believe that leaving people we love is by far the most difficult part of moving, especially when the distance involves thousands of miles apart. When we went to the Philippines as missionaries we left family and friends. Once there, we were continually seeing friends and coworkers, and eventually even children leave us to return to the U.S. The kind of house we lived in and the different environment we had to adjust to really weren't that difficult, but the separations were. We were never certain that we would see each other again in this world, but because of Jesus, we did know we would be together again in Heaven. Hope is one of the greatest gifts God has given us. That was why we moved to the Philippines, to share God's hope of eternal life through His Son Jesus Christ.

Although we moved many times in the US, our biggest family move was in 1962, from Los Angeles to the Philippines. We traveled first by ship to Hong Kong.

The Four Flats families came to see us off before the ship left port. Our tiny cabin for seven people was barely wide enough to walk between the bunks.

Our family waves goodbye to our friends and the life we knew, ready to begin a new adventure in the Philippines.

Getting on and off planes, beginning with our arrival in the Philippines in 1962, has become a way of life for our family and continues even now for most of my adult children.

CHAPTER 12

ADVENTURES WITH FIRE AND WATER

"Honey, why are the fire trucks all leaving when the fire is getting bigger?" I was balanced on tiptoes standing on our bed so I could see out a small window. My husband had been sleeping soundly while I was watching a city block go up in flames not far from our house. I had been trying desperately to keep from waking Dick since I had a reputation for having a weird kind of excitement when it came to fires, but I just had to ask.

Because of several childhood experiences involving fires, I had an unusual fear mixed with the strong desire to go and watch when a building was burning. My poor husband had been dragged out of bed many times to either take me for a closer view, or at least watch with me from a distance. I thought maybe I could watch it alone and not bother him this time, but it was more than I could bear. "They're leaving to go to the river to get water because there aren't any fire hydrants in the area." Dick's sleepy answer showed how unconcerned he was when he replied to my rather frantic question. However, when there was wild pounding and shouting at our gate, he promptly jumped up, dressed and ran to see what was happening.

Our neighbors from the fire area wanted someone to come and keep watch on their possessions that they had rescued from the fire. We lived on a "compound" with several other missionary families and a big, concrete wall surrounded us. But not far from us was an area equivalent to several blocks all squished together with no streets and only narrow walks between the houses. It was similar to a squatter area but the buildings were a little bigger and better, made of wood instead of garbage dump materials. The dwellings were certainly not fireproof in any way and, because they nearly touched each other, there were often fires that destroyed blocks at a time. When possible, people gathered all of their valuable belongings and moved them to a safe distance from the fire.

Unfortunately, the fires weren't the only destructive force. Large trucks with several tough men always showed up to pack up other people's property and drive off with it, never to be seen again by the owners. Although as many as 10 city blocks have burned at one time, the people usually get out unharmed, but lose everything they own. There was just one block between where we lived and the fire.

My fascination and fear of fires began as a four-year-old when it appeared the hospital, just two blocks from our house, was on fire. No one took time to hold my hand as sirens wailed, huge red trucks sped by, and people were shouting as they ran past us. Eight years later as a 12 year old, I was recovering from an appendectomy when the nurses' home, which was attached to the hospital, caught fire. That same year our town had the biggest disaster it had known. Someone lit a cigarette in a large drug store filled with fireworks. Many people died when they were trapped inside. And then there was a gas leak in a restaurant located between two buildings that my dad owned. The explosion was so massive that it almost destroyed three buildings and several people were killed, including one of my best friends.

When I wrote my first book, *Never to Forget*, I declared it would absolutely be the last one. No one had ever heard of a computer or a copy machine, a fax or a cell phone. We used a typewriter and carbon paper, where every mistake had to be erased on both the original and the copy. I have no idea how many times we had to read and redo the manuscript. When we finally finished the book and took it to the printers, we thought we could relax. By this time the whole family and many friends had been helping me. That's when we heard the news: the whole city block where the print shop with my book manuscript was located was on fire. As many people prayed, the fire stopped just before it reached the print shop. Having an experience like this taught me to pray whenever I hear a siren. Someone is usually in trouble and needs God's help.

Dick and I had just reached our home, about 35 minutes from Manila, when we received an urgent phone call informing us that the theater we had just left was on fire. A few months earlier this had been the studio where we produced our television show, but it was now used for live musicals and dramas. Our World of Women Center was located down the aisle in this same shopping mall. We were instructed to return as quickly as possible and decide if the hundreds of books and tapes in the center should be removed. It would be a terrible mess to re-sort and put them back in place.

Upon arriving at the fire scene, we heard people discussing a serious problem the firemen were having. They couldn't seem to find the source of the fire. Because we knew it had been a television studio and had extensive wiring under the floors, we decided to go inside and talk to the fire fighters. This was the closest I ever got to being in a seriously burning building. Our information was what they needed in order to get the fire under control. However, I'm not sure it did anything to help my attitude about fires.

———

When the quartet and wives were traveling through Kansas, we drove through a small town that had been devastated by a flood. There were marks on the buildings showing how high the water had been, and some of the marks were as high as the second story. It was years later when we had our own experience with floods. During our first few years in Manila, we had seen how quickly the water levels could rise. This was especially true when the tide was in and the ground already saturated.

One time Dick and I were in downtown Manila and had been inside a building for a couple of hours. We were aware that it had been raining some, but were totally shocked when we stepped outside. We could barely see across the street and the rain had stronger pressure than our shower at home. Parking had been difficult to find, so we were parked several blocks from where we needed to be. Since we didn't want to spend the night here and we felt concern to be home when our children arrived, we made a mad dash for our car, wading in water above our knees at times. By the time we reached the car the back end was under water.

Although Dick was afraid the car would not start, it did! However, as we made our way home, it stalled a number of times but boys and men always showed up to push us until it started again. When a bus passed us it made waves that literally made us float. On side streets we saw people standing in the doors of their homes with water up to their chests. We looked and felt like we had gone swimming in our clothes and a drive that should have taken about 45 minutes took us over three hours.

We were distressed when we arrived home and found that our children still weren't home from school. It was already two hours later than usual. Although totally relieved when they finally arrived, we were left weak and overwhelmed by the stories they told and thanked the Lord for protecting them. When they got within a few blocks from where we lived, the bus couldn't go any further. The children convinced the bus driver to let them walk the rest of the way home.

Older children carried smaller children, but they came to one place where there was a small bridge crossing over a canal-like sewer. This was usually almost empty except for garbage, but now it was a deep raging torrent. The children formed a human chain and began inching their way across the bridge. The force of the current broke Steve's grip, sweeping him to the other side of the road. It looked like he would go into the canal and be drowned, but at the last second he caught the rail and clung desperately until some men came to his rescue. Everyone arrived home safely, and there was rejoicing with praise to God for His miraculous protection.

Psalm 37:3-4 discusses God's care. **"Trust in the Lord. Be kind and good to others; then you will live safely here in the land and prosper, feeding in safety. Be delighted with the Lord. Then He will give you all your heart's desires. Commit everything you do to the Lord. Trust Him to help you do it and He will."**

I probably could write a book just about the various fires, floods, typhoons, earthquakes, volcanoes, critters we could see (dangerous snakes, monstrous spiders, cockroaches and too many others to name), critters we couldn't see (amoebas, internal worms and other things you probably don't want to hear about), robberies, revolutions, poverty, street kids, begging, cultures, foods, etc. that we experienced during our more than 30 years in the Philippines. We found ourselves on the streets with the Filipino people during the "People's Power Revolution." And we were even caught in the middle of political intrigue.

I guess I can mention that finding a rat swimming in our toilet, or an iguana rearing its head there, did cause some screams. The reactions were the same when I killed a spider whose belly was the size of a ping pong ball. I should have known it was full of a million baby spiders waiting to be born.

However, that's not the purpose of this book. I want to share how attitudes make a huge difference in every experience and how God can change a bad attitude if we let Him. The right attitude did not necessarily take away all fear, danger, heartache, or sickness, and it didn't make us like the poverty, heat, humidity and the unsanitary conditions. But when God changed our attitude, it kept us working where He had led, kept us loving the people and gave us awesome experiences. Sometimes even cultural differences were hard to accept, until Dick Hillis, our mission leader, drilled it into us to change our thinking and attitude from "It's wrong" to "It's not wrong, just different."

Throughout our time in the Philippines we experienced many typhoons and floods, including several like this.

In November 1970 super typhoon Yoling hit Manila with 155 mph winds causing an estimated $80 million in damage, including severe destruction to Faith Academy, which sat on a hill overlooking Manila, receiving the brunt of the storm.

The typhoon blew off the gym roof and knocked down two walls at Faith Academy.

CHAPTER 13

ADVENTURES WITH DICK

Aside from trusting Jesus as my Savior, marrying Dick was the smartest decision I ever made. Actually, I didn't notice him until I heard him sing bass in a male quartet. Besides, one of my girl friends told me she planned to marry him so that took away all interest. However, on one of our choir trips we left the college in cars and went to Portland where we all got into a big rented bus. Dick had a car and was instructed to pick up all the stragglers. As usual, I was one of the late ones and when we arrived at the bus there was no place to sit except with each other. We had plenty of time to talk and discovered that we both loved playing in bands. He played the drums and my instrument was the trumpet.

We got better acquainted one night in the parlor of the girl's dorm at George Fox College when a group of fellas and gals were having a pillow fight, a fairly harmless game until one of the pillows exploded in a virtual blizzard of feathers. The housemother was gone, and after a half hour of hilarious laughter, we began to frantically try to clean up the storm before she arrived. Have you ever tried to gather up feathers? It's sort of like gathering up words you wish you had never spoken.

I had always said, "My special man doesn't have to be tall, dark and handsome, but he must not be short or red-headed." Dick was both short and redheaded. He resembled Mickey

Rooney and at times was even asked to sign autographs. I began to really know Dick and we started to have prayer times together. It wasn't long before we fell in love. He had a car, but not enough money to fill the gas tank, so we often ran out of gas. If we were late getting back to the dorm it wasn't hard for me to climb in the window, with Dick's help, since my room was at the end of the first floor.

I remember one night when we were coming home late from a meeting we were involved in. It was dark and stormy and we were on narrow roads when we suddenly had a flat tire. I wasn't sure of what Dick's reaction was going to be. I had been with guys who got terribly upset if we had a flat tire in the middle of a beautiful day. Dick simply got out of the car and changed the tire. When he finished the job and got back into the car, he apologized to me for making me wait when we were already late. He was soaking wet and a total mess, but I couldn't have been more impressed at how wonderful he was.

Even though I became sure of my love for Dick, I was still a little bothered because he was so short. And it bothered me to be bothered! I tried to project into the future and wondered if it would ever cause problems between us. If I were mad at him, would it make me look down on him? Would I respect and admire him any more if he were taller? I never talked to anyone, except the Lord, about these thoughts.

One night God taught me a valuable lesson. Though it was only a dream, it was as genuine as any waking experience I have ever had and changed my entire attitude. I seemed to be standing on a platform looking out over a vast crowd of people. There was such a large gathering that it was hard at first to distinguish any one person. The Lord said to me, "These are people whose height is according to their character." As I began to look more carefully, I noticed the variety, ranging from very short to very tall. Suddenly I saw one man who was taller than all the others, and it didn't take me long to recognize him. It was Dick! In I Samuel 16:7, the Lord says, **"Look not on his countenance, or the height of his stature. . .For the Lord sees not as man sees; for man looks on the outward** appearance, but the Lord looks on the heart." (KJV) God had given me this privilege to actually see Dick and to be aware of what was genuinely important. So although others may have seen Dick as being short for a man, he was always tall to me. I loved him without question and without reservations!

We didn't plan on being married until the end of our junior year in college, but we couldn't stand to be away from each other. So when my brother Harold and I had a chance to go from Idaho to Twin Rocks Camp in Oregon where the quartet was involved for the week, I jumped at the chance. Even though we would be starting our junior year of college in less than a month and would be together again, I couldn't wait to be with Dick. It was at this time together that we decided we really couldn't be with each other that much without getting into trouble. We either had to go to different schools a long way apart or get married now before college started. Changing schools and being apart didn't have any appeal, so that left getting married. We looked at the calendar and decided that September 8 was the only possibility. I think that gave us about three weeks before the wedding and maybe a week for a honeymoon and moving to Oregon to get settled before classes began. The quartet still had a few engagements, and I wasn't even in Idaho yet. Plus I had the frightening tasks of telling my parents and then planning the wedding. I had the greatest Dad in the world, and although I had absolutely no reason to be afraid of him, I did have some fears. He was strict and had some strong opinions so I wasn't sure how he might feel and react.

I don't know why I was so fearful about telling my parents our plans. They had met Dick and liked him, and we were engaged to be married, so it shouldn't have been a problem. And I knew I had to tell them immediately. However, as soon as Harold and I walked into the house, Dad said, "We've been waiting for you and are leaving immediately for the cabin at Payette Lakes. It's probably our last chance to be there this summer before you go to college. So just put your suitcases in the car and let's go." My heart sank and I was speechless.

Payette Lakes was about a three-hour drive from our home in Nampa. We had a nice cabin right on the lake, with a couple of boats. As a rule we looked forward to having a few days there, but this time it was different for me.

My Dad had a morning routine each day. He took our bigger, faster boat and headed across the lake to the town of McCall. He had a special café where he got a cup of coffee and the daily newspaper. It was a beautiful morning and since mom and I were awake, we decided to go with him, although we stayed in the boat while he went into the town. After he was gone I felt it was a good time to tell my mom our plans to get married Sept. 8th. And then I asked the all-important question, "Will you please tell Dad?" Mom's instant reply was, "I will not! You tell him yourself!"

I didn't have to think about it because my Dad arrived back with his newspaper and Mom said, "Helen has something to tell you!" So as calmly as possible I announced that Dick and I wanted to get married Sept. 8th. Dad didn't reply to me, but he turned to Mom and simply said, "You owe me a milk shake!" My Dad liked to make bets but he always bet in milk shakes. He told Mom that if I went to Twin Rocks and saw Dick, I would come back wanting to get married. Mom didn't think so. It was as simple as that to tell them, but now began the hard part.

Dad's reaction was urgent. "We have to leave now. We don't have time to waste." There were announcements to have printed and sent out, a wedding dress to be made, scheduling the church, cakes to be ordered, flowers, and it seemed like a thousand other details to work on. My parents were absolutely amazing! They really did the impossible and with a beautiful attitude. I had a picture of the dress I wanted, and Mom found a dress designer who would make it in record time. It was made out of parachute silk and was perfect. Our wedding and honeymoon were wonderful. I couldn't have asked for anything better.

While we were gone for just a few days, Dad arranged for a trailer for our car and filled it with every piece of furniture we would need in our tiny apartment at the college. He filled the back seat and trunk of his car with all of our wedding gifts and was ready to take Mom and go with us to get settled in Oregon. My attitude of fear was totally replaced with an attitude of gratitude for my fabulous parents.

———*w*———

When I married Dick I had no idea what my life would be like and I have had experiences that went far beyond anything I had ever even dreamed of. Dick was not only a great choir director, but he was the best husband and father anyone could ever have. He was fun and creative. He made our family life exciting. He included all of the family as much as possible in every part of his life and ministry. He wanted us to be a team and work together, and that's what happened. He was patient with me and helped me to become a better person. If I didn't know how to do something he worked with me. He had far more confidence in me than I had in myself. He encouraged me in every area of my life.

I guess I really don't need to write a separate section on Adventures with Dick. As I've been thinking about this, I realize that Dick has been involved in almost everything I have written. He has either taken me or walked with me through every important experience in my life since the day of our wedding. When we committed our lives to Jesus and then to each other, we became joined together as one. There have been many times in my life when I wanted to give up, especially when it involved writing. "There's no way, no time, no talent! I quit!"

And then Dick would step in. He not only encouraged, prodded, strengthened, reassured and urged me on, but he also took action! He helped with photos and Scriptures, covers and editing. He took care of all the business matters. But most of all, he loved me through the whole process, gave me hugs and let me cry in his arms and told me how proud he was of me. I started writing this book after Dick went to be with

Jesus in 2005. This is now 2014. I've been struggling along for about nine years. Memories of Dick, his files of people and places, and talking to Jesus have kept me going, but it's not the same as having him here beside me, encouraging me and helping. Part of me is missing!

Actually, without Dick, there wouldn't have been all of these experiences and I certainly wouldn't be writing this book. He's the person who made my life exciting. He was unpredictable and at times forgetful, like the day 25 teenagers descended into our home unexpectedly to practice and have dinner. Of course they needed refreshments first, after a long, hot bus ride. He was sorry he forgot to tell me they were coming, but was sure I could come up with something special to feed them. He then added, "We really should start practicing in twenty minutes, and I need you at the piano." Because of a wonderful house girl and great neighbors, I survived.

Dick never lost his ability to sing. I loved having him sing to me. Sometimes we would sit on the couch together, holding hands, and talk about the "little hearts flying all around us." And then he would sing to me: "If Ever I Would Leave You" from the musical *Camelot*.

Never once do I remember being bored after I married Dick. I did have times when I got angry or hurt, but never bored. Sometimes I felt like he expected too much from me, but his expectations and encouragement challenged me and opened up exciting new areas in my life. He was considerate of my feelings, shared news and new ideas with me, corrected me, taught me and let me know how much he loved me. Our relationship, respect and love for each other was satisfying and complete. For two stubborn, obstinate, explosive, vocal and hot- tempered Irish redheads, this was God's greatest miracle in our lives!

Dick served in the Navy during WWII. We met after the war at college and got married in September, 1947. Eleven years later, we had five children.

By the time we left for the Philippines, Dick had assembled the family into a choir. All but Steve had bright red hair, a unique attraction to Filipinos. Our life was filled with endless music, from the Four Flats quartet and the singing Cadds, to church and school choirs.

Our family fell in love with "The Sound of Music" and sang many songs from the movie. We were invited to perform in a large musical review show that Imelda Marcos, wife of the country's president, attended.

Dick and I also sang duets and he was quite the comedian. In one of our favorite routines called "The Little Red School House," I played an elementary school teacher and Dick played an adult student who simply can't move up to the next grade.

As the children became adults, Jon, Steve, and LuAnne often lived overseas or in California. It was, and still is, a rare occassion when we are all in the USA at the same time.

This is one of my favorite pictures of Dick. He was short and a redhead, and often mistaken for the famous actor Mickey Rooney.

In the 57 years I had with Dick I never once felt bored. He was a wonderful husband, father, and a exceptional man. He made life an exciting adventure, not only for me but for our children as well.

This is the last time our entire family, including children, their spouses, our grandkids and great-grandkids, were together for a photo. Since this time we have lost two and added more.

CHAPTER 14

ADVENTURES WITH CHOIRS AND THE FOUR FLATS QUARTET

Dick and I met and fell in love because of a choir trip our first year at Pacific College (now George Fox University). While still a student, Dick became assistant director of our choir and sang bass in the Four Flats Quartet. He also taught music (a choir) for a high school in a nearby town. After graduation from college, the quartet continued singing together and traveled with Youth for Christ until it was time to call it quits. Dick and I moved to Idaho and he taught school and formed the Greenleaf Academy Choir. Although they were the smallest choir from the smallest school, they became so outstanding that they won top honors in the state music festivals. Dick was offered all kinds of jobs, even from the largest school in the state.

All of this time, no matter what else we were involved in, the quartet was in constant demand. We traveled from Idaho to Oregon many weekends and spent some summers singing across the U.S. It soon became evident that the quartet was taking over all of our lives. When Bob Pierce asked them to join him in Asia and then gave them an invitation to be part of World Vision, the four families moved to southern California. The Four Flats Quartet was given several different names and for a few years was known as the World Vision Quartet. However, they never did shake their original name, and even today when memories surface, they will always be the "Four Flats Quartet."

Since a book, "Four Flats and a Pitchpipe," has been written and published, I won't go into most of the adventures we experienced together. As wives, sometimes we went along with the guys—four wives and two babies. Imagine eight adults trying to agree on what restaurant looked best for lunch, or pushing a car for miles when the gas tank ran dry in the middle of nowhere. Together we:

- almost hit an iceberg in Alaska

- ate "country cookin" in the Ozarks

- entered a barbershop contest with our husbands in Oregon

- drank crushed glass in a milkshake in Maryland

- saw street fights and had our food knocked off the table by a raving maniac in Brooklyn

- lost all the suitcases in Kansas

- were introduced to a church congregation as the wives of the wrong husbands in Iowa

- were put in a hotel room with another couple and no space between beds in Washington

- substituted for two of the fellas when they got sick in New York

- suffered morning sickness together in the Midwest

- were guests on the *You Asked For It* television program in Hollywood

- and waited patiently while our men sang for schools, churches, radio, television and presidents in the United States and Southeast Asia.

Our time as a quartet family had a great impact and influence on our personal lives. When the Four Flats and the Four Sharps had 18 little Naturals, they decided it was time to quit traveling extensively. The children were beginning to feel the effects of fathers being gone from home so much. Besides, World Vision had enough of their songs recorded for broadcast that they didn't need them in the studio each week. (The Four Flats Quartet continued to give "Farewell Concerts" whenever they were together, until Dick and Chris died, just a few days apart, in 2005.)

Our lives always included music. When there are five children of various ages and personalities sharing the same back seat of a car, all kinds of situations can erupt. We usually tried to keep one of them in the front seat with us to relieve some of the tension, but even four could cause problems. Dick came up with the idea of singing to keep everyone safely occupied. He also invented music games, and this began adventures with our "Singing Cadd Family."

We let Yvonne and LuAnne sing a song at a missionary conference even before they started school. (The other children were in school and couldn't go with us to these meetings.) It was amazing to see how quickly they made friends and helped us get acquainted faster. We decided it was a good idea to have our children involved in our services here in the U.S. as we were raising support for our work in the Philippines. They were young enough to be cute and they actually became quite good. Four bright red heads and Steve's outgoing personality were also assets.

We hadn't given any thought to them continuing to sing in the Philippines. But when word got around that these five children in one family sang together, they began to get requests. Filipinos love children and families. Most of the Filipinos had never seen red hair so this was clearly an attraction. They probably became more popular than Dick and me as they were invited to sing on television, with the National Symphony Orchestra, programs at the U.S. bases, banquets, conferences, service clubs, etc. Stories of our young family are recorded in a book I wrote over 37 years ago, called "Never to Forget." We were told that eight Filipino families began singing together after they heard us, and some of them became quite well known and popular. I think that's great!

We went to the Philippines specifically to teach music at Faith Academy, a school for missionary children in Southeast Asia. As often happens, other subjects were added when a teacher was needed in another area. Dick often taught different classes beside music, but music was his first love. I was his accompanist. I also taught at times. A first year typing class was given to me. Since everyone brought their own typewriter, we had such a variety that normal typing rules didn't always apply. When I instructed the students to return the carriage firmly, some of the tiny portable typewriters from Hong Kong flew onto the floor. Spanish typewriters were also a challenge. But we had fun and laughed a lot!

Dick's dream was to have a ministering group and go into the Filipino community, so he formed a team of eight Faith Academy teenagers, four girls and four guys. Each student could play a musical instrument as well as sing. They were a very talented group. During one summer a schedule of concerts was set up to travel the island of Luzon and present programs in schools and churches along the way. The trip was so successful that when the question came up, "Do you feel that Faith Academy should have an all-year-round Teen Team?" the answer was a resounding, "Yes, a thousand times, yes!"

Dick became so well known that he was continually asked to teach at other schools and direct different choirs around the city. At one time he managed to get involved with at least seven different groups. He not only had several music groups at Faith Academy, but he also taught at a Chinese school and the American school while directing a Chinese men's choir, a Filipino mixed chorale and a weekly TV program. For my part, I played the piano for most of these commitments. Sometimes my attitude was on a roller coaster of up and down feelings. I hadn't learned the importance of choosing the right attitude and the difference it could make in every activity. When two of the schools scheduled a concert on the same evening without consulting Dick, he began to realize the importance of learning to use the word, "No!"

Returning to the U.S. after five years for a "furlough" was an important requirement of our mission. Dick had learned a good lesson and began concentrating more on his work at Faith Academy. He wanted a choral group that required auditions. His desire was a small group of 16 – 20 singers with an equal number of girls and boys. He wanted them to have a name, not just be "advanced choir." He did a play on words, calling them the Madri-Gals & Guys. However, it wasn't long until they acquired a short nickname, the Mads. He didn't like it, but the name stuck! This group was larger than the Teen Team and was Dick's dream for a ministering choir.

Once again, there is a book with stories of this group over a period of eight or nine years. It involved many different students, since the group changed each year as the kids graduated or left the Philippines. Dick started writing the book "The Madri-Gals & Guys" before he died, and five years later I finished writing about our adventures with them. And we did have numerous adventures.

We sang for special occasions at the American Embassy, the U.S. military bases, churches, schools, service clubs, concert halls, hotels, open-air plazas and banquets. These missionary kids made three trips to the U.S., traveling through Europe on our way to begin the East coast tour. Two of the U.S. adventures took us to the West coast, where once again we performed in high schools, colleges, churches, on radio and television. We probably averaged at least one meeting a day.

One of our crazy adventures was the time the airline made a mistake on our tickets. The plane was scheduled to leave Tokyo two hours earlier than our tickets said. By the time the mistake was discovered, the choir members were scattered in various areas sightseeing or shopping. With no cell phones in those days, we had no way to contact anyone. The airline, the hotel, Dick and the other adult leaders were all in panic. Hotel personnel went into our rooms and stuffed everyone's belongings into random suitcases. And they forgot to check the bathrooms where all personal items were left. Because of the intense timeline, our business manager forgot to pick up all of the money for the trip that he had put into the hotel's safe. This mistake was not discovered until we were flying over the middle of the Pacific Ocean. We had no idea what we were going to do. Bill was supposed to be the only person that could get the money, because he was the one that put it there. We needed money as soon as we landed in the U.S. It also included all of the personal money belonging to the students. Through a number of radio contacts, special arrangements were finally made for the pilot to pick up the money on his return trip to Tokyo in a few days.

Fortunately, when we arrived in Portland, Oregon, Gary Poppinga, Faith Academy's former superintendent, met us. Gary immediately came to our rescue and loaned us enough dollars to meet out needs until the money came from Japan. Our choir members eventually managed to collect their own clothes and other items from the mixed up suitcases. We never lacked anything. If one of the choir members looked cold, someone gave them a coat. Every place we went it seemed as though people couldn't do enough for our students.

Our experiences were so extraordinary, awesome, astonishing, spectacular and fantastic that I can't possibly tell about them here. Besides all the good happenings, we had normal mishaps: The rented bus broke down and had to be pushed by our boys. There was sickness, including measles and a malaria attack. Uniforms were left behind and we had occasional misunderstandings. But each service began with prayer and sharing. And these teenagers had a ministry that continued to change lives long after the concerts. Faith Academy received letters from several pastors expressing their thanks for sending our choir. One pastor told how it had changed their church and brought new life. He said, "I suppose at times you must wonder, 'Is it worth while, sending out these young people, the expense, time, etc.?' To this we say a resounding: YES!!!"

"Refreshing!" "Super great!" "In a class by themselves!" were words often used to describe this unique group of teenagers. They were all children of missionaries in SE Asia and their sparkle and energy were evident in every concert. Another pastor, after expressing how he was ministered to personally, made this statement, "I've never had a group of any age visit a church where I've been pastor that has had the impact this group had on us at Alamitos!" Probably the best compliment we ever received was when another pastor expressed, "The kids graciously stepped aside so that we could see Jesus."

When we were leaving our work at Faith Academy, my husband expressed his feelings. "The years I spent in the music department at Faith Academy would have to be termed the highlight of my lifetime. I have always had an exciting and incredible life, but the satisfaction of seeing young people grow to maturity, both musically and spiritually, can never be put into words. My own children testify to their Madri-Gal & Guys experience as one of the highlights of their lives. Many other students have expressed the same thing. As I look back, I can only thank God that He gave Helen and me the privilege of working together those wonderful years at Faith Academy."

The Four Flats Quartet started out as an award-winning college barbershop quartet from Pacific College in Newberg, Oregon.

The Four Flats eventually became the World Vision Quartet for a few years and traveled to Asia, sang for presidents in the US and Asia, and joined several Billy Graham meetings.

One of the first choirs Dick directed at Faith Academy was called the "Teen Team." They performed in churches and prisons in the Manila area, as well as toured the island of Luzon. Each of the eight members played an instrument.

The 1976 Madri-Gals & Guys rehearse in a recording studio where they made a record for a tour of the west coast of the US.

The Madri-Gals & Guys performed a variety of music from musicals to gospel.

The Madri-Gals & Guys recorded three records over a period of six years with three tours to the USA.

1970 Record Cover for a US west coast tour.

1974 Record Cover for a US east coast tour.

1976 Record Cover for a US west coast tour.

CHAPTER 15

ADVENTURES WITH CAROLYN – OUR FIRST CHILD

D ick and I were married just before starting our junior year in college. Shortly after we began our senior year in college I made the exciting discovery that we were going to have a baby! Although we were both thrilled about this news, it did create a few problems. Besides a full schedule of classes, I was editor of our school's yearbook. In those days we didn't have any of the technology available today. No computers, no copy machines, no digital photos. We did everything the hard way, by hand! We had to depend on our own creativity without the help of the computer.

As music majors, both Dick and I were required to give a Senior Recital. This usually took place close to the end of the school year, but since I would be playing the trumpet, both my size and my breathing created problems. We hadn't told anyone yet, and after discussing it with Roy Clark, our wonderful music professor, we decided to give a very early joint recital and try to keep my pregnancy a secret until after our program. The whole idea wasn't an easy task. We were already overloaded and now we had to learn our music much faster than normal. Although we wanted to tell everyone we met our exciting news, we only told my parents, the quartet and my best friend Mary.

Dick and I never quite agreed on a name for our baby, but we finally decided that if it was a boy he would be David and a girl would be Carolyn. When we had babies in those days we waited for the surprise ending to find out whether it would be David or Carolyn. The quartet was scheduled to travel for the college during the summer months. So it took some special planning in their schedule to make it possible for Dick to be with me when the baby was born, which was supposed to be the last half of July. The arrangements looked good. The guys would come back to the Northwest for meetings in our area three weeks before our baby was scheduled to arrive and three weeks after the date.

This seemed perfect! I would have the baby and then go with the guys to Idaho where my parents and siblings lived. However, the baby did not cooperate, and although we did everything possible to encourage her arrival, she decided to make her appearance the day Dick had to leave with the other three quartet members. That was the 9th of August. Dick managed to stay until Carolyn was born, but then was gone before I was awake enough to talk. Since nothing worked out on schedule (do babies ever stick to our schedules?), my Dad immediately sent my mom to be with me when Dick left.

I had warned Dick that most babies were not very attractive when they are first born. They can be red and wrinkled and not like the cute pictures we so often see. Carolyn came into this world with bright red fuzz on a very pointed head. This was the first and only memory Dick had of his first child until I joined him in Idaho. The doctor assured me Carolyn was perfectly normal in every way, and her pointed head would soon look normal if I placed pillows properly around it. She should have been born at least two weeks earlier and had been too low for too long.

I seemed to be having the after-birth-blues and cried most of the time. I really missed Dick and wanted to be with him. I was also having a lot of trouble nursing Carolyn. When my mom phoned my Dad and told him I was crying most of the time, he drove the 450 miles to Newberg and the next day we were on our way to Idaho. My parents were fantastic! I'm not sure I would have survived without their support and love. By the time Dick saw his baby again her head not only looked normal but she was really cute with her bright red fuzz.

Carolyn was the ideal baby. She didn't cry very often, she entertained herself, and by the time she was six or seven months old I could leave her sitting on the front bench in church while I went to the piano to accompany Dick when he sang a solo. She liked her room organized, she never broke her toys and she sang herself to sleep every night and for naps. Dick and I decided we must be great parents.

—*м*—

Carolyn is the oldest of the 18 quartet children. Along with Chris and Divonna's baby boy, Ronnie, she traveled with us to Alaska, across the U.S. and into Canada. She was eight months old and Ronnie was six months old when the quartet was invited to go to Alaska on a converted WW II minesweeper. Captain Stabbert and his family had turned this old vessel into a floating medical clinic, a chapel and living quarters for staff and guests. They were planning an evangelistic cruise up the coast of Canada on the Inland Passage and into Alaska. Amazingly, they asked the wives and babies to come along.

We were really excited when the guys told us the wives had been invited to go to Alaska with them. This was very unusual. We generally stayed home while they traveled. We met Captain Stabbert and his family on their ship, the Willis Shank, in Seattle on a sunny day in April 1950. In addition to their family there were various other helpers: a volunteer crew, cook, medical person and pastor. Roberta Stabbert had prepared for the two babies with everything we needed for the month long trip. Carolyn and Ronnie each had their own baby beds, while the rest of us slept in bunk beds. There was a slight problem though, because the babies' beds were not built in or bolted down securely. However, the Inland Passage was smooth sailing and beautiful. The weather was cold, but

sunny and lovely. We had great times and wonderful relationships while having new and exciting experiences.

As we traveled up the coast, the ship stopped to visit
small indigenous villages along the way. Since so few unusual
things ever happened in these isolated villages, we caused a
great commotion each time we pulled into a dock. Norval had
his unicycle with him and since there were no streets, he rode
through the town on the boardwalks. By the time he came
back to the ship every kid in town was following him. When
they announced the evening service almost everyone in the
village arrived. The chapel could only hold about 70 people,
so the overflow spread out all over the ship. The people loved
the quartet and didn't want them to stop singing. They were
also fascinated with the two white babies. It was hard to get
them to leave and then they were back early the next morning
wanting more. It was a joy to see many people trust Jesus as
their Savior.

Even with all these great things happening, there were
other experiences where my attitude needed a total overhaul.
God and Dick helped me survive, but I did have to change
or the new fears I faced could have almost destroyed me
and our future ministry. For example, when we needed to go
ashore it was not like the movies where you see people using
wide solid stairs with rails as they leave their luxury liner. To
me it was more like a horror movie, only worse because we
had our baby.

One time the only way ashore was over a board about 10
inches wide stretched from the ship to the dock. Dick guessed
the drop to the water below was about 15 or 20 feet, but what
I saw was a black bottomless pit. Since my balance has never
been great and Dick has always had unusually good balance,
he carried Carolyn. As I watched in terror, he made it safely
across and handed our baby to someone else so he could come
back for me. He inched me across very slowly and I'm still
alive to talk about it. Another time it was just the opposite. We
had to climb a rope ladder down the side of our ship and step
across to another rope ladder on the ship tied next to us. Then

we had to climb up that rope ladder in order to reach shore. Dick had Carolyn strapped to his back and I was on my own this time. There were times when I crawled on my hands and knees across a plank to keep from falling into the unknown.

Once ashore we faced a new fear. Many of the native villagers were infected with tuberculosis. Those were the days when people were often isolated to keep them from spreading the disease. Some of these villagers were sick and were spitting up blood. We didn't have time to think about ourselves being exposed because everyone wanted to hold and kiss our adorable white babies. This was another type of terror and required a strong faith and total trust in God. We were helpless, but God is never helpless and He was in control. We had given our children to Him before they were born and we just needed to do the best we could in caring for them and then trust God with their lives.

The Inland Passage was calm and beautiful, but there did come a day when we had to cross the Queen Charlotte Sound and be in the open sea. Captain Stabbert warned us that it might be rough and advised us to take some seasick pills to calm our stomachs. No one mentioned that we only needed half or even a quarter of the pill, so we swallowed the whole thing. In all my life I had never even had an aspirin, so anything I took knocked me out. Carolyn was in her baby bed and I was in my bunk nearby. In my semi-unconscious state, I became aware that the baby bed was moving across the room and hitting the wall on the other side. I knew this was not safe, so I managed to get my baby and put her in bed with me, hoping that she would soon be asleep in my arms. Carolyn wasn't sick or the slightest bit sleepy; she only wanted to play.

Sometimes parents seem to acquire super-human strength when it comes to their children's safety. Apparently that's what happened to me because I was totally drugged with the seasick pill, but managed to stay awake those hours on the open sea. It was a struggle and I remember thinking, "So this is what it feels like when they torture people by keeping them awake hour after hour!" After we made the crossing and the water smoothed out, we got the call to dinner.

I don't remember much from that point on. I'm told I made it to the mess hall, got my food and fell sound asleep with my face in the plate. Dick said they carried me to bed and I never moved until morning, so he was totally in charge of our baby that night. Although I don't remember that experience, I can recall the snow covered mountains, clear sparkling water, bluish icebergs, glaciers, quaint little villages, friendly and loving native Alaskans, dedicated missionaries, wonderful people on the ship, fresh fish, delicious tiny shrimp we ate like popcorn and adoring audiences.

The Willis Shank would stay in Alaska, so we took another ship back home to fulfill a schedule of concerts. None of us had ever been on a ship so luxurious. The Princess Louise was a cruise ship with all the opulence anyone could ask for. Our room was a suite with a special bed for Carolyn. The meals were beyond our wildest imagination. We had menus with no prices and they told us to order anything and everything we wanted. All was included in the price of the ticket. This was a treat we did not expect, but it made a wonderful climax to an already exciting and memorable trip.

—∿∿—

As a rule, the wives stayed home when the quartet traveled in other parts of the country. But after a taste of traveling with our husbands on the Alaska trip, we weren't as satisfied to just stay home and wait for them. So since we only had the two babies, we all tagged along across the U.S. with the quartet. We had two cars; each carrying two couples, one baby and either a pink or blue potty. Carolyn had her first birthday while we were crossing the United States. This was a memorable occasion, so we bought her a small cake, took her outside and gave her the freedom to do whatever she desired. I think my best description would be that she dressed herself in her birthday cake, beginning at the top of her head. Although it was a mess, it was a celebration.

It was always interesting to travel with a baby, especially when many of our meals were in restaurants. One day in a small café we were seated at a large table and each person had a place mat with silverware and a glass of water. Suddenly, with no warning and with lightening speed, Carolyn grabbed one of the mats and gave a quick, strong pull. The mat came sailing out but the silverware, dishes and water glasses stayed intact, right where they were on the table, but minus the mat. It was all we could do to keep the guys from trying the same trick.

Carolyn was a very cautious child. She was walking around things from the time she was nine months old, but she always had to be touching something. Shortly after her first birthday I took her outside from a very hot church service and put her down on the grass. She totally surprised me by taking off walking as if she had been doing it all of her life. She had so much fun that she didn't want to quit, not even when it was time to go to bed. Our two babies, a bright-redheaded girl and a very blond boy, made friends wherever we went and added a whole new dimension to the quartet travels.

Probably one of the most memorable experiences we had was when we crossed the bridge into Brooklyn. We had always heard about the Brooklyn accent and their street fights. But we thought it was just exaggerated for movies. However, the minute we crossed over into Brooklyn it was like entering another country. They lived up to everything we had ever heard or seen in the movies. Within minutes we saw our first of many street fights. And then we heard them speak, almost a foreign language, but just like in the movies. It wasn't long before we had our own movie-type of experience when we entered a cafeteria to have some lunch.

Dick went through the line before me so that he could take Carolyn when it was my turn to get some food. He was sitting at a table holding our baby when a wild woman came rushing in. As she passed Dick's table, with one sweep of her arm she knocked all of his food onto the floor. From there she went back and began yelling at the workers behind the counter. They evidently didn't respond quickly enough to suit her so she picked up one of the big trays and threw it at them. They managed to duck, but it hit one of the large coffee urns. She suddenly turned and came screaming to where I was standing near the water containers. As I watched in stunned amazement she began picking up the drinking glasses and throwing them onto the floor. Shattered pieces of glass landed all over my legs and feet. We did feel like we were part of a wild movie, but this was reality. She yelled at the workers again and went screaming out the door. The manager came rushing over to Dick's table to make sure our baby was OK. And after he explained that the crazy woman was on drugs and needed a fix, he offered to give us anything we wanted, especially for Carolyn. This was our introduction to Brooklyn.

For months after Carolyn learned to talk she never called us daddy and mommy. We were "Dick" and "Helen" and she always referred to herself as Carolyn. "Carolyn wants a drink" or "Carolyn's doll is sleepy." Her memory has always been phenomenal. Before Carolyn started school, she could quote the whole book of Rudolph, the Red-Nosed Reindeer, and she can still remember most of it today. She also learned Bible verses and numerous other children's books. Sometimes Dick tried to skip a page or two when he was reading to her, but she always reprimanded him and asked him to turn back to the right page. Carolyn did far more than simply recite the books. She also acted out the parts and kept us all entertained.

I do not know what I would have done if any of the other children had been born first. I could always count on Carolyn to help me, even as a tiny child. And when the other babies came along she was my assistant. She was never lazy or demanding, could basically take care of herself and always wanted to learn anything new.

For the six years we lived in California, I always gave the children vitamins. When they were old enough, the vitamins were in the form of a pill. When we were moving from that house someone tipped the chrome kitchen table and hundreds of pills spilled out over the floor. That must have been the healthiest table in the nation because it was full of vitamin pills. After an intensive investigation, we discovered that Carolyn had faithfully been feeding her vitamins into the hollow table leg for six years! She's always been original.

I am probably one of the worst package-wrappers anywhere so I simply gave any package I wanted wrapped to Carolyn to do for me. It took me only minutes to toss a package together, but Carolyn took time to create a masterpiece. She could also make an original costume out of just about anything.

When we went to the Philippines in 1962, Carolyn was 13 years old and in the 8th grade and became my dependable babysitter. It didn't always work with the boys, since they never thought they needed a babysitter and their sister certainly didn't qualify. Yvonne and LuAnne were very happy with Carolyn because she did fun activities with them. Carolyn's dependability came into question during our time in Hong Kong when we were put off the ship.

The night we attended a meeting on the rooftop of one of the 10 story H-buildings we didn't want to take Yvonne and LuAnne. There were no elevators and we had to climb steep stairs. Carolyn agreed to stay with the girls in the hotel room. She not only locked the door, but also put the bolt across it. When we returned we knocked on the door but nothing happened. We really banged hard and called Carolyn's name but still got no response from her. We did get a response from other guests, as heads kept popping out of rooms to see who was making all the racket. We finally asked the desk clerk to please ring our room on the phone. After an hour of calling at 10-minute intervals in attempt to awaken at least one of the girls, everyone in the hotel almost panicked. Even ledges were checked from the rooms next door to see if we could crawl across, but they weren't wide enough.

By this time it seemed that nearly everyone in the hotel had joined us. There were whispers of a gas leak or carbon monoxide in the room and we were getting frightened. Deciding it was time to do something drastic, the hotel got their biggest, strongest men and rammed the door. It broke open, locks and all! The noise was unimaginable, with shouting, phone ringing, banging and crashing a door down.

Not one of the girls moved. We were certain they were dead. We began shaking them and calling their names. Carolyn finally sat up, looked around puzzled at all the people and sleepily asked, "What's wrong?" The phone was on the table right next to her head. Yvonne and LuAnne slept on. I guess they were just completely worn out from the time changes, excitement and activities. We were afraid the hotel would throw us out, but everyone was almost as relieved as we were to find the children alive. We made lots of new friends, but it was an unusual way to get acquainted.

Faith Academy, the school for missionary kids in that part of Asia, was a terrific school. However, it was not easy. The children had to get up very early to catch the bus around 6:30 a.m. The bus ride took almost an hour, and even at that early hour it was hot and sticky. The teachers were excellent and expected a great deal from the students. Even the youngest children often had homework, and high school students were always complaining about too much work.

Since it was a small school most of the kids were involved in some kind of extra activity, especially sports and music. Because we had one of the best coaches and music directors of any high school in the world, we usually had champion basketball teams and our music groups took first place at festivals. However, it did require practice and this took time.

Carolyn was never satisfied with anything less than straight "A's," so she seemed to spend most of the time doing schoolwork. At one point we actually told Carolyn that it wasn't necessary to get perfect grades. We certainly never had to tell the boys that! When the bus brought the children home around 3:15 p.m. they were hot and tired from the long bus ride and needed time to unwind, to run and play and relax, but there was homework to be done. We wanted all of our children to learn to play the piano and other instruments and this also required time. And since the children were becoming popular singing together and were invited to sing in various places that meant time spent practicing as a family.

Years earlier, Dick and I had decided it was important to have a family time each day, so we started reading together after dinner. Once we got into this habit and had found books that kept everyone interested, we all began to look forward with anticipation to this time together. Everything we did required discipline, as well as making choices. We couldn't possibly do all the things we wanted to do. Once again my attitude needed help. It seems like when we get our attitude straightened out in one area something else pops up and we have to start all over again. I'm so glad God doesn't give up on us but patiently continues to teach and love us through all circumstances.

—*vv*—

We were constantly amazed at Carolyn's abilities. She never got over her love of acting and singing. But when she came home with an "A++" in a math class, and the teacher told us Carolyn could probably teach her, we wondered how we ever got a child like this. Besides all of her other activities, Carolyn managed to be Valedictorian and received several scholarships for college.

When Carolyn graduated from Faith Academy with honors on April 28, 1967, the school officials let Dick present her with the awards. The next day he wrote her the following letter:

Dearest Carolyn,

Last night you graduated! It was a wonderful night! You were beautiful and sweet as always. There were so many thoughts that raced through my mind. I remembered how you used to say when you were a little baby just barely able to talk, "When I get to be a big girl I'm going to sing in Daddy's choir." And it came true, along with a lot of other dreams. I doubt if you were ever as thrilled as I have been.

And last night...what a crowning touch to all God's super abundant blessings to me over the years...to get to award to you, my very own flesh and blood, my daughter, the highest honor that can come to a student. I wanted to say so many things. I wanted to say how outstanding you are in music, drama, original ideas, crafts, speaking and just about anything you undertake. I even had some clever things thought up that might make the people laugh. But I did not have to say anything more than a few words for everyone already knew of your outstanding achievements and personality. The handshake was for the dignity that the occasion required, but the kiss was from my heart full of love.

Now that you have made us the proudest parents that could be, we look forward with you to the days ahead when you will excel even more. You will not know, I am sure, what a wonderful feeling it is to have complete confidence in a person such as we have in you. One reason we have this confidence is that we know where your confidence lies...in Jesus Christ.

I could wish no better thing for you as a father than to ask that God will reveal His perfect will to you and that you will settle for nothing more or less. I know you will.

I have not dreaded this day, but I do dread that inevitable day when we will separate our paths. But as life moves on God always seems to be there with that Grace that we need. I want you to know the meaning of my life verse: Gal. 2:20 and also Roman chapter 6.

With much love, Dad

Galatians 2:20 *"I am crucified with Christ: nevertheless I live: yet not I, but Christ lives in me: and the life which I now live in the flesh I live by the faith of the Son of God, who loved me; and gave himself for me."*

———ᴠᴠ———

As I've said before, the most difficult part of being a missionary is leaving people you love. It is especially hard when your children leave home to go to college in another country. With Carolyn she didn't leave us, we left her, because our family was on furlough her first year in college. Leaving her was one of the hardest things we ever had to face. She seemed so young and vulnerable as we walked up the ramp to board the airplane that took us away from her for a possible four years. I probably cried at least half of the way to Hawaii, and even now it's hard to think about. My human emotions ached and hurt, and yet I did have peace that only Christ can give, as the scripture in Colossians 3:15 describes: **"Let the peace of heart which comes from Christ be always present in your hearts and lives, for this is your responsibility and privilege as members of His body. And always be thankful."**

Carolyn spent the summer with our dear friends Norm and Muriel Cook and their girls. We had complete confidence in leaving her in their care until college started in the fall. She couldn't have been in better hands! It didn't take away the hurt of leaving her and breaking up our family for the first time, but it certainly helped ease the pain and concern. Even in situations like this, attitude plays an extremely important part. I'm not sure I could have gotten onto that plane if God hadn't taken control of my attitude and reminded me that we were all still in His hands together, no matter where we were in the world.

Carolyn starred in numerous musical productions, which we could only read about. It hurt to miss her graduation, not getting to watch as she received honors, yet distance couldn't destroy our close relationship. This was probably one of our biggest regrets, missing these important events in her life. The new technology we have now is amazing and has revolutionized our communication, making it so much easier to keep in contact and actually see activities as they are happening. However, we didn't have anything like that in those days and flying back was too expensive and out of the question.

When we did come back for a furlough Carolyn often sang with us as a family again, even though by now she had finished college and was teaching school in a town near us. We were here to help when Carolyn had a bout with pneumonia and missed directing her big Christmas extravaganza. We had constantly read about her dramatic ability in musicals and plays, and we finally had the privilege of seeing her perform in a major program. This was the only time we had seen her on stage since her high school days in the Philippines.

Before long, Carolyn moved to our hometown of Newberg and taught in the Newberg school system until she retired last year. There were times when she taught full-time elementary music, directed the high school musical and instructed a college class in the evening. I found an old newspaper article recently that my Mom had sent me in Manila. The Newberg Fire Department was putting on an annual talent show, and it was considered a great success. But to quote the newspaper article: "Blodgett and other fire department organizers give a ton of credit to a woman not in the department. She is Carolyn Cadd, music teacher at Renee. Without her, I really don't know where this talent show would be." Carolyn and the department representatives auditioned the acts during November, choosing about 30 good acts. We are always continually proud of Carolyn's accomplishments.

Carolyn made two trips to the Philippines to visit us during her summer vacations from teaching. With a group of children, she made several segments for our television show, teaching music and games. But on one of her times in Manila, she became sick with typhoid fever. They had a strong medicine, which helped get rid of the disease, but it wasn't always safe for white people and required constant monitoring. When she began to have adverse reactions, we knew she needed to get back to the U.S., but she was too sick to travel alone. We finally found two strong guys who were going to Oregon, and they were very happy to be her escort and take care of her. Sometimes when I think back on some of the experiences my children have lived through, I am amazed at God's protection and care.

———

When Walt and Yvonne finished their time in the Philippines and a year of special schooling in England, they returned to Newberg to live. Carolyn was teaching in the Newberg schools, and since Walt and Yvonne had an extra room, they invited Carolyn to live with them. It was during this time that Walt and Yvonne decided they probably couldn't have any more children and they really wanted more than one child. Their daughter Miriam was already four years old. After many weeks of filling out papers, interviews and all the other red tape it takes to adopt a baby, they were able to get their second little girl. Hannah was adorable, and just when everything seemed to be going smoothly and everyone was adjusting to the new schedules, Yvonne became pregnant. Megan was on her way.

Although Hannah was still a baby, Yvonne's pregnancy probably wouldn't have been a problem and she could have handled it, but being pregnant for Yvonne meant being sick and vomiting almost every day for nine months. Walt was working and Carolyn taught school full time, but Carolyn was a wonderful cook and so efficient that she came home from teaching small children all day to taking care of Miriam, Hannah and Yvonne, as well as making meals for the family. From the time she was a child, Carolyn came to the rescue of other family members, including me!

Shortly after Megan was born, Walt and Yvonne were approached by the adoption agency to see if they would be willing to adopt Hannah's two younger half-sisters, Annie and Emily. Although the three girls had the same birth mother, they all had different fathers, but the agency wanted to keep siblings together. This would have meant four little girls under four years old for Walt and Yvonne, and this thought at that time was totally overwhelming. But they did have the bright idea that maybe Carolyn could take Annie and Emily. Carolyn was single, but had already gone through adoption classes with the state and the living situation would keep all three girls close. The adoption was approved fairly quickly. Carolyn suddenly became the mother of two little girls: Annie and Emily! This became a continuous adventure that will last for the rest of Carolyn's life.

Carolyn and Yvonne decided their house really wasn't large enough for all the new members that had been added, so they bought a lovely piece of property in the country that had two houses on it. About the same time, God had some other surprises.

—*∿*—

Walt became a friend with one of his coworkers. Ron Brannon and Walt worked in the same office, and when it seemed like Ron needed some special friends, Walt and Yvonne began asking him to their home for dinner. Carolyn and her girls often joined the group and it wasn't too long before Ron and Carolyn became good friends.

The friendship grew and before long we acquired another great son-in-law. The wedding took place in February 1996, when most of our family happened to be home at the same time. Both Ron and Walt are quiet and reserved guys, and I'm not sure they had any idea what kind of family they were getting into when they married Carolyn and Yvonne.

When Carolyn and Ron married, they both got more than just a spouse. They also acquired new family members. Ron had been married before and had two daughters, one of whom, Katelyn, was seven months younger than Emily,

Carolyn's youngest. Heather was already an adult, living in South Carolina.

Around the time Katelyn was in sixth grade, Katelyn's mom, Linda, did not have a job. The two of them were living in a trailer, but needed a new place to park it. Since Ron and Carolyn and Walt and Yvonne had an empty field with electric and water sources nearby, they invited Linda to park the trailer in their field temporarily. Unfortunately, there was no access to the septic system, so showers and laundry had to be done in Ron and Carolyn's house. Ron and Carolyn also invited Linda and Katelyn to share meals with them sometimes. Some people thought it was quite unusual for Carolyn to be willing to have an ex-wife of Ron's be such a close part of her life, but Carolyn believes that when God opens up opportunities to show his love we should take those opportunities. Temporary turned into long-term, and when Annie and Emily moved out, Ron and Carolyn invited Linda and Katelyn to move into the girls' rooms, since the trailer was old now and they would finally not have to walk a block to take a shower. (Later, when Walt re-married and moved away, Ron and Carolyn bought his half of their property and Linda and Katelyn moved into Walt and Yvonne's former house.)

A few years after Ron and Carolyn's marriage, Heather, Ron's oldest daughter, moved back to Oregon and eventually bought a house in Newberg. Heather had a baby boy, Jake, in 2008, giving Ron and Carolyn their first grandchild. But when Jake was three, Heather had an accident in which a heavy metal gutter fell on her head, causing a severe concussion and brain injury. This happened the second day of beginning her Master's program in Speech and Language Pathology. Soon after, Heather's partner left her and Ron and Carolyn suggested that Heather and Jake move in with them while she was healing and attempting to continue the Master's program at a slower pace. She did, and four years later, after therapy and slow recovery and much hard work, Heather graduated.

Annie married and had two children, Alex and Rosalie, two years apart, and Emily had Natalie, who was born four weeks after Rosalie. Since Emily did not have a steady job and Natalie's father left shortly after Natie was born, Emily and Natie also moved in with Ron and Carolyn. They were happy to care for Natalie when Emily went back to school to start a three-year program in Auto Body Repair. Carolyn's attitude has had to adjust to numerous people living with her, but she continues to say that helping out where needed is the right thing to do.

Although Carolyn has retired from full-time teaching, she still works part time as a substitute teacher. On Tuesday evenings, she serves an evening meal for anyone in our extended family who is available to come. She is my only child who actually lives in the U.S., and her home is only a few miles from where I live, So Carolyn is still my helper, and I don't know what I would do without her.

Three sisters: Carolyn, our oldest, holding LuAnne, our youngest, and Yvonne.

All grown up, the three sisters, Carolyn, LuAnne, and Yvonne, were always close.

Carolyn adopted two girls, Annie and Emily, while still single. Later she married Ron Brannon and welcomed his two daughters, Katelyn and Heather, into their home.

Carolyn met Ron when she was in her 40s. She was a single mom with no thought of marriage.

Carolyn with Natalie, one of her four grandkids, who lives in their home.

A Brannon family outing every Christmas includes picking and cutting Christmas trees for the various extended family members.

CHAPTER 16

ADVENTURES WITH JON —
OUR FIRST SON

B ecause Carolyn was such an unusual and perfect baby, Dick and I were still convinced that we had the knowledge and secrets to great parenting. This misconception was totally shattered very soon after our baby boy came. I think he was born with a smile, thinking of all the fun and mischief he could quietly get into.

The summer before Jonny was born we traveled the United States with the quartet. All of the wives were pregnant and we each had a baby within the next six months. Jonathan was the first boy, and he made his appearance less than an hour after I checked into the hospital. This was in Nampa, Idaho, a small town with a small hospital and only one delivery room. If the doctor hadn't been in the hospital at that exact time, I wouldn't have had a doctor or a delivery room. Jon didn't have a pointed head, but his fuzz was even brighter red than Carolyn's had been.

While Carolyn was a very cautious baby, Jonathan was the opposite. He wanted to walk before he was nine months old. He couldn't, but he tried, and was constantly sporting bruises and cuts. I couldn't turn my back on him for even a minute or I would find him in the kitchen sink trying to turn the water on. It was scary when he climbed on the stove and I never could figure how he managed to be sitting on top of the piano when I only turned my back for a few seconds. I think he was born to climb and fly. There was also the time he ate all of the cat's food and smelled like fish for days.

One time, I asked Dick to watch Jonny while I took a quick shower. Dick took his eyes off Jonny for a moment to make a phone call. When I came out of the shower feeling all clean and refreshed, I found my baby quite the opposite! I could barely see his eyes through the garbage covering his hair, face, hands and arms. Carolyn had always been careful and orderly about her toys and her room, but all that changed when Jon arrived. He loved taking things apart, but couldn't always get them back together, although he tried. Watches were a favorite "toy," and if we weren't careful, we would find the parts in various places around the house. One day, he managed to use a hammer on the big plate glass mirror that had been mine since I was a child. The crack was so perfect that not one little portion of the mirror could be salvaged. That may have been the time when Dick and I sat down and calmly (as calmly as you can be at a time like that) discussed the pros and cons of children versus things. Even though we came to the conclusion that children really are more important, I still cried a lot!

Dick loved to play with Jon and often at breakfast he would teasingly crack a hard-boiled egg on Jonny's head. One morning when we were later than usual and Dick was almost tardy for his teaching job, Jonny suddenly grabbed a boiled egg and surprised his father by smashing the egg on Dick's head. It turned out to be one of those rare days when I managed to cook a soft-boiled egg. Dick looked so funny with egg yolk in his hair and running down his forehead into his eyes, but he couldn't say a word! This was a good lesson in seeing how our children imitate what they see us doing and saying.

When we lived in California, Jon went hiking in the foothills with some friends and came home with a baby snake. Later when some people came to see me, Jon proudly showed them the snake he had found. The reaction of our guests was immediate and intense as they instructed us to get rid of that snake as quickly as possible. It was a baby rattlesnake and was just as poisonous as its parents. It just hadn't developed rattles yet, but it could still bite and kill. Dick wasn't home and I didn't know how to kill it, so I flushed it down the toilet.

Jealousy overcame Jonny whenever Carolyn lost a tooth, because she put it under her pillow at night and found some money in its place the next morning. He kept asking her if he could borrow one of her teeth. It didn't really matter whether it was loose or not. He only wanted it on loan; someday he would pay her back.

As a child, I was always car sick if we went over 30 miles from home but only once did any of the children show signs of my problem. We were on an all day trip and the road was narrow and winding. Jonny was just a baby and I was holding him on my lap when suddenly he vomited. Dick stopped the car and we jumped out but Jonny was fine. I intended to clean up the mess, but there wasn't any. We were puzzled, until about ten miles down the road when I reached into my dress pocket to get a tissue. The mystery was solved!

Jon had the rare ability to look wide-awake when he was really sound asleep. He even talked intelligently. One night I had taken my five children to church when the quartet was on a trip. Jon fell asleep and after the service I woke him with instructions to go to the car. Looking perfectly normal, he walked out the door. I was gathering up the other children when someone came and asked, "Are you missing a boy?" Jon had walked out to the first car he came to, climbed into the back seat and continued his sleep. I shudder to think of the panic if those people hadn't happened to look in the back seat of their car before going home and parking the car in their garage for the night.

Jon has always been a paradox. He is without doubt our quietest child, and yet he caused much of the noise around our house. He is not very talkative (which is the opposite of the rest of our family), but when he does start to say something we all stop and listen. Otherwise, we all talk at the same time.

Jon often has a way of communicating which is much more effective than words. He has always been full of compassion, especially for the underdog, and yet he often played so rough with Yvonne and LuAnne that they came running to me for protection. When Jon was in high school, he was the wrestling champion in his weight class and he liked to practice on me.

Jon always loved animals, although he was terribly allergic to cats. When he was little and we lived in the U.S., he liked the normal animals like dogs, frogs, horses, goats, tadpoles, etc. In the Philippines he added lizards, monkeys and guinea pigs, but we never let him make pets of the huge cockroaches, rats, or mice. When Jon moved to Africa to work, his interests expanded to a host of African creatures. However, he did have enough respect for animals like the hippo, Cape buffalo, lions and crocodiles to not get too friendly. Personally, I wanted to keep a very healthy distance from most of the animals and snakes we encountered there.

Even though Jon could fix things that were a puzzle to me, he had a serious struggle with schoolwork. Years later, we discovered that he was dyslexic, but in those days no one had ever heard of such a thing. After taking a child's I.Q. test, we were told that he was almost a genius, but in school he barely passed in most of his classes, which required reading.

Jon graduated from Faith Academy in the Philippines and left to attend George Fox College in Oregon. He only stayed at the college one year before transferring to Portland Community College where he began his Airplane Airframe and Powerplant studies. However, his year at George Fox was long enough for him to meet Cheryl Lewis and fall in love with her. Although Jon and Cher did not meet until they both attended George Fox College, Dick and I were in college with her parents and I sang in a quartet with her mother many years earlier. To make it even more unusual and special, my parents and Cher's grandparents grew up together in a small community in Idaho and remained close friends all of their lives.

The most important affair we attended upon arriving home in 1972 was Jon and Cher's wedding. Cher is lovely, sensitive and talented, with a beautiful singing voice. Their wedding was a "family affair" where Jon's brother and three sisters stood with him, and Cher had her brother and sister as her attendants. The two mothers were candle lighters.

Joshua was born in February 1974, and no baby was ever more wanted and more loved. Jon wrote one of the most beautiful letters I've ever read about his overwhelming love for his new son. Some things we can never understand, and I won't even attempt an explanation. Although Josh seemed to be far above average in intelligence and understanding, he was born with serious physical challenges. Jon and Cher suffered through a constant series of sicknesses and surgeries with their precious baby.

I personally had a terrible struggle during this time, and it hurt to see my kids and grandbaby suffering. So the Lord had to work on my attitude and teach me an important lesson that I have never forgotten. I wanted to help as much as possible and I was willing to pray for them and give money for expenses. But to protect myself and my feelings, and to keep from hurting, I built a wall around myself and I tried to stay away as much as possible. God knew I was selfish and more concerned about my own feelings than I was about anyone else. I needed an attitude change and a strong dose of compassion. I prayed for Jon, Cher and Josh constantly, but one day the Lord spoke very clearly to me. He instructed, "Don't bother to pray for them unless you are willing to be involved in their suffering and emotional needs." This really shocked me. I was willing to give money and pray, but I didn't want to be involved in suffering. I was building a hard shell around my feelings, and God wanted to smash that shell and leave me open and vulnerable. He knew I needed an unconditional love that was willing to be a total part of the hurts and agony. I felt compelled to pray for my children, but the Lord made it very clear that my prayers were useless until I was willing to be involved in their lives, the pain and all. I had already had pain and I didn't want any more, but that's not the reality of life and this was a lesson I needed again! When the Lord revealed truth to me, I did want to change and be totally included in their lives, whatever it meant.

Jon and Cher sent out a letter to family and friends dated November 1976:

It is truly a blessing of the Lord that we can call upon each other. The sharing of concerns in prayer multiplies the praise our Lord receives upon victory!

Joshua is two and a half years old now and his doctors have decided he is ready for his most major reconstructive surgery. . .We feel deeply the need for much prayer support— prayer for the shock and pain Josh will experience; prayer for the success of the surgeries; and for the guidance of the Great Physician in the operating room; prayer for our strength as parents going through a two week or longer round-the-clock stay at the hospital with Josh. We will also greatly appreciate visits.

We are bold in asking for your commitment to this task in the joyous knowledge of the multiple blessings you will receive from His hand because of your faithfulness.

Love in Christ, Jon, Cher and Josh Cadd

This part of Jon, Cher and Josh's life is now history. Although Josh had more major surgeries, God performed many miracles, and today Josh has a beautiful family. He is married to Audra, and they have two lovely children, Raeleigh and Gabriel. They are working with deaf people under Wycliffe Associates in Kenya. Josh has always had one of the most remarkable attitudes I have ever seen. He didn't complain and blame God for his problems or pain. We had the privilege of having both Josh and grandson Jesse live with us while they attended George Fox College. Our days with these guys were filled with joy.

Hopefully, Jon and Cher will write their own book soon. Their experiences need to be shared. God gave Jon his dream of being a missionary pilot, and their first assignment was with Pacific Missionary Aviation in Micronesia in the Pacific Islands. We have both laughed and cried as Jon shared funny and frightening experiences during those days. One major source of joy that changed their lives was the adoption of a newborn baby boy, and they named him Caleb.

Dick and I had the privilege of visiting them on our way back to the Philippines and were amazed at their work and how much the people on the different islands loved them. Because we were Jon's parents, we were treated like royalty.

I want to share some of Jon's experiences while working with P.M.A. in Micronesia. Here's one experience when Jon was flying home to the island of Yap from Guam.

> I've been flying through a lot of rain and clouds. The other night I was coming from Guam and it became dark before I got back to Yap. Cher drove our car out to the end of the runway so I could find the airstrip (since it had no lights)! With the landing lights on the airplane and Cher's car lights showing me the runway, I didn't have any trouble getting down safely. The Yapese radio operator was really scared and said it was the first time it had ever been done in Yap. Well, Mom, I don't mean to make you nervous or anything. I'm really enjoying the work right now. I do thank you all for your prayers and hope you will not stop. I especially appreciate your prayers for my spiritual growth.

Another letter he wrote began, "When a friend asked me to write about the Evangel 4500 aircraft, I told him that I had been a pretty inexperienced young pilot when I was flying one and most of my Evangel stories were not as much about the aircraft as about me trying to get out of some sort of trouble I had gotten myself into. This is one of those times. Hope you enjoy it."

LOST AT SEA

Flying over the ocean is a distinctly lonely occupation, even when there are people with you. Vast openness or sameness as far as the eye can see gives you a sense of small on a grand scale. This is especially true when you are lost. I have only been really lost three or four times in my long flying career. Pilots are not supposed to be lost. Pilots are never lost. They are just temporarily disorientated. We don't have the luxury of Daniel Boone who could say when asked if he had ever been lost, 'NO, but I was a mite confused for a few weeks one time.' A pilot is on the clock much more than the driver of a boat or automobile who, if out of fuel, will not immediately crash. He has just so much fuel and that is all. Then something very interesting is going to happen. Lostness like that is the whole bunch of fear you would have getting lost for weeks in the woods, distilled down to the time it takes to empty your fuel tank. And yet you can get yourself very well lost in a very short time going the speeds the plane is traveling. I heard a story of a passenger who asked the confused looking pilot where they were. The pilot said, 'I am not sure exactly, but we are making very good time.'

Woleai was an island that had not seen an aircraft land since before the end of World War II. It had been a Japanese air base during the war and the Americans had bombed the hell out of it. The runway was totally unusable, peppered with craters over 10 feet deep. But the people of Woleai were anxious to establish air service again. Their only contact with the outside world was the occasional ship from Yap and an HF radio that was used to report the weather and make orders for supplies when the ship was coming. I talked to the U.S. Navy Construction Battalion Seabees on our island who did community projects like this throughout the district, and they agreed this was a worthwhile venture. So after getting permission from higher up they arranged a landing craft and loaded it up with graders and rollers and front end loaders and shipped off to Woleai, some 370 nautical miles away from Yap. A few weeks later I got the call that they had finished. We made plans to go open the airstrip. I was to take the Seabee lieutenant in charge of the project with me. We loaded extra life rafts, food and water for the trip. This was new and exciting for me. I would be the first one to land there since the war and there was a big celebration planned.

On the morning of the trip it was cloudy and overcast. Although the plane was ready to go, I decided to wait for a while to see how the day developed. I took my camera and maps back into the house and put them by the back door— except for the one with Yap and Woleai on it, which I spread out on the table. Cher made coffee and we relaxed while the weather cleared.

Flying over water is different than over land. You can track your progress over land by looking at ground references, but all those waves look pretty much the same after a while. So maps are more for the planning portion of the flight than for keeping you on track when flying over water. So I looked over the map one more time, checking my heading and distance for accuracy and just to see the big picture of the islands in the area. Micronesia is over 4000 islands covering a huge area the size of the U. S., but if you were to squash all the land together it would not even cover an area the size of Rhode Island. This made navigation a very interesting thing in a little airplane with no GPS or even Loran. The way to navigate using 'Dead Reckoning' is to draw a course line on the map between your two points and figure out what the heading is between them. Then you figure out how far it is between the two points and, knowing about how fast the plane flies, you can figure out how long it will take you to do the trip. After taking off you just fly that heading for the correct length of time and you should be at your destination. Sounds pretty simple. Not rocket science. One problem that can change everything is wind. It is impossible to tell its exact strength and direction. Even with a good weather briefing things change rapidly and over the great distance we often flew quite a lot of deviation from course could take place without you knowing.

The weather finally cleared and we went out to the plane to leave. As I checked the Evangel aircraft over one more time I remembered my maps and camera and asked my lovely wife Cher if she would please get them for me. She dutifully ran off and came back with the pile and I stuck them behind the wall between the cockpit and the cabin area. As we took off we could see that it was turning into a beautiful day. The large clouds were breaking up, leaving only scattered puffs with a few big colony piles, giving some depth to the endless blue of the sea. There is only the occasional interruption in blue when flying the Pacific and about an hour out of Yap we passed the island of Lorol, the only island between us and our destination.

I turned to get the map out of the back just to double-check our position in relation to the island, but to my dismay I could not find the one I needed. It was probably still on the table unnoticed, separated from the pile that I had left by the door. I asked the Seabee Lieutenant to climb in the back and check if it had slid back where I couldn't see it. It hadn't! Now, as I have said, you don't always use a map when flying over water. I often flew for weeks without looking at a map. We talked it over and both decided that since there was nothing else to see between us and the island we were going to, and since we had already delayed the day for weather and there was a celebration party waiting for our arrival, we would just carry on without the map. What could go wrong anyway?

Well, I will tell you. As we got to the time when we were supposed to be over the island I didn't even have an island in sight! In my little plane, I couldn't carry enough fuel for a round trip. I needed to find this island! When you have been flying the islands for a while your 'island eyes' kick in and you start to be able to detect these little dots of land from very far away, even up to 50 miles away. It is not by seeing the island itself, but from the little lens cloud that is formed by air rising and cooling just a little bit as it flows over it. You can get people thinking you have the most amazing eyesight with little tricks like that. But I didn't even have anything like this to help me as I scanned the whole horizon. I flew on hoping that the little headwind I was into had slowed me down and I was just not there yet. After about 15 minutes of hard looking I caught a little cloud out of the corner of my eye. Hurray! There it was. I turned the plane to the south shaking my head at being blown off course again. As we approached the island and I could see it better, my heart sank. This was not the Woleai atoll. It was too small and not enough islands. Now I felt I must carry on and see if I could identify where I was. Who knows? Maybe there would be a water tower with the name on it or something. We approached closer and the smallness of these islands gripped me. There were only a few huts and four or five dugouts on the small pieces of sandy ground.

Now I had a big decision to make. I had no idea where I was. The worry constricted my thinking process down to the tiniest passages of logical thought. Should I just land in the water inside the reef and make sure we were at least found? I circled using up valuable fuel. I started to pray. Lord, help me! As I circled, I thought back to the map on my dining room table and tried to bring the picture back to the screen of my mind. All right, this can only be one of two islands, Eauripik or Ifalik. Either way, if I guess wrong I will be over nothing but water when I run out of fuel. Wait! If it was Ifalik, I would have had to fly right over Woleai. I am almost positive I didn't do that. But I have done some pretty dumb things today! No, it must be Eauripik. Now if that is so, remembering back to the picture of the map on my table, it would be kind of Northeast from here to Woleai, maybe 45 to 50 degrees. This is not the way to navigate, especially when you are short on fuel. But I took off on the course I pulled out of my hat and prayed that I would make it. By this time my fuel was already getting low with less that an eighth of a tank on each side. This was crazy! I kicked the rudders to watch the needles on the fuel gauges move more. Yes, there was fuel still there. Not much though. I was still doing a lot of praying.

The next time I kicked the rudders there was very little movement on the fuel gauge needles. I was getting very close to empty now. Wait. What was that little cloud on the horizon? Yes! It was the islands. As I got closer I was quite sure that they were the most beautiful islands in the vast Pacific. A necklace of shiny green emeralds surrounded by stunning turquoise and all set in the deepest sea blue that you can imagine. Now, if I could only make it inside the atoll I could land in the water next to one of the islands. I kicked the rudders again and there was no movement of needles. I was getting short of breath. The island with the air-strip was on the far side of the atoll. I could see inside the necklace.

Remember, this is going to be the first landing ever made on this strip since WWII and lots of damage had hopefully been repaired. It is normal to fly over a strip like this to see if it is fit for landing. We sometimes make three or four passes. I didn't have time for that. I just headed straight for the end of the runway and left the mixture lean, as well as the gear and flaps up until the last minute. On short final, gear lowered and flaps down, I passed over a little sign the Seabees had made that said, 'Welcome to Woleai Jon!' I smiled as I pulled the power back and knew that I had the field made.

Everyone on the island was there! It was going to be a great party. I turned the plane around and taxied back to where the crowd was waiting. But as I rolled right up to the dancing, celebrating people both engines quit. I was completely out of fuel. My momentum carried me quietly up to where everyone stood. The Seabees rolled a couple of drums of avgas up to the plane and started fueling. It was as if there had never been a problem, we were never seconds from ditching in the ocean. Everything was fine. I was covered in leis and surrounded by happy people. I was the hero instead of the dummy. Life isn't always fair. And sometimes that is good!

After spending several years in the U.S. to help take care of Cher's mother, Jon and Cher joined Mission Aviation Fellowship and were sent to Zimbabwe, Africa.

The first time we went to Zimbabwe, we had a several hour layover in Zambia. We had been warned that tourists were an easy prey and were often robbed on the streets. I'm sure a group of guys thought we would be the perfect people to go after, but they didn't know where we came from. We were experienced in this type of thing, so when they couldn't get the bag I was clinging next to my body, they went for the glasses in Dick's shirt pocket. Like lightening, Dick grabbed the kid's hand and held him so tight he couldn't get away. Dick not only told him to put the glasses back, but also warned them to leave us alone. I think they were really shocked and scared because we never saw them again.

Because Jon was a pilot, he had privileges to go inside the arrival area when we arrived in Zimbabwe. It was special to have him meet us and take us through immigration and customs. It seemed that everyone knew him and liked him, so we never had any trouble entering or leaving the country. Jon and Cher were determined that we would see as much as possible of their part of Africa. We had lunch with the monkeys who wanted us to share our food, climbed rock hills, stood in awe of the Baobab trees, met special friends, went on safaris, saw Victoria Falls and went with Jon when he flew a doctor to a remote clinic.

The plane trip with Jon had several surprises. It felt like we were in the middle of nowhere, and as we started to land there was no airstrip. At the last minute, we spotted the grass strip between rows of bushes and trees. When we pulled to a stop, we saw that soldiers with machine guns were lined up on either side of us. Jon told us to wait while he left us in the plane and calmly walked over to the soldiers. I don't know what he said to them, but then he did one of his "magic" tricks. He pulled a coin from a soldier's ear. In a matter of minutes, Jon was surrounded by others who wanted a coin pulled from their ears. We could see that everyone was laughing and having fun, and then Jon asked to see one of their guns, which they willingly handed to him. Now we were free to get out of the plane and go to the clinic with the doctor. Jon's simple magic tricks worked every time.

We were told there were about 300 babies here to see the doctor. Some missionaries lived and worked there, but the doctor only came when Jon brought him. We had another surprise when we had a tour of the clinic. One of the rooms was devoted to dental work, and the one dental chair had a sign on it telling where it was made, A-dec in Newberg, Oregon, U.S.A., our small hometown that seemed a world away from where we were now.

Dick accompanied Jon to a government office, and as they walked in the door the official immediately began to pour out his heart to Jon. When he realized Dick's presence, he apologized and then explained that Jon was the only person he could talk to. He couldn't say enough good things about

Jon, and we began to get a glimpse of how many lives our son was touching. He's a superior pilot, but his influence goes far beyond flying. When Jon and Cher joined MAF, they went from the Micronesian Islands to Africa. This was quite a change, but they loved Africa and spent the next 22 years in the country of Zimbabwe.

The country was beautiful with luscious farms, plenty of food and park-like in many areas. But because of "dubious government policies" which crippled food supplies, when a severe drought came, there was nothing to eat and people were starving. According to the U.S. Agency for International Development, six million Zimbabweans were facing death unless action was taken immediately. The economy had been ruined, they could no longer fly their planes, and this was considered the worst famine Southern Africa had faced in more than 60 years. So Jon and Cher were sent to live in Uganda but work in Congo. At that time it was too dangerous to live in Congo because of rebel uprisings.

One time when we were with them in Zimbabwe, they took us to Fothergill Island where they had lived and worked for a time. I have never loved camping. My idea of fun camping is with all the comforts of home. However, here is the kind of place Jon and Cher's family lived in on Fothergill Island — a small house without doors and only half walls. The walls came up about three feet from the floor. The roof was thatched on poles. This openness allowed the rain to blow right through and the bugs and birds to fly in and out, but it also gave a great view when the elephants came to the fence or the buffalo came grazing at night. The bedrooms were round metal sheds that doubled as ovens in the day. A generator that was turned off at night provided electricity on the island.

Although they weren't living there when we visited, it was a challenge when they did live there. For me it meant a total revamping of my attitude to be there for just a few days. I could either hate it and be totally miserable, or I could love this new experience and have wonderful memories in Africa. With God's help, I chose to love it.

There were a few frightening times. I also had some difficulty getting used to the mosquito nets, but it was unthinkable to be without them. Dick and I had our own tiny hut with the half walls, thatched roof, etc. It's probably better if I don't discuss the problem of needing a toilet in the middle of the night.

Fothergill Island is on Lake Kariba and part of a National Park, so we could expect daily visits from Cape buffalo, elephants, jackals and hyena. We shared the land with impala, zebra, waterbuck, kudu, lions, hippos and hundreds of different types of wonderful birds and not so wonderful snakes! One night Cher and Caleb were trapped in the bathroom by a puff adder sleeping in the dining room, and a baby crocodile lived in their shower for a short time.

Where we stayed was actually a resort, with tourists coming and going, and a great staff. Since it was a resort, I think they must have hired the best chefs in the world, and it's impossible to describe the fabulous, delicious meals served there. Dick had a hard time waiting for the next meal to start. Every place we went with Jon and Cher, we found they were so well known and loved. During the few days we were on the Island, Jon must have arranged for us to have every possible kind of safari.

There was the walking safari when Dick was so engrossed in taking pictures that he didn't notice the rest of us were following the guide and very quietly walking away from an elephant that was too interested in our group. We kept very quiet while the guide carefully guided Dick back with the rest of us. The safari by truck seemed a little safer than walking, especially when we needed to watch for snakes. As we got into a rather small metal boat, we noticed another boat like ours near the dock with a big hole taken out of its side. We were told, "Don't worry. Hippos don't do this very often." But we did get closer to hippos than I wanted to be. We had a wonderful education about the various animals. Jon made sure we had a super safari by plane, and I was more comfortable with this distance away from many of the animals.

One thing we found interesting and fun was the "tea time." Because of the British influence, it didn't matter where we were, when it was time for tea (and there was an exact time), we stopped whatever we were doing for our tea and "biscuits" (cookies to Americans). The safari leaders were always prepared, even in the back of the truck and in our little metal boat. We really liked this tradition and thought maybe we should carry it on at home.

Later, in another location, we had a safari in Jon's car. This time we had a picnic with the monkeys. Actually it was a battle to see who got the most food. And we also saw some different animals, such as ostriches. Cher decided she wanted an ostrich feather, so when one came to the window of the car and had its rear end in the right position, she rolled the window down just enough to reach out and grab a feather. Without a change in attitude, I would have missed all the joy of this part of Africa. There was a baby rhino whose mother had been killed by poachers for its horn, so humans raised the baby. Jon had a picture of him sitting on it, and I decided I wanted a photo of me like that. However, we couldn't find the right rhino, and you don't want to make a mistake!

We had numerous adventures with Jon and Cher and their friends and their work and their animals. We only had the opportunity to visit them when they were in Zimbabwe, so our unusual and great experiences with them were in that country. Almost everything we did involved animals, because Jon and Cher love animals. I think Cher was born a veterinarian. She just didn't get the normal Vet education and official title. Jon would often bring her an unusual animal, especially if he saw that it was being mistreated and needed some tender loving care. Here is Cher's story of Bruce Mongoose:

I like animals. Not just to look at or keep in the yard, I want them sharing my everyday life. So when I met Jon's plane and he said, 'I brought you something' I was thrilled when a tiny, little banded mongoose leapt out of the basket and installed himself tightly in the springs under the passenger seat. Jon fished him out and we were introduced. Thus began more than 13 years of life with an intelligent, affectionate, inquisitive cyclone named Bruce.

Jon was in Mozambique when he spotted a small boy dragging a baby mongoose by a string tied around a grossly swollen back leg. 'Hey, that kid has a mongoose!' and the driver did a U-turn right there and pulled up by the boy. Bruce was purchased for about 25 cents and Jon popped him inside his shirt and took him back to where he was staying. He had to fly the next day so he just left Bruce in his room. When he returned, all the floor molding had been stripped off one whole side of the room. Bruce had been looking for the termites he must have smelled. That right there should have been a clue that the little thing would be trouble.

Bruce was inquisitive. He neeeeeeeeded to know what was in that huge 50-kilo bag in the broom closet. It was corn meal. Then he neeeeeeeded to know if maybe there was something hidden in the corn meal. After getting it all out onto the kitchen floor he was satisfied that he hadn't missed out on anything interesting. Small holes in upholstery held the promise of getting through to something more interesting inside the furniture so he would tentatively pick at them a bit. This would evolve into actually getting into position for better viewing and leverage. Then when the hole was big enough, he would get right down to digging, tearing, removing fabric he saw no use for. Bruce could find every single loose piece of parquet flooring. And remove it and its' near neighbors.

Bruce was also observant. He knew what item would get the biggest rise out of each of us when it was peed in or turffed out: pee down the hole in Josh's guitar and in Caleb's school hat, without which he would get a demerit. So many demerits and you got a caning. When I incurred his wrath he dumped all my African violets out of the pots and spread them around liberally.

Well, I could write a whole book about Bruce. Jon says I should. There is so much more to tell, but for now I will close. Next time I will try to convince you that he was lovable.

When visiting our kids, we thoroughly enjoyed Bruce's antics. He loved eggs. To get them opened, he held the egg in his front paws, spread his back legs apart and threw the egg like a fast football, against a hard surface. If he wanted more eggs than he was given, he sometimes managed to get into the refrigerator and help himself. They might find him happily exploring other foods stored in this cold place to see what tasted good to him. He learned to like tea, so if we weren't paying attention, we might find Bruce drinking from our cup.

On our first visit to Zimbabwe, our grandson Josh had a snake in a cage. They assured us that it wasn't a poisonous variety and that it couldn't get out. I still never felt very comfortable with it. And then the unthinkable happened. We came home one day and the cage was empty! That could only mean one thing: there was a medium size snake loose in the house! Jon's family wasn't the slightest bit concerned. It was harmless and they would find it soon. I'm not sure how Dick felt, but my feelings were very close to the panic stage. As much as I tried to hide it, I'm sure it showed. Think about it; if I sat on the couch, it could be under one of the cushions. Or it might even crawl into bed with us. The possibilities were unlimited, and although I don't like to admit it, I hate snakes, even the tiny garden garter variety the children pick up and play with.

At this point in time, I wasn't interested in an attitude change. Both Josh and Caleb searched the house thoroughly. Everyone was looking in every conceivable place, but the invader was nowhere to be found. We finally had to go to bed, and I'm not sure I slept. I certainly didn't want to get up and go to the bathroom in the dark. This went on for several days, and then one morning a happy shout went up from the bathroom. Someone in the family was washing their face, and as they looked down, the friendly snake poked his head out from the tiny overflow hole in the sink. This was great news that the snake had been found, but there was a problem as to how to persuade him away from his hiding place. Someone finally enticed it out.

Jon and Cher and their two sons lived in several different locations in Zimbabwe. When living on Fothergill Island, Jon wrote the following about his thoughts and feelings:

> We love our lives here, with the thatched huts, Africans, flying, beauty of nature and opportunities for sharing Christ. These are truly some of the best years of our lives. The trick is to keep our eyes on the Lord and the blessings, because if we don't, thatched huts become a lack of privacy and Africans are a frustrating, difficult cultural mindset and flying is just a lot of hard work and the nature is hazy skies that hurt your eyes and keep you from seeing the elephants and impala that have just walked onto the airstrip in front of you.
>
> The opportunities to share Christ become a duty or drudgery and easier passed by. Sometimes we are so excited to be here we can hardly contain the joy and sometimes we think, 'I'm too tired to take another step.' I think what I want to say is that we are terribly human and weak and could do nothing without the Lord living in us. And that is a daily or hourly decision we make and we make the wrong choice so much. We need your prayers so that we can say with Paul, 'Christ in me is the hope of glory.' (Col. 1:27b)

I understand exactly what he is expressing. This can apply to all of life and wherever we live and whatever our circumstances happen to be. I had these feelings at times in the Philippines, even though it was far more modern and was nothing like Africa. Probably we feel this way when living in a culture so different from what we grew up with. However, Ephesians 4:23-24 gives us these instructions: **"Now your** attitudes and thoughts must all be constantly changing for the better. Yes, you must be a new and different person, holy and good. Clothe yourself with this new nature." Philippians 2:5-6 even tell us, "Your attitude should be the kind shown us by Jesus Christ, who though he was God, did not demand and cling to his rights as God." Once again, attitude makes the difference, and the Bible indicates we have a choice.

All of my children have lived in great danger at times, and as I've been reading these letters from Jon and Cher, I remember a conversation Jon had with me when they had been home on furlough and were preparing to go back to Africa and more danger.

Jon put his arm around me and quietly said, "Now Mom, I don't want you to worry about me. I do want you to pray for me, but don't worry. I'm indispensible until God's through with me here, and then I get to go and be with Him. And what's better than that?" I mentioned earlier that I learn from my children, and the Lord used Jon to give me truth, so that with God's help I gained a new attitude. With this new attitude, fears (and probably ulcers) were replaced with peace and a stronger trust in God. I honestly don't think I worry about my children, but I certainly do pray! Even if they were sitting next to me in my living room, I couldn't protect them. God is the one in control, and He has taken care of them in every kind of situation.

This letter came when Jon and Cher were living in Uganda, but flying into Congo.

> I just got back from a couple of days in Congo and it has been very interesting. I don't know if you have heard about all that is going on here, but it is in international news. Militia groups are really pushing and attacking big targets. One group who are Tutsis have attacked right outside of Goma where there are tens of thousands of refugees coming into town. People were running out as they were coming in and even the airport was abandoned at one point. We were scheduled to take a

load of medicines and mosquito nets and doctors in when all of this was going on and didn't know if we would be able to go, but the rebels allowed a corridor for aid. I was able to take two loads in. It was interesting seeing the same stuff that was on the news—only much more from my vantage point up higher. A cell phone tower was blown down, but no one was shooting at me, so that was good.

You can pray for wisdom. It is going crazy everywhere. The LRA (Lord's Resistance Army) is taking over in the north of the country where we fly. Lots of massacres and terrible things. They go into a village and put all the men in a group and beat them and hack them with machetes. If you run, they shoot you in the back, which many choose. We are supposed to fly 11 tons of relief there, but it is too hot to get there right now.

—⁓—

While living in Zimbabwe, much of Jon's flying was into Mozambique during the rebel war there. On one flight he was taking a doctor and nurse back to their mission hospital. They had to descend closer to land because of clouds coming off the ocean when "all of a sudden, the loud crack of bullets going by the plane at the speed of sound got everyone's attention," Jon said. "The doctor said it sounded like someone was throwing gravel against the side of the plane, but the unmistakable rhythm of automatic weapons kept me from turning to see where the sound came from. Although this doesn't happen every day, it is always down below us."

Jon mentioned they often didn't know if they were being shot at unless they got hit or saw flashes. Another time they were shot at and hit, and his passenger got a bullet in his hand. It could have been so much worse! Jon often rescues people when rebel armies are only a few miles away. When flying doctors into remote areas, Jon has helped during surgeries and once even repaired some broken equipment on the floor of the operating room while a surgery was taking place. His experiences have included being charged by an elephant on takeoff, time with the pygmies in deep jungle areas, meeting Princess Diana and flying some of her staff and having dinner with the president of Burundi.

—*∿*—

Although Cher doesn't get to share in some of Jon's experiences, she is an essential part of his ministry. Jon explained:

> I was wondering why it should be so much better to fly here in Africa than other places that I have flown, and then my wife's lovely voice came over the radio and it hit me! It is that I get to talk to my wife all day long. She is actually part of my life while I fly. What a privilege! Cher is always there, checking the weather, calling to arrange passenger pickups, getting supplies for the missionaries and most of all a comfort to me. Her voice, the voice of the woman I love repeating back my position report and telling me how her day is proceeding. It is such a joy to me. I know that she often thinks it is me that does the real mission stuff here. But she is such a part of everything I do that you cannot separate me from her. Although I'm not a poet, I wrote a poem as a tribute to her (and the other MAF wives).

FLIGHT FOLLOWER

Mine she is, and light her hair
Who comes to me upon the air.
She follows me while I'm in flight
And makes sure everything's all right.
No one could ever really care
As much as Cher, my lady Cher.

Smooth it is, her voice so fair
It comforts me just being there.
With rain and lightning all about
Or even when the sun shines out.
While over rugged land or sea
She comforts me, she comforts me.

"MAF, it's niner-eight!
I'm gonna be a little late.
Will you please make this call and see
Then do these other things for me!"
A servant life is now your fate
My lovely mate, my precious mate

Mine she is, my lady Cher
A joy to me upon the air.
I thank God for her day and night
Who follows me while I'm in flight,
Who follows me while I'm in flight.

Cher is truly a remarkable woman. She has one of the most beautiful singing voices I have ever heard. She can fix almost anything and is extremely creative, thoughtful, talented and generous. In Cher's introduction to her section of Jon's blog, she has given the best description of how the right attitude can take any location, any situation, any experience, anything and everything and turn it into a life of adventure. In a nutshell, Cher has given the purpose of this book, to show the key to unlocking your adventures. A word of warning—the key is almost impossible to turn without the help of God. But God offers that help. **"God loved the world so much that He gave His only Son so that anyone who believes in Him shall not perish but have eternal life."** This comes from God's Word, John 3:16.

Now here is Cher's introduction:

Don't get your hopes up. My stories aren't as exciting as Jon's. I am Cher, the Bush Pilot's Wife. The first time we sat down in private to chat, Jon asked me how I would feel about being a missionary's wife. I think I said that if that was what God wanted for me it was what I wanted as well. Whatever I said, it must have been the right answer because here I am, 38 years later, testing him out on his promise to 'marry me and I'll show you the world!' I am happy to say that he is doing well.

We started out in Oregon, living in a tiny little old 1950's trailer which we bought off the side of the road for $400. I can see it in my mind as clearly as I can the house we just left in Kampala four months ago! Since then we have lived in the U.S. for a while, for 2 years on Yap in Micronesia, 22 years in Zimbabwe and Mozambique, four years in Uganda and now in the Democratic Republic of Congo. While living in Yap we visited Jon's family in the Philippines and on our trips to and from the USA we have traveled in Europe. Our work in Africa has also taken us to Zambia, Lesotho, Botswana, South Africa, Malawi, Tanzania and Kenya.

But more than all the places, we have learned to really SEE the world! And, oh, there is so much out there! Whole dramas are played out in tiny insect footprints in the dust. A huge, wrinkled whole-body print illustrates an elephant lying down against a sloping anthill. Here a snake has passed by. There a lion has left a pug mark in which I can lay my whole hand. From the air the Ituri Rain Forest looks like God's broccoli patch. Cultivated land divided by hedges and thorn barriers looks like a stunning crazy quilt all done in 'natural' colors. We peer down into streaming volcano craters and fly above mother whales piggybacking their babies through shockingly blue tropical waters. And faces. Young, old, outrageously wrinkled (OK, that's the mirror), smiling or recoiling in horror at our funny white faces, laughing at how we talk. Clothes that celebrate the best and brightest in the color palette. Fabrics sporting anything from chickens to Coca Cola, envelopes, handprints, the faces of African leaders inevitably placed on ample backsides. Shoes made of tire tread with pointed toes that curl up and back like the footwear of Genies. In these pages I hope to give you a glimpse of the world through my eyes.

I have to admit that sometimes as we were traveling the world, all I saw was the dirt and grime. I felt stifling heat or shivering cold. The smells were foul, rotten, or sweaty. However, God did open my eyes to really see and feel and love most places and experiences.

I found one more letter from Jon that needs to be shared.

As I landed at Fingoe, the crowd started to gather and by the time we were out of the plane there were 50 or more people and more coming. One little boy stepped forward and handed me a stone. This happens because I do sleight of hand tricks, pulling 'vanishing stones' from peoples' ears. I did a trick and a loud cry of excitement went up from the crowd. Now it was time to walk into town, and the crowd walked and talked excitedly all around me. One of the soldiers looking at the enthusiastic crowd said, 'Today you are Jesus Christ.'

His words cut into me as if he had taken the bayonet from his belt and stabbed me. I want to be Jesus to these people every day. I wanted to be Jesus the day I saw the funeral procession coming down the road with a little four-foot-long coffin, women throwing themselves on the ground and putting dirt on their heads in grief. And like Jesus, 'when He saw her' (the widowed mother of the dead boy at Nain), 'his heart went out to her.'(Luke 7) I wanted to raise the dead in Jesus' name! I wanted to be Jesus last week when we flew into a village recently 'liberated' from the MNR bandits where people were starving to death. Instead of just giving my three little rolls and chewing gum as far as they went, like Jesus, I wanted to break the bread and have everyone be satisfied. I want to be Jesus when I see people steeped in spirit worship and spiritual darkness without the knowledge of our Savior and what He did for us on the cross. But we don't speak the same language and love is the only communication I have.

Maybe my biggest problem was that I don't think it was Jesus they saw in me. Just me. I read today in John 12:21 of the Greeks who came to Philip and said, 'Sir, we would like to see Jesus.' That is still the heart cry of the world today, even if they don't know what it is their heart cries for. I ask you with all my heart to pray for me that 'Christ in me, the hope of glory' will be a reality in my life. That I will have the heart of my Lord Jesus in every moment of my life. And that I will be totally usable to God. That His glory will be safe with me.

I am thankful, excited and filled with joy at what my children are doing for others wherever they are in the world. This would not be possible if I lived with an attitude of fear, but I am so grateful that **"God has not given us the spirit of fear, but of power, love, and a sound mind."** (II Timothy 1:7) (NKJV)

For more of Jon's adventures, check out his blog at http://captainsblogafrica.wordpress.com

Jon and Cher, with their sons Caleb and Joshua, lived in Zimbabwe 22 years working with Mission Aviation fellowship.

Jon is passionate about wildlife and the African bush. His life in Zimbabwe included much contact with wildlife, from buzzing elephants off the airstrip, to keeping a human-raised rhino away from the MAF plane.

Jon and Cher continue with MAF in DR Congo, and Cher flight follows most every day.

Cher is a lover of animals, and her pets have included a mongoose, red-tailed monkey, a Duiker, rats, turtles, dogs, and multiple birds.

Jon loves flying and his passion is obvious to his many passengers. When he takes to the sky, he will often turn to the passenger seated next to him and say, with all sincerity and a big grin, "It's a beautiful day at the office!"

Jon and Cher have lived in the Democratic Republic of Congo since 2010 where Jon is the Program Manager for MAF. Although his job doesn't allow him to fly as much as before, he still manages to get out to the bush and entertain the children on the ground with little magic tricks at the airstrips where he lands.

CHAPTER 17

ADVENTURES WITH STEVE

The first sight of my new baby boy was as the nurse laid him in my arms, cleaned and wrapped in a blanket. But my first reaction was that this was a mistake. They brought me the wrong baby. Instead of the expected bright red fuzz, this adorable black-eyed little boy had a full head of thick black hair that stood straight up and almost seemed to go too far onto his face. "No, he can't be mine!" But he certainly wasn't the wrong baby, and we would have wanted to keep him even if he hadn't been ours. Although he was a total contrast to Carolyn and Jon, we immediately fell in love with Steve.

One day in the hospital after they had brought the babies to us for feeding, I looked up to see a nurse standing in the doorway carefully scrutinizing me. After a time of silent staring she said, "I just wanted to see what the mother of little 'Leather-lungs' looked like! He is louder than all the other babies put together! If we could find a soundproof closet for him, we'd have a relatively quiet, organized nursery. As it is, we have bedlam! Good luck!" With that encouraging remark, she turned and left the room. It seemed incredible that this sweet little baby, nursing peacefully, could possible cause any trouble.

Although Steve didn't have red hair, he attracted as much attention as our cute little redheads. This was because of his big dark eyes and outgoing personality. He wasn't afraid of anyone so he made friends instantly. The nurse was right that he did have a loud voice, and he is the one person I know of that can get by without a microphone.

We were in a car accident when Steve was not yet three years old. His collarbone was broken and required a cast that fit him like a T-shirt. The cast was extremely upsetting to him, so Dick set out to change Steve's attitude. As Dick knocked on the cast, he'd growl, "Knock, knock, knock. Let me come in." Steve's high pitched voice would respond, "No, No, No! Not by the hair on my chinny-chin-chin." Even in children, the right attitude can turn disaster to delight.

Complications arose when Steve came down with both mumps and chicken pox during the time he was in the cast. Everyone that met Steve signed his cast, and Dick's games became so much fun that when it was time to have the cast removed, Steve wasn't at all sure he wanted to give it up.

During one of our moves Steve wanted to help me unpack, and when I was out of the room he picked up my only antique; a beautiful, rare, expensive, large cut-glass bowl. It was too big and too heavy for him, so when he dropped it on the cement floor it shattered beyond any hope of repair. This was a special gift to me from my great Aunt Ella and was one of a kind. Although I cried, our decision that children were more important than things made me thankful it was only a dish!

I have no idea how Steve learned to whistle when he was still a baby. But Carolyn and Jon were envious and continually tried to learn from their baby brother. Even before Steve talked, he was imitating sounds. He could barely walk, but he could make a sound like a duck, and because he was so little everyone wanted to hear him do his imitation. He still has the uncanny ability to imitate almost any language, person, animal or other noise he hears, and he has used this talent for numerous ads on radio and television, as well as in theater productions. Steve kept us all entertained from the day he was born, but his younger sister Yvonne became his most faithful fan. Even if no one else was impressed, he could always count on a response from his little sister.

If Dick spanked both of our boys, Jon never made a sound and Steve could be heard a block away before Dick ever touched him. Steve had good advice for Jon, "If you yell and cry loud enough, Daddy won't spank you so hard." The nurse was right. He can be very *loud*!

All our children were full of adventures but Steve's were often a little more dramatic and louder since he seemed to be a born actor. Before we went to the Philippines we were required to have certain inoculations. Although Dick and I hate shots as much as the children, we carefully hid our feelings and calmly explained that we must have vaccinations before we could leave for the Philippines. "It will sting for only a moment and then it's over! The shots will protect you and keep you from getting awful diseases later on." The children were all prepared to be brave and assured us they wouldn't even cry.

I held Yvonne and LuAnne, one in each arm, while the Dr. administered their shots. They were fine, with no tears at all. We hadn't been paying much attention to Steve, and he managed to watch the whole procedure. When he saw the needle go into Yvonne's arm, he went into panic.

First, we had to find him. As we pulled him from the tiny dressing room, he cried, "I saw what the doctor did. He put that needle all the way through Yvonne's arm. I saw it with my own eyes!" We told him it only looked that way, and even Yvonne's assurance that it didn't hurt much didn't convince him.

Now we had to begin all over again with why we were doing this. Nothing worked. We tried bribery and then threats, but he was convinced that nothing could be as bad as that needle. He begged and pleaded and cried. Finally, in desperation he got down on his knees in front of Dick and grabbed his daddy around the legs. Looking up into Dick's face with those big brown eyes he pleaded, "Daddy, if you love me, don't let the doctor do that to me." We felt sick and didn't want to subject Steve to the shots when he was so afraid. But it was the deadline before leaving and could not be delayed even one day. It could even be a matter of life or death. Soon after arriving in Manila a boy just one block away from us died of cholera. We couldn't make Steve understand and it took both of us to hold him so the doctor could proceed with the vaccination. It really hurt us, and Steve felt betrayed.

I personally learned an important lesson when the Lord reminded me of this experience a few years later. I was going through a time of unreasonable fear: afraid for Dick, afraid for the children, afraid of robbers, afraid of diseases, afraid of accidents. I was consumed with fears. During my devotions one day I read I John 4:18. **"We need have no fear of someone who loves us perfectly; his perfect love for us eliminates all dread of what He might do to us. If we are afraid, it is for fear of what He might do to us, and shows that we are not fully convinced that He really loves us."** I thought, "That's great, if only I could grasp it, make it mine, believe it!" That's when God brought the experience with Steve and his fear of the shots back to my mind.

I felt the Lord question me, "Helen, do you love Steve?" My quick reply was, "Of course, Lord! You know I love Steve!" God responded, "But you made him have those shots." My declaration was, "You know why we did that! It was required and probably saved his life. We knew what was best for Steve, but we just couldn't make him understand." And then my Heavenly Father gently, but clearly asked, "Helen, is your love better than mine?"

All of a sudden I was overwhelmed with the meaning of the scripture! "Oh no, God! My love is imperfect and often selfish, but I do love my children so much I would never deliberately do anything to hurt them. I only want what is best for them. I want to protect them. I make so many mistakes, and my knowledge is so limited. But You know everything and You don't make mistakes. Your love is perfect; so perfect you gave your Son to be our Savior. You are in control, so why should I be afraid?" Then He spoke tenderly and I felt submerged in the warmth of His love as He whispered, "Yes, Helen, I love you. I see everything from the beginning to the end and I don't make mistakes. Often I can't make you understand, even though I try. Sometimes all you can see is the 'needle' of my protection. But try to remember, my love for you is perfect. You never need to live in fear again!"

Sometimes I forget and revert back to the control of fear, but I've sincerely asked God to keep reminding me. The obsession of fear cannot overcome me if I truly trust God and believe His love is perfect. Thank you, Lord!

—◆—

It seemed as though our children waited until we were traveling to need a hospital. On our first trip through Europe, Yvonne was hit by a car and seriously injured. The next medical emergency was with Steve. At first we thought he had an upset stomach, but it didn't go away. We were living in a tiny RV and staying in campgrounds. About 4:30 a.m. we realized Steve was very sick, and it suddenly dawned on us that this sounded like a severe attack of appendicitis. We decided we couldn't wait to get help for him, but it was a problem because the way out of the campground was locked until later in the morning. We had to wake up the caretakers and have them unlock the gate so we could go to the hospital.

A doctor on duty felt Steve needed immediate surgery, so by 6:00 a.m. Steve was in the operating room. His appendix was on the verge of rupturing. As I mentioned earlier, Steve was both loud and dramatic, and the anesthetic made him nauseated. You could literally hear him all over the hospital and the Catholic sisters were trying frantically to make him vomit quietly, but it didn't work. For some reason, every time Yvonne came to see Steve after surgery, the minute she walked into the room Steve and Yvonne began to laugh. However, it hurt Steve to laugh and he informed Yvonne she couldn't come to visit him again.

Carolyn and Jon were already in the U.S. for college, so we only had our three younger children with us. Fortunately, we didn't have a set schedule or deadline, and we happened to be in one of the most charming cities in Switzerland. The city of Lucerne was next to a beautiful lake and was surrounded by spectacular mountains. Steve's bed was next to a window with an incredible view of a famous mountain peak, so one day during a no visiting time, we took a train trip up the mountain. Steve was only in the hospital a few days when the doctor decided he was well enough to continue traveling if he was careful. Once again we began more adventures.

It's hard to know where to start again, what to include, and where to end in telling our experiences with Steve. I mentioned earlier that Steve kept us entertained from the day he was born, and we probably lived and worked with him longer than with the other children. I found an article written in an old Faith Academy newspaper about Steve, and I think it is worthy of reprinting here. This was printed in 1998 and titled:

STEVE CADD: Whatever became of him?

Few students from 1962-1972 will forget him. More school rules were instituted because of his outlandish mischievousness! Steve was active in music, wrestling, girls and sometimes studies—not necessarily in that order!

Following Faith graduation, Steve studied at George Fox University in Newberg, Oregon. He took his practice teacher's training under his father, Dick Cadd, who was then music teacher at Faith. By this time Steve had married Shelley, a fellow student of George Fox, and they had a boy named Jesse. Both of them had a great interest in mission work, so they stayed on in the Philippines, joining Action International Ministries.

Steve organized a Filipino evangelistic music and drama team that traveled in the Philippines for several years and did three tours in the USA. During this period he was asked to direct an evangelistic film for the first time. Steve felt he had found his calling. After two years of study and top honors at the London International

Film School, he returned to the Philippines with his wife and children, two boys and two adopted Filipina girls.

Steve launched into film making with vigor and passion. He produced and directed TERESA, THE LONG ROAD HOME, SNATCHED FROM DARKNESS and others. SNATCHED was translated into Spanish, Vietnamese, Cambodian, Indonesian and Thai. His burden continues to be the production of culturally relevant evangelistic films in the local language. After 17 years with Action, Steve formed Sword Productions, which is registered in the USA, Philippines and United Kingdom.

Steve is also active in theater. He is the only foreigner included in the popular Philippine Christian theater group TRUMPETS. Acclaimed by the secular press for the 'Best musical production of the Year,' these professionals have brought the gospel to the Philippines in a most unique way. Steve has pastored this group holding weekly Bible studies.

His children are following in their father's footsteps. Jesse, 1993 graduate of Faith, recently graduated from George Fox University with a major in computer science. He also received awards for his outstanding dramatic ability. Benjamin is a junior at Faith and loves drama too. He has performed in commercial ads and Faith Academy drama productions.

Currently, Steve is directing the *700 Club* Asia television show on Channel 7 in Manila. He is leading a nationwide evangelistic push. His gifts and talents are being put to work in a strategic video project targeting a hostile unreached people group. The objective is to show what Christian life looks like in that culture. The ever-active Steve is also making films, doing voices for ads and preaching frequently.

Steve married Shelley in June 1974. He had often had what he thought was back trouble throughout his life, and in December of 1974 the pain became unbearable. One night he awoke, feverish and retching. Christmas Day he was admitted to the hospital and after one unsuccessful attempt to salvage his left kidney, it was removed. Through several miracles, Steve's life was saved and the entire bill for two major surgeries was supplied. Steve and Shelley's first child, Jesse, arrived in June 1976. When their baby was only 2 1/2 months old, they came to Faith Academy in the Philippines so that Steve could do his student teaching under Dick. They lived with us during that time. It was a fun, blessed and exciting time – a special privilege. God's miracles continued for them as He kept them safe through what might have been a disastrous car accident.

Although Faith Academy asked Steve to replace Dick when we went on furlough, they felt the Lord was leading them to join Action International Ministries and begin to develop a music-drama ministry. Instead of returning to the United States, they remained in the Philippines as full time missionaries.

While with Action International Ministries, Steve followed his desire to form a music-drama group and appropriately called them "Action Company." This group of vibrant, spiritually-alive young people came from different backgrounds. Steve's training for them as singers and in drama was demanding and thorough. He wanted them to be the best!

Objectives were two-fold: the internship program was designed to train these students not only in music and drama but also equip them to go back to their local churches and use their talents to train others. It wasn't long before they were involved in outreach to schools, churches, jails, hospitals and open-air concerts throughout the Philippines. This unique group eventually made their way to the United States three different times as they presented Action International Ministries work in the Philippines during a delightful program of music and drama.

—w—

At this time Steve and Shelley were caring for Christopher, a Filipino baby boy. Christ for Great Manila (CGM), who rescued street kids and abandoned children, found Christopher but didn't have a baby home so they asked Steve and Shelley to take him. Christopher had an older sister, Nikki, who was seven and often living on the streets, and they took her into their home as well. One night they woke to find baby Christopher dead. From his history of lack of care as an infant, he most likely had a damaged immune system. Steve and Shelley were heartbroken. Soon after, a Catholic Sister came to their door with a tiny, severely malnourished baby girl who needed a home so they accepted Milei. A few years later Shelley gave birth to another son, Ben. Now they had two girls and two boys.

—⁓—

During this time in Steve's life, he was asked to direct a film *Six Who Died*. Although he hadn't worked in this area before, the experience basically changed the direction of his life. He totally enjoyed working with Action Company, but directing the film grabbed him in such a way that he couldn't escape the urge to learn more. He had a vision of how quality Christian films in the local language could reach thousands with the good news of Jesus, but he felt the need for more training and experience in producing and directing movies. It was a huge decision to leave Action Company and move to London where he could study at the London International Film School. In August 1984, the family of six packed their suitcases and began a new adventure in England.

Although there was constant pressure at the Film School, the Steve Cadd family put up with visits from parents, siblings and friends. London was a fun city to explore and with their help we learned to ride trains, buses and the famous underground system. We had come from the Philippine unstructured transportation system, but it didn't take long to realize the British were on a set time schedule. If we weren't right on time for our chosen transportation, it didn't wait for us like our Filipino jeepneys.

While learning to make movies Steve won the "Governor's Award" several times, as well as receiving a "Winner's Medal" in a Fuji Film contest. He participated in making 15 films, including directing, scriptwriting, producing, lighting, camera, sound and editing, and graduated with "Distinction in Direction Award." Because of his outstanding performance at the school, Steve had some tempting offers in the secular world of movies. However, he never lost his desire to use the media in the local Philippine language in order to help people understand God's love and Jesus' sacrifice for them. Dick and I were thrilled to have them back in the Philippines and we were hoping to have some adventures learning about the movie industry and working with our son. It didn't take long to discover the complications, hard work, spiritual battles, technical difficulties, expenses, locations, scripts, actors and deadlines in producing a quality film.

By now we were living in the U.S. We felt it was important to be where we could get acquainted with our grandchildren here and Dick was 75 years old, with occasional health issues. Steve needed a U.S. Home Office for Sword Productions, and we were thrilled to be in charge of this and be a vital part of our son's mission.

There was a time when every one of our children was on a different continent and we were flying around the world to be with each one while making documentaries for several mission groups. My greatest desire in life had always been to have our family live near each other, but now they were scattered around the world. I needed a total revamping of my dreams and special help with my attitude. I had lessons to learn and the Lord often used my children as the teachers, although they probably weren't aware of that role.

In 1998 Dick and I left on a six-month trip to many parts of the world. Our first stop was the Philippines to help with the film that Steve was shooting. I wasn't really expecting to be actively involved, but Dick had numerous jobs. Often perfecting the story takes the longest time, but they did have a great script. So when we arrived, Dick immediately went with Steve to search for the right location.

Three hours out of Manila Steve found just the right little town. It was very provincial, with a typical market place, a country school, tiny jailhouse and very old pre-war houses. Everything about the small town seemed to be exactly what was needed for the movie and they came back excited and ready to actually begin filming. Steve already had his cast and crew. One of the unusual and gratifying results in all of the plans was the cooperation of five different mission groups who contributed lights, cameras and personnel to help make this film possible.

Dick and others thought Steve must be crazy when he announced the shooting schedule was to take only seven days. There were more than 40 people involved in the cast and crew. They needed to not only provide transportation for these people, but also house and feed them on several different locations. There were vans filled with lights, tracks, crane, dolly, stands, cables and items too numerous to even remember. It took a truck and trailer to carry their own power system, since the lighting required so much energy. Dick was available to assist Steve wherever needed and use a smaller video camera to shoot "behind the scenes." I didn't realize how important it was to do Dick's job, but I also had no idea that scenes weren't shot in sequence. Later, if it was discovered that a portion of a scene needed to be redone, it required watching Dick's video to make sure everything was the same so that it would fit in, such as placement of furniture, hair style, clothes, etc.

I really didn't plan to even go along for most of the filming. I expected to visit with Shelley and friends, do some shopping and have fun. The group was having a final meeting in Steve's living room before leaving the next morning and I was just walking out the door when Steve suddenly exclaimed, "Mom, stop! You can't go anyplace! We need you. You are now our new talent coordinator." One of their major crewmembers had an emergency and couldn't do the job.

I was very skeptical as I asked Steve, "What is a 'talent coordinator'?" Since they were in the middle of an important meeting, Steve simply replied, "Oh, you'll learn. We'll talk later, but sit down and join us so you'll know our plans and schedules." That was the end of my free time and the beginning of an adventure I never dreamed possible and a responsibility that at times almost led to panic. Steve didn't have time to talk to me, but did manage to inform me that my job was to see that all of the actors got to the right locations on time and were wearing the proper clothes. This was not just giving them the information they needed, but I had to arrange for their transportation. The entire cast didn't come at the same time, but only the ones involved in the scene being shot. Being 'Talent Coordinator' was a major job and quite difficult even in the best of circumstances.

We were doing most of the filming in a location three hours from where the cast members lived in Manila. This alone presented serious problems because even in Manila phones were not totally reliable, but in the province they seldom worked. By this time, we had cell phones, but hills and trees surrounded the small town, so it was almost impossible to get a working signal.

I had a very impressive chart of each scene, where it would be filmed, who needed to be there and the costumes they should be wearing.

Each of the cast had the same information, so all I really needed to do was to call and remind them and be certain that they had a way to get there. I also had a list with the names, addresses, and phone numbers of all of the talent involved in the movie.

The nightmare began when we fell behind in the shooting schedule and everything changed! The schedule was revised constantly, so Dick began driving me around while I kept trying to find someplace where I could get a dial tone. If we heard that someone in the area had a phone that actually worked, we tried to become good friends with them. But even the best phones didn't always cooperate, and we had to travel to a bigger town closer to Manila. Although we had a car and driver available to pick up people, changing his schedule sometimes was impossible. By the time we were through shooting the movie, I felt like I could easily perform the job of talent coordinator in Hollywood, with a lot less stress!

Dick wrote to someone and said, "The accommodations were primitive." The word primitive doesn't come close to describing some of the places we stayed. Toilets were rare. Sleep was wishful thinking. One of the best places we stayed did have a bathroom. However, it was a tiny room at the far side of the house and the only thing in it was an unusual toilet and a bucket of water with a dipper attached. As far as I could tell, there was no running water so I have no idea how they filled the bucket. But that bucket was essential for "flushing" the toilet and washing our hands.

We had our own private bedroom in this one house, and we each had a single bed. Because of the constant heat, the windows had nothing but steel bars on them. Although everyone had bars on their windows to keep robbers out, sometimes people had blinds or curtains, but we had nothing to keep anything out. Because I was so tired I fell asleep immediately, but when it began to get light I woke up feeling like someone or something was lying right next to my body and it wasn't big enough to be my husband. When my eyes focused enough to see, the "something" turned out to be a dirty stray cat that had come in through the bars for a comfortable body to curl up with. Actually, it could have been far worse, like when we shared our bed with a rat! After I got over the shock of this little stranger, I decided it was really funny. We found that having the right attitude involved humor, and being able to laugh at situations rather than getting upset or angry kept stressful times under control.

One night when we were filming a swarm of thousands of flying termites descended on us. We had a fairly nice house where the female actresses were staying, and the termites were attracted by all of the lights in the house. Unless you have been caught in a cloud of these insects I doubt if you can even imagine what it was like, but all of a sudden the place was filled with screaming girls racing to get out of the house. The bugs were everywhere, in their hair, down inside their clothes, in the beds! As long as there were lights on our invaders had no intention of leaving, and none of the girls had any intention of going back inside of that house. Although this was totally against my nature I covered my nose and mouth, fought my way into the thick black flying mass and began turning off all of the lights. It was adventures like this that destroyed the best-laid plans and schedules.

The one thing that kept us going was our prayer and praise times, which began each day by 7:00 a.m. When it seemed like the enemy was attacking us, we met these times by stopping to praise the Lord and pray. One day we had to move all of the people and equipment to a special location that was very difficult to reach. The only way to get there was down a steep hill and then up the other side. Everyone made it safely except the truck pulling the heavy generator. It got stuck at the bottom of the hill and refused to go up the other side.

This created a tremendous problem and blocked the road for other vehicles. We were in a very small town and had no idea what to do, so we prayed. Dick and I were given the job of searching the town to see if there was a big truck anywhere that could push or pull our vehicle. After driving through every street and asking every person we saw we came up with nothing! Then someone suggested we find a fire truck which could attach the fire hoses to the generator and pull it up the hill.

If a small town even had a fire truck, it had probably been retired from a larger city and was usually worn out and tired. Dick and I set out to research what sounded like a crazy idea. There actually was a fire truck, but we needed to find someone in charge, someone with authority. Besides all the other problems, we were on a deadline, the filming had to be finished before dark and there wasn't much time.

People were hungry and our plan was to go to another town down the road where we could sleep. After more searching and questioning people, we finally found the one person who could give us permission to use the fire truck. He was very reluctant to use their fire truck in this way, and we couldn't blame him. He was also concerned about what would happen if there was a fire and the truck was needed. But he finally came to look at the situation, and by this time most of the town people had gathered to watch the show.

Because no one had any other suggestions, the man in charge finally gave his consent to use the fire truck and hoses, and immediately all of the men and boys from the town came forward to help. It suddenly became the town project and they all wanted to be involved. There was a special time of cooperation and sharing and bonding. We became friends. It wasn't easy, but with the fire truck and everyone pushing and working together, the job was accomplished.

We often were filming until the early morning hours, but the last night was an all-nighter. Amazingly, we finished on time and headed home. Steve was under tremendous pressure with many things going wrong, but he never lost his cool. He is greatly loved and respected by all who work with him. It would be nice if I could say all of our problems were over and everything went smoothly to finish the film. However, there is a sequel to the story about losing an important videotape, plus the new camera jammed and had to be sent back to the factory, with the tape still in it. Eventually it was finished, and the Lord has used this movie in miraculous ways to bring many people to Jesus.

With all these experiences, I keep thinking back to the time when I wouldn't dream of eating at a restaurant unless it displayed a big "A" in the window; or I had to examine a motel room to make sure it was clean enough before I consented to stay there. I remember the quartet guys telling Dick he was crazy to take me to the Philippines. I wouldn't last a month, they said. And I probably wouldn't have made it through those first few months if the Lord hadn't helped change my attitude. The change didn't happen all at once, but God made it fun to have new experiences and see the humor: a cat curled up next to the meat in a cooler, or a colorful jeepney that always had room for one more, even when it meant they were on the outside hanging on for dear life. I do admit that if some of the experiences had happened those first few weeks, like the rat that ran across our bed in the night or the robbers making their way through our house, I might have collapsed under the weight of disgust and fear. Because God knew how much I could handle and He graciously taught me gradually, I not only survived the 30 days, but also found it extremely hard to leave after 32 years. I wouldn't trade the fascinating adventures, even the unpleasant ones, for all the five-star hotels or grade "A" restaurants or clean beds you could give me. God's help with my attitude made the difference.

There were times when my stubborn will and pride got in the way of what God wanted to accomplish, so He had to teach me some very difficult lessons. Some of the adventures were painful to go through, but really fun to talk about later. Other things I encountered were so devastating that I still can't think about them. But I changed. Often God gave me a glimpse of what I was like, and it was shattering to see that I was just like the people I couldn't stand to be around because of their actions and attitudes. Sometimes we need to see a reflection of ourselves in other people, and often it's not a pleasant sight. I guess I've said all of this to conclude that if God asks us to do something, He always makes it possible. However, we always have a choice and since God doesn't force us, we can ruin His best plans for our lives. But He doesn't give up on us.

In working with Steve we discovered there would be excitement, spiritual battles, often danger and always something unexpected. It has never been difficult to work with our children, even when they are in control. Even now, Steve is my "boss" since I took over Dick's job when he died. Dick was Steve's U.S. Vice President of Sword Productions and the Home Office here. Steve is a strong spiritual leader, but gentle, kind and loved by those who work with him. He is even patient with me. However, Steve went through agony for at least five years, but didn't tell anyone what was going on in his private life.

—∿—

With Steve encouraging her, Shelley went back to school and earned a degree in counseling. No one knows exactly what happened or why, but we believe Shelley developed a delusion against Steve. In her mind, he became a drug addict and even a drug "king." For her benefit, Steve had numerous drug tests and was told by drug specialists that he was the "cleanest" person they had ever tested. As time went on, there were more delusions and serious accusations.

Over a period of two months, every allegation and complaint was thoroughly checked out by Steve's Sword Board and found to be false. There was never found another witness against Steve. The Bible says an accusation against a fellow Christian must be supported by two or three witnesses and the Board could not find even one. Although Steve was strongly advised and urged by a lawyer to divorce Shelley, he felt it was not an option. However, Shelley suddenly divorced Steve in 2004.

Although Steve was proven 100% innocent, he went back to the Philippines feeling depressed and lonely and that his reputation had been irreparably damaged. He wondered if God could ever use him again. Steve's Sword Board and his family expressed complete confidence and trust in him and that we must not let the enemy destroy this ministry. Arriving back in Manila Steve found the same assurance and acceptance. At first he wanted to stay away from people who had heard the accusations, but soon found he had the full support of everyone.

It's not surprising that Satan would try to destroy this ministry, because Sword Production films were being used powerfully to rescue people from sin and darkness and bring them into the glorious light of the Kingdom of God.

Steve's films were being used not only in the Philippines, but also throughout Asia and translated for the Spanish-speaking world.

All of these experiences took place at a time when the Lord was opening up unusual opportunities for Steve to use his expertise and talent in closed countries that had very little knowledge of the wonderful good news of Jesus and His love. When God wants to do a great work, it usually turns out to be a big spiritual battle. For this reason, we plead with Christians to pray for anyone doing God's work, especially in countries and areas that have been under the devil's control for many years. Satan doesn't give up his territory without a fight. Our family and the Sword Board felt that Steve should return to Manila and continue his work. After several months we received this Breaking News!

When I first got back to Manila I had no intentions of getting involved in any relationships. I simply wanted to get back to the work that God has called me to do and allow Him to heal me from the awfulness of the past several years. I received an email from Shelley at that time which contained the following line, '. . .the Lord has made it clear that all ties are cut in the Spirit between us and that His dealings in our lives are now separate.'"

Soon afterward I had a long talk with the head pastor of my church here, and he told me that sooner or later I would probably meet someone and eventually get married again. He wanted me to know that as a church they were ok with that. In my case I was considered the "offended party" and was free to remarry. It was those two incidents that allowed me to start thinking differently about my future.

I began to notice that I was especially enjoying Mayen Bustamante's company whenever we were at the same gathering. It bothered me at first so I went to another one of our pastors and the man I hold myself accountable to. He reaffirmed that I was free to remarry and there was nothing wrong with the feelings I was having. He encouraged me to talk to Mayen and see if she felt similarly. Mayen is a very prayerful and Godly woman so when I told her that I was beginning to have feelings for her, she responded that she needed time to pray and ask God. Mayen is Filipina and we have known each other for about 10 years. She is an actress with *Trumpets* so we have been together in many Christian musicals over the years. We served together for a time on the spiritual committee of *Trumpets*. We have always had a deep respect for one another and a good friendship; always with appropriate boundaries.

To make a long (and very fun!) story short, we both agreed that we felt we should spend some time getting to know one another better. It didn't take us very long to decide that we both felt the same. Our core values are the same, our vision for what we believe God is calling us to do is the same. We both have the same heart for reaching unreached people. This past month of shooting the movie in Mindanao, Mayen was the lead female actress and the acting coach. So we worked side by side every day for a month in a very pressured environment. What we discovered is that we work very well together as a team and we get along fantastically! We both know now more than ever that we are meant for one another.

We are planning on a wedding October 1 of this year! I talked to all of my family very early on in this relationship. They have been so supportive and are thrilled for me that the Lord had brought a wonderful partner into my life. The church family here is supportive as well and have embraced us as a couple.

Since Yvonne and her three daughters had a chance to go to Manila, Steve and Mayen decided to move their wedding plans forward in order for Steve to have some of his family present. So on August 18, in a beautiful and simple ceremony with only a few family and friends, Steve and Mayen were officially married.

They spent the next two weeks with Yvonne and her daughters, taking them to famous places. This included the Banawe Rice Terraces, Sagada Caves, Baguio and Subic Bay. They actually swam with whales, even danced with them. It also meant hundreds of miles in a very crowded car and, to quote Yvonne, "It's the first time I have ever gone with a couple on their honeymoon." Instead of a wedding, on Oct. 1, Steve and Mayen still planned a celebration reception for their friends and then a trip to New Zealand for a real honeymoon. We would love to have gone to the wedding, but it wasn't possible at that time.

Mayen is the perfect partner for Steve. She thinks he is wonderful and she is not only a professional actress and singer, but she teaches acting and has produced shows. She is a worship leader, as well as a leader of outreach groups and has discipled leaders who are now leading others. Mayen has a heart for the lost and a real desire to see the unreached nations of the world come to know Christ. She loves working with Steve and is a terrific asset as they work in various nations. She not only trains the actors, but also has an unusual ability to pick up new languages much faster than most people and this is extremely helpful.

—◆—

Although Dick worked with Steve on many projects, from producing films and videos to being in charge of banquets and providing unusual entertainment, when Dick went to Heaven, I claimed the privilege of adventures with my son. There's no possibility of doing some of the jobs my husband did with Steve. Both of the guys had technical ability and I have trouble turning on the television. I have learned some basic programs on the computer, but if anything goes wrong (which it assuredly does!), I need someone nearby calling out, "Attitude Check,

Helen!" For me, the computer has been an entirely different type of adventure, and it's certainly been a challenging one.

Because technology was changing so rapidly, I remember Dick saying, "Steve, someday in the near future you will be changing from using film and going to video." Dick was already using video for his work, but Steve was adamant, assuring Dick that "video will never be good enough for shooting a movie. It can't get the quality and depth and I will never use it for my movies." I'm not sure that Dick lived long enough to see that change, but it did eventually happen.

Steve started Sword Productions, an international movie production company, communicating the gospel through film in Asia. Their movies tell relevant, gripping, life-changing stories to people in their own language and culture. They strive for excellence in movie making to ensure the movies are of the highest caliber and are the "must-see" films for the younger generation in that country. Through movies, hundreds of thousands of people have been reached in the Philippines, Vietnam, Cambodia, Mongolia, Malaysia and beyond.

In one generation, media influences such as movies and television, have dramatically impacted the culture and beliefs of the young people who watch them. If the leaders in the entertainment industry were Christians who wanted to change the direction of their entire nation, imagine how the Gospel could spread! This is the work Sword Productions is doing. They are helping to train a new generation of local filmmakers, scriptwriters, directors and actors to continue to reach their cultures for Jesus through powerful and exciting movies. They take in their professional equipment and team, and as they are teaching and training they are also making a major movie. This is a more expensive ministry than some because they leave their equipment behind and set up a Christian Media Commission. When the training is finished they have a fully equipped production company, complete with their first major motion picture.

After the Philippines they were invited to Mongolia, then Cambodia and Nepal. Their work more recently is in Myanmar

(Burma), Vietnam, Sri Lanka and Laos. The invitations continue to pour in from other Asian countries. My involvement keeps me in the U.S., sending out letters and receipts, money and equipment and taking care of any request Steve sends me. Every country and each movie has its exciting moments and battles as Satan uses every trick possible to try and destroy their work. Although I am only a small part of it, Steve's life is one adventure after another, and I love being included in the overall picture. My son-in-law, Ron Brannon, is a CPA. He assists me in jobs for Sword that I can't do.

I may not be actively involved in most of my children's adventures but, as their mother, I am always with them emotionally. I go with them in prayer but, far more important, I know God is there. And He can do so much more than I could ever do to help them. The most amazing and awesome assurance I have is that the Lord is with each one wherever they are in the world, and He is also with me. I'm certain they haven't told me about some of their most dangerous experiences, but here is one of Steve's episodes.

I have SO MUCH to tell you!! Let me start first by reporting on this past month of shooting the movie 'Raising Heaven' in Mindanao — (Southern Philippines with lots of Muslim Terrorists.) For the most part, the shooting went very well even though it was rainy season! It was a full month of shooting from early morning until late at night. The team (about 20 cast and crew) got on very well and the non-believers on the crew frequently were moved by the experience of making a movie where people didn't yell and scream at them and where everyone was treated with respect, no matter how big or small their job.

The last week of filming was the most eventful with some of our hardest sequences saved for the last few days. The most difficult scenes for me to film are ones that involve shooting in very public places where we have hundreds of onlookers who are very difficult to control. We had a small contingent of security people with us all the time, due to the uncertain conditions in Mindanao. But when we were shooting in the local public market w had an additional 30 to 50 security personnel to help control the crowds. On one of these days of shooting in the market, we were working at the back of the market in an area that was basically the red-light district of the city. There were a string of brothels and nightclubs that were built out over the sea that came right up to the back of the market. We had been having trouble that day with one particular place that didn't want to turn off their karaoke and it was interfering with our sound. So our producer, Nenette, had gone inside to try and nicely talk the owner into turning the karaoke off.

Meanwhile, I'm out in front getting ready to roll on a scene we had been rehearsing. I had asked our security to please clear out the area of onlookers so we could roll cameras. A few minutes later there was a terrible crashing sound followed by screams! The entire floor of that nightclub had given way and the people had fallen into the sea about 15 feet below including our producer! It was low tide so there were many exposed rocks and broken boards with nails sticking out. In addition, and perhaps worst of all, the establishments in that area had no sewage facilities so they just let the raw sewage from toilets, etc. fall directly into the ocean so the whole area was a giant stinking toilet!

A few moments later the people were pulled out, along with Nenette who looked awful. We laid her on the ground and called for an ambulance, unsure whether or not there were broken bones or if she would go into shock. After she was taken away to the hospital we gathered around and prayed and then continued shooting.

A news crew from a local TV station showed up and started shooting interviews with people. We were concerned that they might try and blame the incident on our filming. But as we watched the segment on TV that night, it turns out that all of those places were built illegally and the city had wanted to get rid of them. Our incident may well be the trigger to pull all of those places down! We heard later from the hospital that Nenette was fine, just a couple of small bruises and the temporary loss of her dignity! She said she was more worried about the filthy water than anything.

Then a few days later we were shooting the last sequence of the movie—the kidnapping and car chase scene. I shot the beginning and the ending of the scene first, as they were the most complicated. The final scene is when the kidnappers are run off the road and crash into a shed on the side of the road. It involved a carabao (water buffalo) cart, a motorcycle/sidecar and two speeding vehicles. We had no stunt men or stand-ins. Our actors and crew were doing it all! I had been concerned throughout the day that our actors were getting caught up in the moment and had started to drive like madmen! I had told them several times that they were going too fast and to please slow down. The crash scene went fine with no incident. We then started setting up for some shots of the two cars going past the cameras. On one of these passes, the two cars were going particularly fast and I tried to signal them to SLOW DOWN as they passed the cameras and I called CUT into the walkie-talkie. The first vehicle braked quickly as the road was approaching a curve and a large crowd of people who had gathered to watch. For some reason he decided to make a U-turn in the road. The second vehicle came speeding down the road and couldn't stop in time and was heading for an impact directly into the side of the first vehicle.

I watched in horror at the impending crash. At the last second the driver of the second vehicle swerved suddenly and crashed into a low stone retaining wall on the side of the road and just clipped the front end of the first vehicle. But someone had been sitting on the wall, exactly where they had hit. I ran up the road to see who had been killed and how many people we had to take to the hospital. I could hear people yelling the name of JESS, our production designer. He was the one who had been sitting on the wall. As I approached the gathered crowd and started asking what happened, I learned that NO ONE had been hurt. Jess had been sitting exactly where the jeep impact had happened but for some unexplained (!) reason, he had flipped backward off the wall and landed unharmed on the grass. It all happened so fast there had been no time to think, but a split second before the jeep slammed into the wall, Jess simply felt pushed off the wall! The reason the jeep had not been able to stop in time? NO BRAKES! Their brakes had suddenly gone out. The only damage to the vehicles was a left wheel bent under the jeep and the bumper of the other vehicle torn off. It was already 5 p.m. so we called it a day and the two vehicles were repaired and ready to go the following day.

The next day we still had a number of road shots to do which mostly entailed the two vehicles driving past the camera on the side of the road. We did several setups and then while I was waiting by the side of the road for another pass I got a call on the walkie-talkie that the jeep brakes had failed AGAIN! So I went in search of someone to fix the brakes and passed our producer who wanted to know what was happening. I told her that the jeep brakes had failed again and she immediately responded that we would not shoot any more. She was not willing to take a chance on a vehicle whose brakes had failed twice in two days. So that was how the movie shooting ended. It was only 10 a.m. and we had planned a full day of shooting but we packed up and went home for lunch.

The following Monday, when we were preparing to leave for the airport, Romy, the head of our security detail, told me what had happened after we packed up. He received word that REAL KIDNAPPERS/BANDITS had been seen on the road where we were shooting. They had been casing us out and had apparently decided that we would make a good target. They came back to where we had been shooting, but we weren't there. So what I had thought was a problem with the brakes was actually God watching out for us and clearing us out of the area before anything serious could happen.

In the space of just five days we witnessed three times that the enemy had tried to cause us harm but each time God had protected us! I will now be working on editing the movie in the coming months. Please continue to pray as I work on all of the myriad of details in post-production. In addition, we have the Cambodia project that is taking shape very rapidly and will require that I take another trip there in the next month. We have also been asked to do a joint project of a new evangelistic Tagalog movie which we'll start researching on right away. Thank you for praying for us! PRAYER WORKS!!! GOD BLESS! Steve

---

One time when my mom was voicing her concern for Steve, he put his arm around her and assured her that when he gave his life to Jesus, he had already died. His life belonged to the Lord, and he (Steve) was no longer in control.

The doctor's orders of "No stress, No pollution, No excitement" doesn't fit Steve's life! He rides a motorcycle in some of the most polluted areas possible, or on some of the worst and most dangerous roads in the world. However, the safest place anywhere is where God has asked us to go. If I didn't believe this, I would be a worrying wreck, but God is in control, not me! And I trust Him!

Brothers Steve & Jon

Steve and older brother Jon were partners in mischief and best friends, both as children and adults.

(Above) Steve and Mayen trained a team to make a Christian movie in Nepal in 2013 called "Bijay!" (Left) Steve and Mayen vist Steve's eldest son Jesse, wife Kerri, and grandson Rowan. Jesse and family have lived in Kuwait, Germany and Japan.

During preproduction for the Nepal film, Steve coached the actors as they rehearsed scenes while also training the two Nepali directors on camera angles.

In 2014 a group of Christians in Laos invited Steve, Mayen, and the team to train them in film production. Steve taught media and directing while Mayen trained possible actors for a Christian film.

Mayen became a US citizen and, knowing she was a musician, the organizers of the ceremony asked her to sing the National Anthem for the event.

Two of Steve's children, Ben and Milei, live in Portland, Oregon so he is able to see them when he returns to Oregon for visits. His daughter Nikki lives in Florida, and Jesse in Japan.

In 2015, the Christian group 'Trumpets' wrote and performed a musical stage version of the C.S. Lewis classic "A Horse and His Boy." Both Steve and Mayen performed in the show.

CHAPTER 18

ADVENTURES WITH YVONNE (FAMILY ACCIDENTS and SICKNESS)

It's time I talked about these difficult topics. These are experiences we go through in life that are adventures into the unknown, during which we hang on and hope and trust God. According to my mother, my adventures with sickness began within days after I was born when I managed to get whooping cough. With the church and community praying for me, I survived. Then when I was about four years old I had a battle with mastoiditis. I still remember with horror those trips to the hospital when they put me in a straight jacket and punctured my eardrum—not just once, but several times. There was no such thing as the wonder drugs of today, and they didn't give me any kind of painkiller.

The doctors finally told my parents the only hope of saving my life was to operate. But that meant great risks at my age, and it could either kill me or leave me with brain damage because it was so close to my brain. (Dick jokingly said, "I see you didn't die!") The night before the scheduled surgery our church had a night of prayer for me, and when Mom came to take me to the hospital she found I was covered with big red blotches all over my body. God had answered prayer and took the poison out evenly throughout my body rather than letting the doctors release so much pressure all at once near my brain. I recovered, but it did leave a hole in my eardrum, which eventually healed, leaving scar tissue. Years later in Manila, I went swimming in a contaminated pool and when my damaged ear became infected, it burst like an explosion. This has left me basically with no eardrum in my right ear.

While in the Philippines, I had an allergic reaction to a medication for a kidney infection. This caused a terrible itching and then I began to swell so much that Dick had to file off my rings. It was not easy to do this when the swelling almost covered the ring. I was afraid they might need to remove my whole finger. When I awoke the next morning, the first person that saw me screamed—my ears were huge, my eyes, nose and face were totally swollen in such a way that I looked like a monster. It was getting hard to breathe, which meant that my throat was swelling too. Dick phoned our friends who were doctors and was told to get me to the hospital as fast as possible. Again, this was not easy because we lived out in the country, near Faith Academy and traffic could be horrible. When we arrived at the hospital they were standing in the doorway ready to give me an injection to counteract the medication that caused the problem.

Aside from having my appendix out and having five babies, I don't feel like I have been sick very often, but apparently it's been serious when it has happened. When we were coming back to the Philippines from England, we had a layover in Malaysia. There wasn't time to go to a hotel, so we just stayed in the airport most of the night. It just happened that the airport was under construction at the time, and no water was available to flush toilets or wash our hands. There was no such thing as bottled water in those days. We ordered some food at the restaurant and realized they also couldn't wash their hands or the dishes. Back in Manila I got very sick, and when I turned a bright orange we discovered I had come down with hepatitis, probably from our night in Malaysia.

Our family of seven had its share of colds, flu, cuts, bruises and all the normal sicknesses and accidents that happen to

everyone throughout life. The most memorable accident happened in Holland when Yvonne was hit by a car. It was 1967,
the year we took our family through Europe on our way to
the U.S. after five years in the Philippines. We were traveling
in a camper we had purchased in England.

As we crossed into Northern Holland from Denmark, we
were all excited. The whole family had been looking forward
to visiting this tiny country, which you can drive through
in one day. Carolyn's best friend from Faith Academy, Dora
Nijman, was from here. We wanted to visit Dora's married
sister in Enkhuizen, but it wasn't easy finding her house and
we arrived just before dark. Although they were happy to see
us, neither one of the couple was fluent in English, but with the
help of an English-Dutch dictionary we managed to carry on
a fairly intelligible and enjoyable conversation. They showed
us to a campground on the edge of town where we grabbed a
bite to eat and tumbled into bed. We wanted an early start in
the morning because we were headed for Alkmaar (about 30
miles away) to see the famous cheese weighing market.

The next day was cloudy, but it wasn't raining. While
driving along the narrow brick road, we couldn't resist stopping to take pictures of three beautiful windmills. We discovered too late that cars hurtled down this tiny road as if racing
to win the Grand Prix. Steve was already across the road and
turned to watch Yvonne look both ways before crossing, but
neither one saw the approaching vehicle. I had just snapped a
picture of Dick when we heard the screech of brakes. Whirling
around, we stared in horror as a speeding car slammed into
Yvonne. I must have been in shock for a few seconds, because
I suddenly heard Carolyn saying, "Mom, it doesn't do any
good to scream!" I snapped back into reality and raced with
the others to Yvonne's crumpled body.

Yvonne lay in the road motionless, her eyes rolled back in
her head, blood gushing from her mouth and nose. We could
find no pulse. To the people who began to gather, we cried out
"Doctor! Hospital! Please help!" until it dawned on us that
no one spoke English. A dim recollection of long past First

Aid training warned us not to move Yvonne, but we were afraid she might be hit again while lying there on the road. Since there was no communication and apparently no help, we carefully picked up Yvonne's broken body and laid her in the camper. Dick jumped into the driver's seat and tried once again to get directions to the hospital—but the people only looked puzzled and spoke words we could not understand. The driver of the car that hit Yvonne was running across the field.

We took off in the same direction we had been heading—toward Alkmaar. Jon was helping watch for signs while Dick had the car at top speed, lights on and horn blaring. Steve and LuAnne were huddled together crying and praying. Carolyn and I bent over Yvonne and all we could do was cry out, "Oh God, help us!" In our mad race Yvonne began to moan, which gave us new hope. Until that moment, we weren't even certain that she was alive.

With some relief we finally saw a sign pointing straight ahead to Alkmaar, 2 kilometers, when Dick suddenly shouted, "Something is wrong! Everything on the car is dead! We're just coasting!" What a time to have car trouble! This was a new car and we had never had any kind of problem with it before now.

Dick was frantically trying to get the motor going again when he caught a glimpse of a service station up ahead on the right. We coasted into the station and Dick jumped out to find help when he noticed a policeman standing by a telephone. Without even thinking about language difficulties, Dick's words tumbled out about our terrible plight. The officer slowly replied in broken English, "Calm down. I get help." He then made a phone call and assured Dick that an ambulance would arrive in a few minutes.

After what seemed like hours instead of minutes, the ambulance arrived and Carolyn and I rode with Yvonne to the hospital. Dick stayed behind with the other children to see if they could get the car started. As Dick watched the ambulance leave he was surprised to see that it didn't go down the main highway but instead it went on a little side road directly across from the service station. Dick was still pondering the significance of this when he turned back to the car—and had another surprise. In all of Holland, we knew only two people—the couple we had met the night before! And there they were pulling into the gas station! When Dick informed them of the accident they immediately changed their plans and proceeded to help us in every way possible. Their assistance with details, language, and as prayer partners was invaluable!

Dick was really anxious to get to the hospital so, with the help of our friends, he explained the strange behavior of our car to the station's mechanic. A car might be hard to get started but it is rather rare when a speeding car suddenly quits for no visible reason. We had plenty of gas and nothing appeared to be wrong. Dick got in to see if he could start the car and it started up instantly and sounded perfectly normal. The mechanic couldn't find anything wrong either. Dick and the others arrived at the hospital shortly after the ambulance.

Yvonne was hit about 9:00 a.m. and it was after 4:00 p.m. before we had any idea of how seriously she was hurt and even whether she would live or die. Yvonne's upper left leg was completely broken and required traction. The lower portion was also broken, but not as seriously as the upper part, so it was put into a partial cast. Prayer has always been extremely important in our lives, but at first we found it difficult to talk to God in a rational way. Yet we discovered that God isn't limited by what we say or don't say to Him. He understands our thoughts and emotions much better than we do ourselves.

During those hours of waiting we wanted to put our minds in neutral— to somehow form a vacuum. Instead, our thoughts kept returning to the scene of the accident to relive it over and over again, and then our imaginations raced forward to torture us with uncertainty about the future. Through it all we somehow knew that God was still with us— and we had already discovered a few ways He had been working on our behalf.

To start with, there was the policeman who could speak English and quickly got us an ambulance. We never would have found the hospital on our own. Then there were the two friends who "just happened" to come by at exactly the right time and place. But the thing that startled us the most was when we were informed that if we had followed the sign pointing straight ahead into Alkmaar, we would have been routed around the city and out the other side because it was "Cheese Market Day" and no through traffic was allowed. It might have been the difference between life and death for Yvonne. We were amazed to find that the little side road across from the service station was the only way to the hospital on the special market day. Sometimes people are credited with intuition in times of stress, but I never heard of a car with that particular gift. Yet for no apparent reason this car stopped at the only possible way to the hospital and started up again after it accomplished its mission. We call that a miracle!

Although Yvonne was seriously injured, we were told that everything could heal without permanent damage, though it would take time. The doctor said she would be six to eight weeks in traction before she could be put into a cast and moved. Many questions began to plague our minds. Should Dick go on ahead to the States? What about all the camps and churches in the U.S. where our family was booked to sing and speak, beginning in about two weeks? How were we going to pay for everything? Through the first long night I kept hearing the screech of brakes and seeing Yvonne in the road. I didn't want to stay awake, nor did I want to sleep and dream. Dick was also restless.

So we got our Bible and began to read. We just read on and on— anything and any place. It was the only way to relieve our confused minds of the turmoil. And then we came upon Colossians 3:15, and it seemed as though a light was shining right on this verse, just for us! **"Let the peace of heart which comes from Christ be always present in your hearts and** lives, for this is your responsibility and privilege as members of His body. And always be thankful." This doesn't say "peace when everything is going great, but "peace, always present." We did not have peace, so we asked Him for it, and He gave it to us! We did have a struggle over the last part, "And always be thankful." That took some work and a total change of attitude.

I cried when Yvonne's first words after surgery were, "I'm awfully sorry to cause you so much trouble. I thought I looked both ways, but I didn't see any car coming." Her first consideration was always of others. She was a mass of bruises, cuts and scratches, and was completely miserable — but she was alive! And her injuries weren't permanent. She did have a slight concussion and her mouth and tongue were cut. That's why she was bleeding, but there were no signs of internal injury or brain damage. It's always hard to understand why things like this happen, but we do know God is always with us in every circumstance of life, and we trust Him.

I think that Dick and I always had a secret fear that we might not be able to keep Yvonne for long because she was more like an angel than a normal child. We have always loved every one of our children equally, but as far as disposition was concerned, Vonnie was the one person in our family that everyone could always get along with. One reason was because she was so unselfish and never thought of her own desires, but always thought of the other person. Six years earlier when we still lived in California I had a horrible dream of seeing Yvonne lying on the ground after a car had hit her. It was such a vivid dream that I lived in fear of it for months. Although I forgot it over the years, it instantly came back to me when I saw her lying in the road.

Since our thoughts were concentrated on Yvonne, we didn't even think about the driver, except that we saw him running away. Later in the day he came to the hospital with a policeman. He hadn't really run away, but was racing to the nearest farmhouse to find a telephone. Naturally, he was terribly shook and felt awful about hitting Yvonne. The blame automatically went to us because we removed Yvonne from the scene of the accident. That was a Dutch law. Although our ignorance of the law was not considered an excuse, we could not have left Vonnie lying in the middle of the road under any circumstances. And we had no idea why the man was running away.

The driver admitted he had a dental appointment and was late for work, so he was in a hurry. We were told there was a slight curve and rise in the road at that point, so Yvonne didn't see the car and he didn't see her. Our Dutch friends advised us to just accept the blame, or we might have to stay in the country for a court case — which could take as long as a year. And we did move Yvonne — which was against the law. Also, a foreigner's chance of winning anything in court was extremely slim. When we pled guilty, it meant that we had to pay for the car that hit Yvonne to be repaired. The expenses weren't enormous, but he hit her so hard that it broke the headlight, bent the bumper and dented the front of his car.

A couple of days after the accident, some of the nurses became concerned about Yvonne's other leg, so they ordered an X-ray. (They had the authority to do this without a doctor's order.) They discovered this leg was also broken in the lower part — but not as serious as the other leg. We did believe and clung to Romans 8:28: **"And we know that all things work together for good to those who love God, to those who are the called according to His purpose."** (NKJV) We did find that God's grace was sufficient.

We were at the hospital constantly for the first couple of days after the accident, but then the hospital staff told us we needed to follow their rules for visiting times. Visiting hours were very limited — one hour in the afternoon and only 30 minutes in the evening. We soon found this was unacceptable in our situation. Steve and LuAnne were too young to even go in and see Yvonne. No children were allowed into this part of the hospital. Jon and Carolyn were old enough to come and visit. However, no more than two people could be in the room with a patient during visiting hours — so we had to share our limited time between four of us.

I tried to put myself in Yvonne's place: just a child; seriously injured; suffering pain; scared; in a strange country with an unfamiliar language; and family forbidden to see her except for one hour and 30 minutes each day. When Yvonne came out of the groggy stage, but still felt miserable, she needed us and we needed her! She cried most of the time and it took us half of the visiting hour to get her calmed down. Then as we had to leave she almost got hysterical. This totally upset us, and so I went to the head nurse (the only one who spoke much English), and I tried to explain our situation. However, she was adamant, "Hospital rules can not be changed under any circumstances!" We felt that our unusual circumstances warranted a little consideration. Yvonne really needed us, emotionally and for communication. The nurses complained of being terribly short handed and too busy, so they also needed us! But "rules were rules!"

I really didn't like asking for special privileges, but for Yvonne's sake, I decided to talk to the doctor in charge of her case. He said it was fine with him for us to be there as much as possible, but nothing moved the head nurse until I told her our request was going to the highest official of the hospital. My determination caused her to relent a little and allow me to come in for 45 minutes in the morning. Although this wasn't enough, it did help and we didn't want to antagonize the hospital staff any further.

The hospital (Ziekenhauss) was large, new, well-equipped, clean, and situated in Alkmaar in order to serve all the towns within 30 miles. Except for the visiting hours, we had no complaints. Differing from U.S. hospitals, the nurses had more authority than the doctors. Visitors were supposed to bring fresh fruits for the patients and it was not only acceptable, the hospital personnel expected it.

Earlier I mentioned the Scripture, Colossians 3:15. We found that we could not ignore the last tag-on, **"And always be thankful."** At first I thought it was terribly out of place. But we discovered it was the whole secret of the first part in having peace. I think God was gracious to give us peace anyway that first night, because we weren't very thankful for all things. We had too many questions. I don't think one learns to be thankful in one easy lesson. It isn't easy, but we tried to be teachable. I'm glad God is patient.

At first we had to deliberately set out and find things to be thankful for, but our surprise was genuine at how long the list became. The most obvious entry on the list was:

1. YVONNE WAS ALIVE!

2. She had no permanent injuries. Although Vonnie looked worse than any of the other children, she was better off than the majority of the children in the hospital. I had no idea so many children had such serious diseases.

3. As a family, we were drawn closer than ever and were brought face to face with what was valuable in life. I hope we never forget what is truly priceless. We still had each other!

4. Friends! From around the world, we were being showered with notes of love, prayer and concern.

5. Excellent hospital and staff.

6. Miracles.

These were only a few of the most important and impressive items. The list was long! And when we truly started thanking God, a whole lot of "little" miracles happened, although it took a few days for us to notice them. Actually, these were probably the greatest miracles of all, because happiness replaced our depression; hope took over our fears; concern for others made self-pity disappear; laughter succeeded complaining; new friends — doctors, nurses, patients and their families — filled in the loneliness; gratefulness did away with bitterness; and we honestly felt surrounded by love.

The mission organization we were with at that time was Overseas Crusades, now called O.C. International. They were fantastic. Just as soon as our office in California received the cable we sent, they phoned our main supporting churches to request prayer. We also sent a letter explaining the injuries, expressing our confusion over schedules, and asking about expenses. Dick Hillis (our mission leader) must have answered it the moment he read it. His assurance that "With God there are no accidents, only incidents!" proved to be a great comfort. Instructions were for us to stay together as a family; churches and camps would understand. They didn't want Dick to leave me here, and I agreed 100%. Dick's letter left us so relieved and happy that we were crying and jumping around hugging each other all at the same time. As soon as the office received the letter we sent, they printed it and mailed it to quite a few churches and individuals. We soon began to receive mail, and we were overwhelmed to hear some of the ways God was working.

In Seattle, some friends of ours awoke one morning thinking about us. They couldn't get us off their minds, and their feeling was one of heaviness. Although they had no idea of our whereabouts, they felt an urgency to pray for us. A day or so later they remembered about our mission representative in their area, so they phoned to inquire if there was any recent news from us. Only a few minutes earlier the man had received word about the accident and could give them information. God's communication plan far surpasses any man-made system.

The doctor, who seemed to be excellent (except for missing that one broken leg), still thought Yvonne would need to be in traction for eight weeks. However, he assured us he would X-ray her at the end of four weeks, and if enough calcium had formed to heal sufficiently, he would put on a cast and send us home to the U.S. He was not encouraging, but we thought God just might do another miracle. So we decided to ship our car the next week. That would give it two weeks to arrive in the U.S. in case we could leave around July 10th. It was very important for the car to be in New York when we arrived, and yet we wanted to avoid paying storage charges, so we needed perfect timing. One reason it was such a big decision to send the car early was because it was not only our means of transportation—it was our home! We hadn't decided what to do when the car was gone.

Because of the hospital's strict rules on visiting, Steve and LuAnne felt left out and had to entertain themselves while we were in the hospital. Carolyn and Jon had visiting privileges, but the four of us could never go in to see Yvonne together, and visiting time was too short to share. Dick and I did share with our older children, but most of the time they found children who had no visitors. The Dutch children were excited to have American teenagers spend time with them and Carolyn and Jon had a wonderful time making new friends. Although most of the nurses did not speak English, the children usually had taken a year or two of English in school. However, much of the time they were too embarrassed to try using a language they had never really spoken. Except for Kurt.

It was love at first sight when we met 13-year-old Kurt. He seldom had visitors, even though he was incurably sick with a blood disease. His parents were divorced and lived too far away to come every day, so Carolyn and Jon spent much time with Kurt. His English wasn't perfect, but he was not afraid to try using it, and he took it upon himself to be Yvonne's interpreter. He wasn't like most patients who must remain in bed constantly, but he had freedom to roam the hospital at times. When we were gone he took care of Vonnie. Carolyn shared the Four Spiritual Laws with him one day, using the simplest language possible. In Revelation 3:20 Jesus said, "Behold, I stand at the door and knock; if anyone hears My voice and opens the door, I will come in to him." Carolyn explained, "Jesus is knocking at your heart, Kurt. He wants to come in, but you must open the door and invite Him in."

For the first week they took great precautions with Yvonne because of the concussion. It was hard for her to move with one leg in traction and the other in a partial cast, but she couldn't even have a pillow or be raised at all the first few days. Her meals consisted mainly of yogurt, but often with sugar or a topping. The yogurt there was different. It could be poured from a quart jar and was much milder. I thought it was wonderful.

The first few nights we parked our camper next to the hospital, but then we found a lovely campground about five minutes drive away. Besides having showers and bathrooms, it gave the other children a chance to run off some of their energy. Alkmaar is famous for their open-air cheese market, and we enjoyed watching wooden shoes being carved there. We discovered a beautiful cathedral and we weren't far from the beach. Actually, nothing was very far away in Holland.

Scripture was a solid rock for us to stand on — we couldn't survive without it. II Samuel 22:31 told us, **"As for God, His way is perfect. The word of the Lord is true. He shields all who hide behind Him."** And Nahum 1:7 reminded us that, **"The Lord is good, when trouble comes, He is the place to go! And He knows everyone who trusts in Him!"** We were learning to trust Him more and more.

We were astounded at the amount of letters and packages that Yvonne began receiving. The hospital staff was also amazed and jokingly told us that they needed to hire more help in order to handle Yvonne's mail. But it was the best medicine she could get. We were overwhelmed to see how much people cared and how they took time to write and pray. Nothing in the world compares to belonging to God's family.

I mentioned that Yvonne was crying a lot at first. Many things began to happen to improve this. First of all, she began feeling better and everything wasn't as strange any more. She began to make friends with other children and the nurses. They tried to teach her some Dutch phrases and she helped them with English. Mail was a marvelous therapy. And then there were the tape recorders. When we went through Hong Kong on our way to Europe, both Dick and Carolyn bought cassette tape recorders so that we could talk through tapes when we went back to the Philippines and left Carolyn in the

U.S. for college. We decided this was a good time to break them in. Yvonne had one in the hospital and we had one with us. Every evening we talked to Yvonne. This was LuAnne and Steve's only means of communicating with Yvonne since they never got in to see her.

We sang to Yvonne family song and choruses, told stories, read the Bible and just talked. Yvonne also had a tape recorder, so she recorded to us, and then each day we exchanged tapes with each other. These tape recorders probably did more to break down language barriers than any other thing. All the children who could walk around in the hospital liked to come and talk and hear themselves. Nurses and children began to learn the choruses we sang and they also taught us some of their songs. Yvonne could turn on the tape and hear our voices whenever she got lonely. One tape was both touching and funny when through obvious sobs and tears, Yvonne expressed, "Your tape makes me so happy!"

The day came when we shipped our car to the States. That meant we walked! We probably spent about five hours every day just walking. For a family who hadn't walked in years, this was a traumatic experience. People seldom walked in Manila because it was too hot and humid and crowded and dirty. I remember being so tired I could hardly feel my legs. But I knew they were there and had to get me home, so I kept telling them when to move. We had tried to get a room closer to the hospital, but every room in town was reserved beginning the first day of July. This was because all over Europe the building/construction workers took their vacations at the same time. Our campground only had four campers in it until July 1. Then it had over 80 tents and people continued to pour in.

It was a good thing we couldn't get a room, because we discovered we didn't have enough money anyhow. Alkmaar sponsored a "Camping Fair" the week before we shipped the car and it was an ideal place for us to see many tents all set up in one place. We had a very limited amount of money, so although our choice was restricted, we did find a satisfactory covering for our family of six. The tent was large enough for all of our sleeping bags to lay out flat. It had a plastic floor, the price was right, and the thing that made it super special was a separate little tent within the bigger tent. Dick and I had our own private bedroom.

After paying the price, we proceeded back to the campground to prepare our new home. That's when we discovered why it was so reasonably priced! Enthralled with the many advantages of this particular tent and the low price tag, we neglected to notice its height: no one could stand up in our dwelling place. This may not sound so bad, but six people trying to dress while sitting down was inconvenient, not to mention quite hilarious! All things may be possible, but all things are certainly not easy. At first we didn't really think it was funny, but when we learned to maneuver our bodies in the most unusual positions and became adept at crawling on our hands and knees, it wasn't so bad after all. A change in attitude helped us be able to laugh at each other and the silly situation. I didn't think I could get a meal sitting on the ground, but it wasn't so hard when there was no way to cook anyway. Our meals were quite interesting, though a little odd.

We discovered places called "Automatiks" shortly after Yvonne's accident. These were just what the name implied: tiny places with a few stools to sit on and a place where we put money into a slot to get warm food. But the best part was that they made wonderful sandwiches of ham or roast beef in a bun. They were really yummy; the taste and the price were great, and we hadn't had anything like this for years. The children were also delighted with the potato frits, another name for French fries. These were also a treat and were served in a paper cone with a glob of mayonnaise on top. These were foods we did not have available in the Philippines at that time. Every day we feasted on these specialties for lunch.

Before shipping our camper, we usually cooked something for our evening meal, but with no car now and no way to cook, we ate ham or roast beef sandwiches for supper also. My figures indicated that during our time in Alkmaar, the six of us devoured nearly 300 of these delectable sandwiches. (We had discovered that our whole family could eat at the Automatik for the same price as one person could eat any place else in town.) After about 40 similar sandwiches, Dick began eyeing a big chunk of ground beef in the cooler of our familiar little eating-place. No one spoke English, so we just pointed to what we wanted. But by now they knew us so well that they could start making our sandwiches as we walked in the door. Dick had evidently been thinking about that hamburger for several days and finally decided it was worth the extra money. Once he made that decision, his whole body quivered with anticipation at the thought of this luscious change in menu.

The girl registered surprise when Dick walked to the counter and pointed — not to the roast beef or ham, but to the big ground beef patty. Then it was our turn to exhibit surprise. "Shock" would be a more accurate word. The waitress simply picked up the raw meat, plopped it on a bun and handed it to Dick. We all gathered around this rare object and produced varied observations. "Maybe it's already cooked." I carried on a little private investigation and discovered they didn't have any way to cook food, other than the potato fritz. Dick gathered his courage and took a bite. Sure enough! It was just exactly what it looked like — cold raw meat! We couldn't bear to waste such valuable meat, so Steve came to the rescue and "licked the platter clean." He never committed himself as to whether or not he enjoyed it, but he usually liked anything edible. However, everyone went back to the ham or roast beef sandwiches after that.

Before long, strawberries came into season. They were huge, incredibly delicious, and another food we hadn't seen for five years. Every morning someone came through the campground selling strawberries for 10 cents a basket. Someone else came about the same time with fresh pourable yogurt. Sometimes we added cereal (Corn Flakes or Rice Krispies were the ones available), and our breakfasts were special.

In traveling through Europe we discovered that not every town had a laundromat, but we were delighted when we found one in Alkmaar. Once we sent the car away, we had to carry our dirty clothes in a big bundle as we walked several miles into town. With the camper, we had only been about five minutes away from the hospital. But we were much farther from the town, and we were now walking everywhere. The owner of the laundromat often attempted to visit with me, and we did learn to communicate without understanding the different languages. He was very helpful in familiarizing me with the city. While people were extremely friendly, they spoke so little English and we spoke so little Dutch, that it was hard to get genuinely acquainted. We found that junior high students made the best interpreters.

We had to ship our car from Amsterdam, so on that day Carolyn stayed with Yvonne and the rest of us went to the big city. We had kept only our bare essentials with us in Alkmaar and shipped everything possible in the car. After leaving our vehicle at the proper place, we proceeded on our own sightseeing excursion. We watched as they dredged a canal and brought up not only bicycles, but also a car! The number one place for the children was the intriguing Anne Frank house. Since the car was gone, all we had left were our feet. That was the beginning of our walking days and we almost collapsed. For some reason Jon's and my shoes didn't fit right for this kind of exercise and we both developed blisters. It took me a few minutes longer than it took Jon, but we both came to the same conclusion—who cares what anyone else thinks if we go barefooted! It wasn't so obvious for Jon, but I was wearing a dress and heavy winter coat. If they could have seen my broken blisters, they would have understood.

As we rode the train back to Alkmaar, Steve suddenly shouted, "Hey, look! There's a ship above us!" The canal with its dike was higher than the road and train tracks, so the ship was there beside us—only much higher than our train.

After being here a while we weren't so shocked at how many accidents occur, but our surprise came at the number they seem to avoid! We constantly heard the screech of brakes, and we probably witnessed more accidents here in three weeks than in the past 10 years anywhere else. Even walking was dangerous. It was hard for us to distinguish between the bicycle and walking paths—but it was almost unforgiveable and deadly to walk in a bicycle road. We had never seen so many bicycles anywhere, and they did not appreciate anything in their path.

After Yvonne improved enough for us to leave her alone in the morning, we consented to sing and speak at a meeting for our Salvation Army friends. It was hard to adjust to singing without Yvonne and even more difficult emotionally. However, we again found Jesus to be sufficient, and He helped us—even in our need for an interpreter. Another day we left early and treated the children to a morning at Madurodam. This is a miniature city containing Holland's principal sights and buildings all scaled down perfectly to 1/25 of their actual sizes. Everything worked, from the tiny cars on the highways to bands performing in the park. It really is a full city, and we could easily have spent the whole day wandering trough the delightful area, but we needed to arrive back at the hospital in time for the afternoon visiting hours.

Earlier I mentioned about Kurt, Carolyn, The Four Spiritual Laws, and Revelation 3:20. When Carolyn visited Kurt the next time, his first words were, "Jesus knocks - I want!" Carolyn questioned him thoroughly, and he seemed to really understand his decision.

One of our camping neighbors was an Englishman who married a Dutch girl, and his hobby was pipe organs. One evening he took Jon and Dick to an organ concert at a beautiful cathedral in Haarlem where international artists came to perform their own compositions. Mr. Walker couldn't do enough to help us, and we loved getting acquainted with others this way.

Although the doctor was certain Yvonne couldn't be healed enough to put a cast on, he kept his word and took X-rays after four weeks in traction. Since this was tourist season, we had gone ahead and made plane reservations even before we knew the outcome of the X-rays. We informed the man at the KLM desk about Yvonne, telling him that both of her legs would be in casts. We asked for the seats with extra leg space. We made reservations for the next Friday and then wrote to Dick and Ethel Hamilton, the World Vision representatives for the East Coast, telling them we might come in if Yvonne was healed enough, but not to meet us because we had no assurance that we would arrive. The Hamiltons were the only people we knew near New York, and we couldn't make hotel reservations because we didn't know any hotels in New York or even the specific date we would be arriving. Suddenly everything happened so fast that my heart, my stomach, and my emotions were tumbling all over each other.

Since we were foreigners in Holland, the hospital informed us that all bills must be paid before we could leave, even though we had insurance coverage for anywhere in the world. Our O.C. office in California had told us to let them know anything we needed; so after much figuring, Dick decided we could probably manage with $500 in addition to the money my parents had sent from our bank account. We still had a little money with us, and doctors and hospitals were much less expensive in Europe than in the United States. The sympathetic doctor told us we could pay him later if we didn't have enough cash with us.

Yvonne's X-rays were scheduled for Thursday, so on Wednesday Dick phoned Palo Alto to relate our financial needs. The mission treasurer answered the overseas phone call, but the instant he heard Dick's voice he remarked, "Wait a minute. I think someone with more authority should talk to you." Before Dick could stop him he laid the phone down and was off searching for some elusive executive. All of this time we were paying for an overseas phone call and Dick was about to panic. After what seemed like hours (but was actually only seconds), Walter Paul came back and slowly reported, "I'm sorry Dick, but I can't find anyone else. They're all at a conference so I guess you'll just have to talk to me." That was Dick's intention in the first place, so he quickly relayed his message and our need for $500. He asked that the money be cabled to a certain bank in Alkmaar. This conversation took place on Wednesday evening.

Early Thursday morning before we arrived, Yvonne was X-rayed. When we arrived at the hospital the nurse greeted us with the thrilling news that Yvonne was healed enough and the cast was already on! The doctor left word that we could take her home just as soon as the cast hardened. Excited beyond words, we literally ran to Yvonne's room; but at the door we stopped short. One look and our world caved in.

Yvonne did not have two leg casts as we, in our ignorance of medical things, had anticipated. Instead, she was encased in a huge body cast. It extended from under her arms all the way to her feet. Her legs were spread apart and held firm by a bar in-between. We tried to cover our shock and regain some composure as we walked over to Yvonne's bed where she was sobbing as though her heart would break. The cast was so tight she could hardly breathe and of course crying only made it worse. When Yvonne could control her crying enough to relate all the happenings of the morning, she explained that the metal pin in her knee had been stuck. With no anesthetic, they pushed and pulled and twisted until it broke loose. Vonnie thought the pain of that experience far surpassed anything else she had been through. And no one had prepared any of us for a body cast.

Yvonne felt as though her body was in a vise and she was slowly being strangled to death, while Dick and I were positive she could never fit on an airplane—or anything else! Her legs were spread so far apart there was no way to get her through any normal sized door. And the nurse informed us that we could move her home in a couple of days. But where would we take her? And how could she be transported anywhere? I didn't cry during our visiting time with Yvonne, but once outside—well, that's another story!

Dick and I didn't sink quite as low as we did the day of the accident, but we weren't far behind. It's amazing how fast we forgot all that God had done for us. We felt that everything was hopeless. But we managed to retrace our steps to the KLM airline office.

We explained Yvonne's condition and the clerk exclaimed, "Oh! She's a stretcher case!" Dick quietly asked, "What does that mean?" The clerk had no idea, but after searching in a large book of rules and regulations to find what it involved, his voice registered shock as he read, "There must be a signed statement from the doctor giving conditions, reason for travel and assurance that it is safe for the patient to go by plane. An ambulance must take the patient to the airplane and see him safely situated. A stretcher case requires nine airplane seats!"

Dick and I spoke together, "Nine seats! What does that cost?" He continued reading until he found the answer and replied with obvious relief, "It only costs one extra adult fare, but you must go on a plane that does not have a full load." He informed us that the date we had reserved was completely filled and since tourist season was in full swing, our total number of 15 seats didn't give us any choice. In fact, the only plane with available seats during the next few weeks was to leave the following Monday morning. If we didn't go then, we might be in Holland all summer, and yet it was five days earlier than we had planned to return to the U.S.

Problems loomed so high we couldn't see over them! By now it was late Thursday afternoon and the Post Office was closed, so we had no way to phone overseas or even send a cable—all that kind of business was taken care of exclusively at the Post Office. The $500 we had requested to supplement our own money wouldn't begin to cover hospital expenses, ambulance to the airport and an extra adult plane ticket. Besides that, the $500 had not yet arrived and might not come for several days. If we didn't have enough money by 3:00 p.m. Friday afternoon, we couldn't make it. The bank closed at 3:00 p.m. and didn't open again until 9:00 a.m. on Monday. We had to have our bills paid and leave for the airport by 8:00 a.m. in order to make the airplane on time. We could see absolutely no way! To say we were depressed is a great understatement! We did pray, but with very little faith because we couldn't figure out any way for God to work this one out. We thought God needed our help, and we had none to give.

Friday morning Dick made his way to the bank to see if any money had arrived. None! Even if we phoned California, it was too late to cable money and have it reach the bank before closing time. At the hospital Yvonne was feeling a little better, but the whole family lay under a dark cloud of apprehension. We made the reservations to leave on Monday morning, but were absolutely certain it was impossible.

In spite of us, God was working and never once held back his miracles. Our tent was sold to a family in the campground, but they told us we could use it as long as necessary. By Friday afternoon Yvonne was adjusting to the cast and felt it might be endurable; she actually smiled again. Dick suffered the heaviest load now: money. Well, not really money, but the absence of it! He decided to go to the bank and just wait. Maybe the $500 would come, although we weren't certain how much good it would do. Our bills exceeded twice that amount.

It was almost closing time at the bank, and Dick was still sitting on a bench where he had been most of the day. As he was about to leave, he heard the bank teller call his name. "Mr. Cadd, how much money were you expecting?" Dick sort of shrugged his shoulders and mumbled in a dejected voice, "I guess about $500." "Really? Someone must like you! $1000 just came in for you." I'm not sure that Dick did handstands and summersaults at that moment in the bank, but he certainly had the inspiration for it. This was an impossibility, but incredibly, it really did happen.

Once again, God was there working, in spite of our depression and lack of faith. We had forgotten what He said in Matthew 6:32-34: **"But your heavenly Father already knows perfectly well what you need, and He will give it to you if you give Him first place in your life and live as He wants you to. So don't be anxious about tomorrow. God will take care of your tomorrow too. Live one day at a time."** I wonder why we worried. Even though all the men with authority were attending an out-of-town conference, Walter Paul, our mission treasurer, made the momentous decision to send an extra $500, just in case we had some unexpected expenses! God had arranged another miracle without our help!

By the time evening visiting hours came, the hospital had been paid, arrangements were made for an ambulance, we confirmed reservations on the airline and, best of all, Yvonne was feeling great! Saturday and Sunday were a maze of packing, washing clothes, visiting, thanking, praying and praising God. During our four-week stay we had acquired friends throughout Alkmaar and had become familiar with the cheese market, parks, laundromat, windmills, bicycle paths, stores, hospital, canals and camps. Actually, we truly felt as though we had lived in Holland! We could travel like the residents and even Amsterdam wasn't strange to us now.

When our neighbors at the campground found out we were leaving, they bent over backward to help us. And we had some problems, which we couldn't solve ourselves. Yvonne had a ride to the airplane in the ambulance, but there were six more of us, with baggage and sleeping bags, who had no way. Mr. Walker, the Englishman married to a Dutch lady, attached a small trailer to his tiny Volkswagen. Crammed into the trailer were all of our belongings, and the rest of us planned to squeeze into the car. However, the ambulance attendants consented to allow me and two of the children to ride with Yvonne. Steve and LuAnne were selected because they hadn't seen Vonnie for a full month. I was still wondering how they would manage to pass Yvonne through a door, into an ambulance, or onto a plane! It was very simple: they just turned her sideways!

Oh yes, there was another phenomenon people were constantly talking about: the weather. From the day we shipped our car and began walking everywhere, until we had all of our baggage loaded and covered in the trailer, it didn't rain one drop. However, it did rain almost every day before we shipped our vehicle and began again the moment we all got into the car, ready to leave. People were amazed at the unusual weather, because they said it always rained every day that time of the year.

Yvonne was treated like royalty with everyone being extremely kind and helpful. It seemed as though no one could do enough. The stretcher didn't actually take nine seats, but they had to allow that many in order to take care of her and keep strangers from sitting next to her. Six seats were laid down flat, two each from three consecutive rows, and the stretcher locked into special fittings. Our family was free to use the extra three seats alongside Yvonne, so LuAnne and Steve made up for a month of missing her. The plane stopped only once before landing in New York.

We had been so preoccupied with leaving the Netherlands that we hadn't even given one thought to what lay ahead. As we progressed rapidly over the Atlantic toward the U.S.A., our predicament suddenly dawned on us: no one knew we were arriving on this day; we had no place to stay and no available transportation; we knew absolutely nothing about the East Coast; our money was nearly gone; and we were responsible for five children, one of them in a full body cast! We didn't know anyone around New York, except the Hamiltons from New Jersey, and Dick had met them only once, when the quartet was in the area. Dick had told them that we might be coming on the following Friday, and this was the earlier Monday.

Once again we realized our complete helplessness, but this time we were confident God had something special ready for us. Through the whole episode, He had not forgotten one tiny detail, and this emergency loomed huge. We weren't certain if an ambulance would be meeting Yvonne on the ground, but the Captain came to us before landing and assured us he had radioed ahead to have one waiting. This is all standard procedure for stretcher cases traveling by plane.

None of our family had ever seen the Statue of Liberty, and after being away from the United States for nearly five years, our emotions ran high. Each country we visited was special, and we loved the people. Almost everyone was pleasing, agreeable, friendly and helpful. But there is no place like home and no country like your own! Every single person at the Kennedy Airport seemed concerned about us. One of the airport officials was assigned especially to help us. As soon as Yvonne was safely in the ambulance, the rest of us were whisked through all of the immigration procedures. We began to feel a little foolish when every person we met asked the same question, "Where are you going to take the little girl in the ambulance?" We couldn't come right out and say, "We don't have any idea!" But that was the whole truth! However, we became very adept at mumbling something unintelligible. And we kept praying!

As we approached the final customs inspection, we looked up into a huge glassed waiting area and saw people who were meeting friends and relatives from the plane. It's always fun to view the excitement when loved ones meet after a separation. I was watching as one after another caught the eyes of those they had come to meet, when suddenly, someone started waving, and it appeared as though they were looking directly at me. I turned around to see if someone was behind me, but there was no one. When I glanced up again, I was shocked to see a large banner stretched across the waiting room that read, "WELCOME HOME CADDS!" This was impossible! Nobody knew we were on this plane, and I had never seen these people before. The strain of the last few days must have been more than we realized, and I burst into tears. The customs inspector was trying to ask me questions, and I managed to explain that we were missionaries who were returning after five years—and an injured daughter was waiting outside in an ambulance. He hurriedly stamped all the bags without opening anything. We dashed out the door and found that our welcoming committee was Ethel and Nancy Hamilton with one of their World Vision staff members.

As unbelievable as it sounds, these people had an unusually strong feeling that they should meet this particular plane. Hundreds of airplanes arrive at Kennedy Airport each day, and they had no reason to think we would be on this plane. But it was such a forceful impression that they had to come from New Jersey and brought along an air-conditioned car for

Yvonne, a big station wagon for baggage and a welcome sign! God doesn't do anything halfway!

Airport police broke the rules and let the Hamiltons park directly in front of the terminal until the ambulance came around from the back side. Once Yvonne was moved from the ambulance to the car, we realized this was the first time since the accident that she was completely in our care. It was a little frightening and yet a tremendous relief. It took some careful maneuvering to get Yvonne, six of our family, all our baggage, and three World Vision people into the two cars before heading to New Jersey where the rest of the Hamilton family was expecting us. We were treated to showers and a wonderful meal. And after sleeping on the hard ground in a dirty sleeping bag for several weeks, it was the height of luxury to crawl into a real bed between clean sheets.

We discovered the camper hadn't arrived yet, so we really didn't know how to plan. One very important job we needed to do was to take Yvonne to a doctor and find out if she could travel with us across the country in the camper or if I should take her by plane to my parents' home in Idaho. We didn't want to impose on the Hamiltons. Seven extra people, with one in a body cast, is fairly imposing any way you look at it. Dick and Ethel Hamilton and their children were the most gracious hosts anyone could ever have, and we were cared for like royalty. If we took the rest of our lives trying, we still couldn't repay them. I'm sure they had no idea just how much they were doing for us, emotionally, as well as physically and materially.

Psalms 62:1-2 and Psalms 77:13-14 expressed our feelings of the past few days. **"We stand silently before the Lord, waiting for Him to rescue us. For salvation comes from Him alone. Yes, He alone is our Rock, our rescuer, defense and fortress. Why then should we be tense with fear when trouble comes?" "O God, Your ways are holy. Where is there any other as mighty as You? You are the God of miracles and wonders! You still demonstrate Your awesome power."**

We were overwhelmed with gratitude to God and also to people. But there is more. We took Yvonne to an orthopedic specialist, and he sent her to a big hospital in New Jersey to have X-rays. He wanted to compare them with all the X-rays we had brought from Alkmaar. While we were waiting for the X-rays, a Chinese intern came up to us and said he noticed from our papers that we were from the Philippines. He also was from Manila. As we talked, we found that he was the brother of one of the men in Dick's Chinese choir. He himself had been in the same choir the year before Dick took over this group. Sometimes the world doesn't seem so big!

When the orthopedic specialist examined the new X-rays, he assured us she was doing great and that she had been well cared for in Europe. He felt there was no reason why we couldn't travel in our camping car with Yvonne since there was plenty of room for her to lie out in a bed. This great specialist didn't charge us anything. Yvonne was so happy to be with the family again. It took two of us to pick her up and carry her, but no one minded at all. In fact, it was a privilege, and she was so good-natured and fun to be around. We learned to turn her sideways to get in and out of doors, and the cast gave her plenty of protection.

The Hamiltons were absolutely wonderful! They kept us — two adults and five children — until our car arrived. But it was much more than giving us a comfortable place to sleep and feeding us three great meals each day. They did everything possible to make us feel special. One night they arranged for us to take Yvonne to a band concert in a nearby city park. Vonnie had been in the house too many days and needed the fresh air and a change of scenery.

When we arrived, there was no place to park where we could see and hear the band. We were about to give up and leave when two friendly police officers approached and asked if we needed help. We explained about bringing Yvonne to the concert and immediately they made some phone calls and arranged for us to drive our car on the grass and park directly in front of the band. Yvonne had a perfect view and we all benefited. Later, as we were driving across the United States, one man chased us 15 miles because we had forgotten a couple of 10-cent ice cream cones where we had stopped to eat. When Dick pulled to the side of the road to change drivers, three different carloads of people stopped to ask if we needed help. This sort of kindness and help happened every place we went, from New York to Kansas to Oregon.

Another beautiful, appropriate Scripture is from Psalms 84:5-7: **"Happy are those who are strong in the Lord, who want above all else to follow Your steps. When they walk through the Valley of Weeping it will become a place of springs where pools of blessing and refreshment collect after the rains! They will grow constantly in strength and each of them is invited to meet with the Lord in Zion."**

When we arrived in Idaho to spend some time with my parents, we took Yvonne to another excellent orthopedic specialist. He X-rayed her legs and found her bones to be completely healed. This meant she had spent four weeks in the body cast instead of the eight predicted by the doctor in Holland.

Taking the cast off presented some problems because the Europeans didn't line the cast with padding like Americans do. When the doctor began cutting through Yvonne's cast with the electric "saw," it was impossible to keep from cutting her. Evidently the European's have special cutters for taking off this type of cast, but there was no such thing available in Idaho. Consequently, Yvonne had a slight cut, like a deep scratch, all the way down one leg. But she was so happy! She was finally released from a body prison. Because of the lack of padding, the cast had rubbed against Yvonne's leg near the knee causing an abrasion all the way to the bone. She had been immobile for eight weeks, so her legs were useless at first. The doctor kept her in the hospital one week for special physical therapy.

Visiting hours were certainly different in the U.S. We were asked to please come as early as possible and stay as late as we could. Children adjusted better and seemed to get well faster when someone in the family was with them. It also released the nurses for more specialized tasks.

After whirlpool baths, massage, and gradual bending of the knees limbered up her legs, Yvonne actually had to learn to walk again. Our Dutch doctor told us not to expect Yvonne to walk normally until about Christmas, but by September she was walking "normally" to school. I don't pretend to understand why accidents like this happen. I only know that God doesn't make any mistakes, and His love is perfect. Humans make mistakes, but God showed His great love and concern and care, even in the tiniest little details. We learned many lessons as a family and had some beautiful experiences. The Lord taught us how to appreciate each other and not take life for granted. He opened our eyes to the needs of others. People came to Jesus.

We needed to get special shoes for Yvonne before she could attempt walking, and yet we had no way to try them on her. I traced around her feet, but when I went to the store to find the shoes, the owner said, "Here, take two pair and try them. Bring back the ones that don't fit. You can pay me when you come again." He didn't even ask my name! We were certainly back in "small-town America" where people trusted people.

Once again, the Lord talked to us through His Word. **"These troubles and sufferings of ours are, after all, quite small and won't last very long. Yet this short time of distress will result in God's richest blessing upon us forever and ever! So we do not look at what we can see right now, the troubles all around us, but we look forward to the joys in heaven which we have not yet seen. The troubles will soon be over, but the joys to come will last forever."** (II Corinthians 4:17-18)

And again in Isaiah 43:1-3: **"The Lord who created you says, Don't be afraid, for I have ransomed you, I have called you by my name; you are mine. When you go through deep waters and great trouble, I will be with you. When you go through rivers of difficulty, you will not drown! When you walk through the fire of oppression, you will not be burned** up— the flames will not consume you. For I am the Lord your God, your Savior, the Holy One of Israel."

—*m*—

Elizabeth Elliot made the statement: "It is always possible to be thankful for what is given, rather than resentful over what is withheld or taken away. One attitude or the other becomes a way of life."

Adventures are not necessarily fun or enjoyable—especially at the time we are having them. But they are memorable! Our attitude and reaction toward them will determine how they affect the rest of our lives. Some adventures are inevitable and we usually try to avoid them at any cost. I can't think of any sickness that is enjoyable, but God can teach us valuable lessons if we have an attitude of listening and learning. Of course, the ultimate adventure is death, where we walk into an unexplored area—into the unknown. Some people thrive on exploring new and different territories, but very few of us look forward with anticipation and excitement to this final adventure.

When we were much younger, Dick wanted to talk to me about things I should know and do if something happened to him. I couldn't talk about it. We had five young children, and I was sure I couldn't survive without my husband. I was in love with Dick and I didn't ever want to be without him. We had a great life and I must have thought that talking about it meant it might make it happen sooner. I reacted so badly that he didn't bring it up again until we were in our seventies. By that time I was mature enough to have an intelligent discussion. Dick had made a folder as he tried to prepare everything I would need in case of his death. I was surprised at his reactions when I suggested that I might be the one to die first. He was so certain that I would outlive him that I feared for him emotionally if something happened to me first. We always hoped that we would die together, but we did try to face the reality that we were not the ones in control and had no choice in this matter. One day death would come and we would be separated for a time. However, we did have the assurance that we would see each other again and spend eternity together in Heaven with Jesus. I don't know how people survive without this hope.

The men in Dick's family had a history of dying young. This haunted me when I thought about it, but his mother lived into her eighties and so this was my focus: he could take after her instead of his dad and brothers. We tried to eat right most of the time, and we walked almost every morning in the hills around Faith Academy. We went swimming when possible and thought everything was fine. We were living, working, loving, and having a great life still serving in the Philippines. We actually had tickets to return to the U.S. for a short furlough when Dick suddenly had heart problems. We did not know if it was an actual heart attack, but the doctor wanted to do an angiogram and set up an appointment for one the next day.

For some reason neither of us felt right about this procedure. And then several unusual things happened. Someone gave me a new magazine with an article about angiograms, warning that they were greatly overused and could have serious side effects. Another person informed us that when we came to the U.S. the doctors here would not accept the one performed in Manila, but would insist on a new one. An urgent phone call came from another missionary who had just returned from the United States with recent and updated information about heart health. All of this information had an impact on our decision to cancel the angiogram and come back to Oregon as originally planned. We were also having serious conversations with the Lord.

The Manila doctor gave Dick some nitroglycerine pills to take if he felt he needed one. I packed and took care of all the loose ends so Dick could rest. Neighbors and friends were available to help in every way possible. We were uneasy, but felt like this was the right way to go. Dick was tired and weak, but otherwise felt OK. Yet, I'm sure he was concerned.

I was apprehensive about being "trapped" on an airplane for so many hours with the possibility of Dick having a serious heart attack at any time. However, we had total prayer support and were convinced this was God's plan. We were more comfortable being in the U.S. at this time, and several of our children were also there.

Since Yvonne was a nurse and they had room to keep us, we stayed with her family. At first Dick mostly rested, but before long he felt like being up and more active. He saw a heart doctor who wanted to do an angiogram and probably surgery. But once again several unusual things happened. A relative insisted that we must read a book about "chelation therapy." This was something we had never heard about before and while we were still contemplating trying it, a friend of the family just happened to meet us in the parking lot of a grocery store.

He informed us that he had been praying for us and insisted that Dick must have "chelation therapy." He had been through the angiogram and surgery for his heart several months earlier and declared that it was terrible and he was still trying to recover. Since that time, he had heard about chelation and studied everything he could find about it. He was totally convinced it was the solution to heart problems and only wished that he had heard of it sooner. Since it was not readily accepted by the standard medical world, the best place to be treated was in Reno, Nevada. Since our friend was so certain this was a much safer and better way to treat heart problems, he offered to make an appointment and pay for our trip to Reno.

After studying everything we could about chelation and praying constantly for the Lord to lead us clearly, we made the decision to try this treatment instead of the standard angiogram and surgery. This really was a momentous decision because we were going against the doctor's advice and, even more importantly, our family's. Everyone was scared for Dick and wanted him to have the standard treatment.

However, after much discussion and prayer, we agreed with each other. We realized it might be an emotional battle to go against family and friends, but we had made a firm decision. We followed through with our plans and were satisfied it was the right way for us to go.

We loved Reno and were there at the perfect time of year. We lived in our small RV and often parked at one of the large hotel parking lots made especially for this kind of vehicle. Dick had his treatment each morning five days a week. Then we were free to do anything we wanted to do. A river ran almost the whole length of the town, and it was like a lovely park along either side. This was nice for walking, but we also discovered there were concerts in various areas almost every day.

We were close enough to go to Lake Tahoe and there were numerous conventions to attend. One of our favorite events was a Hot Air Balloon show. People came to this from all over the country and there were more than 100 balloons of every size and shape. One morning they held a "Dawn Patrol." While it was still dark, a number of the balloons went into the air, and it was a spectacular sight to see the glowing shapes lighting the sky.

At the time we were in Reno the hotels and casinos were doing everything possible to attract customers. It wasn't long before we discovered we could eat wonderful meals that were almost free. There were so many adventures that we actually felt like we were having one of the best vacations we had ever been on. Dick was feeling stronger and healthier every day and tests revealed his arteries were now clean instead of clogged. By the time we left Reno we were ready to go back to Manila.

—*ᴧᴧ*—

Dick's heart experience, however, was a "wake-up" call. We began to realize that we were no longer young and were vulnerable to age-related problems. Besides some of our children, we had several grandchildren in the U.S. that we hardly knew, and we felt it was time to get acquainted. So we made the difficult decision to leave the Philippines permanently and officially retire. Leaving the Philippines was not easy. This had been our home for most of the last 33 years and we loved the people and our work. We stayed several more months, but the focus was tying up all the loose ends of our ministry and preparing to move back to Oregon. Besides selling, packing, or giving away all of our possessions, there were numerous farewell dinners and parties, with lots of tears and hugs involved.

One of the hardest goodbyes was when we had to tell Luming we wouldn't be coming back. Luming was our incredible house girl who had been with us from the day we arrived in Manila. I don't know of anyone who had a house girl as long as Luming was with us. She had become part of our family. She was a vital part of our ministry and she learned to know how I thought. She seemed to anticipate our needs and kept our home and guests perfectly cared for. Because of Luming, I was free to do all of the various jobs I experienced during our time in the Philippines. I could have a ministry both outside of our home and also in our home. Luming was very flexible and could manage surprise guests at any time—even produce a meal for 20 hungry teenagers when Dick brought his special choir home for an unexpected rehearsal. When people heard we were leaving permanently, Luming had people pleading with her to come and work for them. However, she had been able to save enough money to buy a home in her province, so she returned there and didn't work for anyone else—until Steve's family returned to live in Manila. Then Luming was happy to work for members of our family again.

It's interesting how quickly we can forget lessons we have learned in the past. We should have had maintenance chelation therapy, but we forgot about it. At one time strong cayenne drops had been an important ingredient to help us keep a healthy heart and free flowing blood. Sometimes when we feel healthy, we forget the things that helped us get that way. Life became normal and we began doing all the things we had always done, except that we didn't go back overseas to live again.

After returning to live in the U.S. we spoke for churches and groups. One summer, we were involved in a missionary conference in California. We had driven a pickup truck from Oregon, where we were living at the time. LuAnne was with us because she wanted to move from California to Oregon and bring her belongings back in the pickup truck. We dropped LuAnne off with her friends and took the truck to the conference.

The day Dick and I were asked to speak and sing, he had trouble getting out of bed. He didn't hurt, but he fell and needed help getting up. We had no idea what was wrong, but we managed to get to the meeting and struggle through several services, where we were the featured part of the program. Dick seemed to get better for a while, but later in the day he began dragging his leg and was extremely tired. I think we both thought of the possibility of a stroke, but we were in serious denial and didn't even say the word. However, it meant I needed to drive the truck to go and meet LuAnne and load up all of her things. I had never driven any kind of a truck before and here I was, driving in the L.A. traffic on roads that were totally unfamiliar. This adventure left me tight and tense, and I was also becoming more concerned for Dick.

When we finally met up with LuAnne, she insisted we take Dick to a doctor her friends were recommending. This was when we heard that awful word: stroke! The doctor insisted that Dick could not go back to Oregon any way except by airplane. That meant LuAnne had to drive the loaded truck back by herself. I needed to be with Dick. By this time he required a wheel chair, which the airline supplied. Dick did recover from this stroke fairly soon, with no apparent problems.

Life soon became normal again, although we did have a partial health checkup each year through a group that came to our town and did tests for aneurisms, osteoporosis, circulation, etc. We knew Dick had an abdominal aneurism, but it wasn't considered serious for several years. In many ways, we settled down to a typical American life. However, we were always restless to be back overseas in cross-cultural ministry. We knew age was catching up with us, but we continued to be active in the work God had given us to do. We finished some major documentaries and picked up the US administration of Sword Productions, our son Steve's mission in the Philippines.

—∿∿—

We managed to move several times during the next few years. And we began to get acquainted with our grandchildren who lived in the U.S. It was pure joy to have two of our grandsons live with us while they attended George Fox College, the same school where Dick and I met, married, and graduated from. This was an interesting time watching Josh and Jesse get acquainted with each other. Josh (Jon's son) was raised in Africa and had been home-schooled. We were amazed when he walked to college barefooted in the snow. Jesse (Steve's son) lived in the Philippines and graduated from Faith Academy. They were as different as day and night, grew up in entirely different cultures and had never really known each other, but they instantly bonded and became special friends.

—∿∿—

Even after moving back to the U.S., we made several overseas trips. We were asked to go to Haiti and make a documentary for one mission group, but while there we also filmed for other organizations. Although we had been to many third world countries and seen extreme poverty, Haiti was different. There seemed to be a form of depression over the country. From the day we arrived we faced death in some way, even to seeing a baby die in a church service. Every night we went to sleep to the sound of voodoo chants. We met wonderful people doing remarkable work in schools, churches and orphanages, but we couldn't shake the feeling of heaviness. It was hard to keep a positive attitude.

When we went to different countries to make documentaries for one group, we were almost always asked to make videos for other missions too. It wasn't hard to do this since we were already in the area, but it did require more of our time in the country and extra editing when we arrived back home. Although we missed living overseas, we were content and happy. Actually, I was always satisfied any place we lived as long as I had Dick. He was always positive, busy, and we were still madly in love. He continued to include me in whatever he was doing, except for gardening. I was always a disaster in that area.

———∿∿———

It was December 23, 2004, just two days before Christmas. Steve was staying with us at the time and most of our other children were in the area. We were getting ready for bed when suddenly Dick couldn't talk or walk. I don't remember how we got him to the hospital, but he was having a massive stroke. After the doctor examined him he came to talk to us. All of the family members who lived in the area were there by that time. We were informed that it wasn't very hopeful for Dick to live through this stroke but, if he survived the night, they would transfer him to a hospital in Portland where he could get better care. Dick did live through the night, and although he was paralyzed in the lower part of his body, he was able to talk and use his hands. The doctor was amazed, but still felt Dick needed to be in a place that was better equipped to take care of him. An ambulance transported him to a large hospital in Portland.

After numerous tests, a different doctor came to explain what happened. He made interesting drawings on a blackboard and concluded by telling us that Dick was very fortunate to be alive. The clot seemed to take a different route than it had been previously going and stopped before it would have killed him. However, it did do a lot of damage, especially affecting the use of his legs. But we had much to be thankful for. Since the next day was Christmas, we wanted it to be really special for Dick. I went home and made some cinnamon rolls and other foods for our breakfast with Dick. I need to include Steve's letter, which describes our wonderful day.

Yesterday was Christmas day and it was a truly wonderful day.

We started out with LuAnne, myself, Mom and Dad in the hospital room. We had brought Dad's favorite Christmas music on cassette and cranked up the volume on the little boom box as loud as we dared, then boosted it up a few more notches. The song is a version of Joy to the World done with a massive choir and orchestra. The finale is the word 'joy' repeated five times, each one building louder until the final JOOOOOOOOOOYYYYYYYY!!!!!! is sung with a chord so rich and full it gives you goose bumps and the orchestra playing furiously under this sustained chord with bells chiming and cymbals crashing and tympani pounding and trumpets blasting! We of course were singing along with arms raised in worship and tears streaming down our faces. It's amazing how worship can transform anyplace into the throne room of God, be it a prison cell, a hospital room or an ordinary living room.

After a breakfast of cinnamon rolls, etc. (shared with the hospital staff), we exchanged gifts among the four of us. Then we left Dad to get some rest and we all went to my sister Carolyn's house for Christmas lunch. A few hours later we packed up the rest of the meal, another PILE of presents and we all headed back into St. Vincent's in Portland. There were about 15 or so family members so we took over the little waiting room on Dad's 6th floor and he was brought in by a wheel chair. We played games, told stories, laughed, ate, laughed, opened presents, laughed, etc. It was so much fun. Dad would often wipe tears from his eyes, sometimes from laughter, sometimes just because he was glad to be there.

All of this pretty much exhausted Dad so we brought him back to his room and sang a few Christmas carols with Dad holding down the bass section all on his own. After we had 'rehearsed' a few songs and asked permission from the staff, we walked up and down the long halls, singing carols to the open doors we found. It was a deeply moving experience as people in the beds would join us in singing songs about Jesus: Joy to the World, Silent Night, Angels We Have Heard On High and my favorite, The First Noel. We often encountered tears, sometimes in the people we were singing too, but just as often in our own eyes. In one room, all we could see was the bottom of the bed, but the feet were moving in time with the music. In another room, a croaky voice joined us behind a curtain.

Once we were about to call it quits about halfway through (these were LONG hallways) and a nurse came running up to us and begged us to come and sing in one more room. As we stood in front of the open door, there sitting on the edge of the bed was the tiny frame of a frail elderly woman. She smiled radiantly as we sang. After that we decided we couldn't stop until we had sung for EVERY room. In one room, the gentleman on the bed sang with such gusto and after the song he wanted to talk to us. It turns out he was a Presbyterian minister and had served short-term on the island of Chuk in the South Pacific. He asked if we knew a missionary by the name of Juanita Simpson! Of course we not only know Juanita Simpson, but our families are nearly joined at the hip! Juanita's kids were at Faith Academy with us (Sandy and Angela) and lived with us during school breaks when they couldn't go home.

Over and over patients and staff would thank us for doing this. The funny thing was, it was the best part of the whole day for us! It is so amazing how God designed it so the giver would gain more than the receiver! Is this why God delights so much in giving to us? I learned again on Christmas that for Christians, when we face adversity or trial our response is SING LOUDER! WORSHIP WITH MORE INTENSITY, LOVE WITH MORE ABANDON!

It couldn't have been a better day.

In just a few days Dick was transferred to a rehabilitation nursing home in Newberg, just a few blocks from our home. This was not a fancy place, but adequate and he had great care. They taught him how to dress himself and worked with his legs, showing him how to get from the bed to the wheel chair and finally helping him take a few steps with a walker. This all took time, and it was several weeks at home before he could use the walker. He was mostly confined to a wheel chair. I learned how to put it up and take it down and put it into the back of our car.

During this time while Dick was gone, specialists came to our home and helped install bars around the house to help Dick. A friend came and installed a ramp over the front steps. Family, friends and neighbors all came to work and prepare the house for Dick, so that when he came home he could function and be pretty independent. A trained therapist came to our home three times a week to continue Dick's rehabilitation. We felt loved and taken care of. However, our lives would never be the same.

Dick did everything possible himself. I think he tried to make things easier for me, and he was wonderful. He never complained, but only thanked me for every little thing I did for him. I know it must have been terribly hard for him because he always wanted to take care of me, but if he was depressed it didn't show. He loved gardening, so I took him outside in the wheel chair. He got down on his hands and knees as he planted flowers, a vegetable garden and took out weeds. He had a cell phone, and if I was in the house when he got tired and needed to come inside, he called me to help him back into the wheel chair. Dick kept busy during this time. Besides weeding and taking care of the outside, he did a lot of writing. He had always told me that if he died, I wouldn't have any friends because he wrote all the letters. He also wrote receipt notes and finally put his life story into writing.

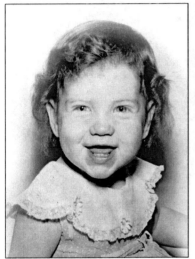 

Yvonne was always a happy baby, and even as an adult she could light up a room when she walked in.

When Yvonne was hit by a car in the Netherlands, she was put in a body cast that took nine seats on the airplane.

 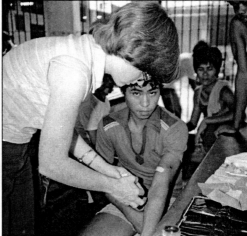

Yvonne became a nurse in her early 20s, and continued in the profession for most of her life. When she and Walt spent several years in the Philippines, Yvonne held clinics in the prison and for the nearby squatter community.

Yvonne loved to travel and saved up her money to take her girls on many trips around the US and overseas, including the Phillippines where her eldest daughter was born. Her children include Miriam, Hannah, and Megan.

I joined Yvonne's family for Christmas caroling at Friendsview Manor in Newberg.

CHAPTER 19

ADVENTURES WITH LUANNE

I had this part called "Adventures in Eastern Europe (with LuAnne)." But as I began thinking about LuAnne, I decided that she brought adventures to our family from the day she was born. It began at Phil Kerr's Monday Musical in the Pasadena Civic Auditorium. I had gone with my husband because the quartet was on the program. They were on the platform and I was in the audience. I was very pregnant and noted for having my babies pretty fast. Phil Kerr announced publicly that the quartet might have to leave suddenly because Dick's wife might need to get to the hospital if their baby decided to arrive. I realized that LuAnne was on the way, but managed to stay until the end of the program. However, there was no time to waste and it was difficult to get to the car because people wanted to hug me, give me advice and pray for me. I appreciated this, but was in no condition to stop and talk. By ignoring red lights and speed limits, we made it to the hospital just in time. This was one time when we seriously wanted to be stopped by a policeman and get a police escort to the hospital. Before I get into my adventures with LuAnne, I want to let you see what she wrote about herself:

My Life in a Nutshell

I don't like talking about myself, and most of my friends and family already know about my crazy life, but for those who don't, here is a semi-brief history.

~ Grew up in the Philippines as a missionary kid from age 4–18, with 4th and 9th grades in Oregon. My amazing father and mother were music teachers at Faith Academy, a school for missionary kids. From as far back as I can remember, the five Cadd kids made music together — everything from gospel to musicals. I went back to the Philippines for a year at age 21 and worked as a co-host on a Filipino television show.

~ Took about 10 years to get my bachelor's degree in Journalism, a combined effort of three universities, and 15 years to get my masters in teaching.

~ Love to travel and love foreign cultures. It is perhaps my top passion in life. I have traveled to over 50 countries and lived in six. I spent 16 months traveling around the world by myself from 1989 – 1990.

~ For over 20 years, off and on, I freelanced in Los Angeles as a location scout/manager for national TV commercials and movies. As a photojournalist on an anti-apartheid newspaper, I briefly had the privilege of witnessing the power and insanity of South Africa a year before Mandela won in the historical elections. For two years I observed the fallout of war in Bosnia a year after the peace accord as I worked on a UN project to repair war-damaged homes. I took my very first full-time teaching job at an international school in Saudi Arabia where I learned a great deal from unique and talented students from around the world.

~ I left my teaching job and returned to Oregon to help care for my sister Yvonne who was dying of breast cancer. It was a life-changing experience, excruciatingly painful at times, but mostly an incredible privilege to help my sister on her journey to the end of her life. She died December 7th, 2009. We all miss her beyond description.

~ I've had boyfriends but no husband or children — the biggest disappointment of my life. However, I've been incredibly blessed with the best parents anyone could wish for and brilliant siblings. Yvonne's family adopted me as their own, and I feel in some ways like I have my own family. The world is full of the dear friends I have made from childhood to now.

~ I am currently living in Democratic Republic of Congo (DRC) with my brother and his wife, Jon and Cher Cadd. I am partly recovering from the last year and a half with my sister and partly trying to figure out what to do with my life.

As a P.S. to this very condensed version of her life, LuAnne worked at Virunga National Park in Congo for two years and was evacuated at least six times because of rebel fighting in the area. She is now living in Kenya, working as a roving journalist for Mission Aviation Fellowship (the same mission as her brother Jon). Check out her blog at luannecadd.com.

LuAnne was our fifth child and, during her first week home, she was exposed to whooping cough. When the doctor gave her a preventive shot she screamed louder, longer and harder than I have ever heard any baby do before. The doctor commented about her redheaded temper, and she certainly did express her anger. Later at home, I discovered what turned out to be a hernia. There had been a weakness and her temper tantrum had broken it loose. LuAnne needed surgery, but the doctor wanted to wait about three months. I was instructed, "Don't let her cry!" That was almost the same as saying, "Don't let her breathe!"

Dick fixed a bottle cap, turned it upside down and taped it to the weak place on LuAnne. The only way to keep her from crying was to carry her and, whenever she started to cry, I would push on the bottle cap to keep the hernia from popping out. I had been warned that gangrene set in quickly if it popped out and strangulated from her crying, so I developed one arm methods of cooking, cleaning, doing the laundry and taking care of my other children. All this time LuAnne was getting more spoiled and I was becoming more tired.

When it came time for my baby to have surgery we took the family and went to Idaho where my parents lived. That way we could have our family doctor and much needed help from my mom and Dad. Dick was home as much as possible during all of this time, but he still had to go with the quartet to their engagements. The guys were working full time with World Vision and Bob Pierce.

After LuAnne's surgery and recovery we decided to "unspoil" her. I kept her close to me and watched to make sure she was OK, but I let her cry. She cried so hard that she completely lost her voice for a time, and when it came back it was low and raspy. For several years people commented about LuAnne's unusual voice. She woke up every hour from 10:30 p.m. until at least 3:30 a.m. until she was three years old. Consequently, I had big bags under my eyes, felt about 90 years old and completely changed my idea of having a dozen children.

Dick and I have always felt like LuAnne was special and that the Lord showed His love for her and for us as He kept her alive numerous times when she was in serious danger. She has survived being on a ship in the middle of a typhoon, car accidents, a bus ride on the dangerous roads in the mountains of Pakistan with a drugged driver, attempted kidnapping in Africa, robbers who held a knife over her, ruptured appendix, riots, war, land mines, a hike in the Himalayan Mountains and much more.

Before we left for the Philippines, we were having a picnic in a park with my brother Wayne and his family. The older children were playing a short distance away, but across a small street in the park. LuAnne suddenly took off and started running across the street. It wasn't supposed to be a major road, but a speeding car came racing by. Wayne happened to be standing near the edge of the road and, without really seeing, reached out his arm and grabbed LuAnne from in front of the car. Just remembering this makes me weak.

When Carolyn was born we felt it would be impossible to love another child as much as we loved her. But then Jon came along and we made the marvelous discovery that, although we didn't lose any of our love for Carolyn, our capacity for love was increased enough to love Jon the same way. The identical thing happened with Steve and Yvonne and LuAnne. God didn't require us to divide our love. He just multiplied it many times. And every one of our children has their own unusual, sometimes terrifying, wonderful, often painful, exciting stories.

While home on furlough in 1972-73, we spent weekends holding meetings somewhere in Oregon and Washington. But during spring vacation, we traveled into Southern California. One evening, LuAnne felt sick and from all appearances it was the stomach flu. By morning she seemed a little better, only still not well. We had one free night and had planned to spend it attending Calvary Chapel in Costa Mesa. LuAnne attended the services with us, although we had to leave early and find a motel where she could go to bed. Through the night she continued to feel worse and then developed a severe pain in her side. Appendicitis loomed into our thinking, so we left Steve and Yvonne in the motel, but decided to drive LuAnne to La Mirada where we could ask our friends from Granada Heights Friends Church for advice about a doctor and hospital. Besides, we had meetings scheduled in that area for the next few days. About 5:00 a.m. we arrived in La Mirada and phoned Rev. Verle Lindley. He advised that we go to a certain hospital in Whittier and ask for Dr. Lohnes.

We found the hospital, but in an emergency room you don't get any specific doctor. You just take whoever is on duty. Evidently the doctor on duty was tired from a difficult night and acted as though LuAnne was faking sickness. As her parents, we knew LuAnne far better than that. She was seldom sick and hated showing it no matter how bad she felt. Instead of taking the usual blood count, the doctor began punching Lu's abdomen. He didn't attempt to be gentle, and at one point she screamed out in terrible pain, but soon after that the pressure was released and she had no more localized pain. However, she still felt very sick all over her body. Finally, the doctor decided to take a blood count, which turned out fairly normal. He gruffly instructed us to "Take her home; she's all right!" We knew better than this, but had no place to go and didn't know what to do.

After we phoned Verle Lindley, he had dressed and come to the hospital to see if he could help. Being completely frustrated and dissatisfied with the doctor's diagnosis, Dick and Verle were standing in the hallway talking about the situation. Verle happened to glance out the small window leading outside to the parking lot. He exclaimed, "Wait a minute! There's Dr. Lohnes, the man I recommended to you." He ran out and in a few minutes came back with the doctor we'd asked to see in the first place. After our explanations about LuAnne, he went in to check on her.

I heard the other doctor tell him LuAnne wasn't really sick, but as Dr. Lohnes came back to us after examining her, he stated, "She's one sick girl. Because her blood count is quite normal now, we can't tell for certain if it's her appendix, but quite often when appendix rupture, the blood goes back to normal for a few hours." He suggested putting LuAnne in the hospital with intravenous feeding and antibiotics. Since he couldn't get the operating room until 1:00 p.m. he wanted to observe her during the morning. In case she didn't improve, he wanted to do exploratory surgery. I balked at this, but he gently told me, "I'm very suspicious she has ruptured appendix. If it were my daughter I certainly wouldn't take any chances." That was convincing!

LuAnne did not improve by 1:00 p.m., but only seemed worse. Dr. Lohnes took her to surgery, and when he came out my heart nearly stopped as he said, "Her appendix was ruptured and peritonitis was evident. But we scraped and cleaned her thoroughly. She's young. I think she will make it!" That was our first inkling of how seriously sick Lu really was. If we had taken her home, she would have died. Let me recount some of the miracles. Verle Lindley didn't have to come, but he did, and he came just in time to glance up at the right second in order to see a busy doctor who had come to the hospital for an emergency, but was now leaving town for the day. The doctor, who was too busy to accept new patients, canceled his out-of-town engagement and stayed home just to take care of LuAnne. Every place along the line took split-second timing. LuAnne recovered beautifully, but only because God intervened. And when it came time to pay the bills, Granada Heights Friends Church covered everything above our insurance on the hospital bill. Dr. Lohnes limited his charges. We were overwhelmed with gratitude to God and His people. It truly is an adventure to follow the Lord and trust Him to be in charge. It's also great to be in the family of God!

LuAnne provided us with many other adventures when she was still at home with us, such as the time we had a serious robbery and she woke up and began talking to the robbers. She probably was still half asleep and didn't realize what she was doing. She knew better than this because, in Manila, if they think you can identify them they will kill you. Again God's intervention and timing probably saved her life, but we could no longer let her be alone in our neighborhood.

Psalms 50:14-15 says, **"What I want from you is your true thanks; I want your promises fulfilled. I want you to trust Me in your times of trouble, so I can rescue you, and you can**

give Me glory." God has certainly rescued our family many times, and there is no way we can thank Him enough.

As I mentioned earlier, having LuAnne has always been an adventure. When she graduated from Faith Academy and left home she decided that she wanted Dick and me to have new adventures. So every time we were with her she planned something exciting, something we had never done before. One time it was a hot air balloon ride in California. She has also taken us to Catalina and on a Caribbean Cruise. Another time it was an African safari when we both happened to be in Kenya at the same time. She offered to take us on a whitewater rafting adventure on the Colorado River, which we graciously declined. It was unusual for her to even tell us what she had in mind because she always wanted to surprise us. We both felt we were a little too old for that kind of rafting and we told her we absolutely refused to go bungee jumping. I guess we lost some of our adventurous spirit. However, some of our most exciting and interesting adventures were still to come with LuAnne.

When we left the Philippines for a short time in the U.S., we decided to go by way of Africa in order to see our kids who were working in Zimbabwe. It was an exciting plane trip just to get there. One plane was late, which made us late for the next plane connection. This happened to be in Pakistan and it was very important to be on this plane because it was the one that went to Kenya (which was on the way to Zimbabwe) and it only went once a week. LuAnne was in Kenya at that time on her year of travel around the world, so we planned to stay there a few days to be with her. When we learned we were late getting to Pakistan, we were told it would be impossible to make the plane even if it hadn't left yet because there was so much government red tape that it took a long time just to get through immigration, etc. Then on our next flight we really were powerless to do anything. We couldn't make the plane fly any faster and we couldn't phone ahead to make other arrangements. So we prayed and waited to see what the Lord would do next.

This is what the Lord did next. The stewardess made everyone stay seated until we were off the plane. Someone met us and ushered us straight through immigration. They never even looked at our tickets or passports, and people told us that had never happened before. They usually didn't care if you missed your plane. We were taken to a car and they told us the plane was already at the end of the runway with the engines running, but they were waiting for us. The car raced to the plane and hurried us on board. Everything was very rushed and I don't remember how we got onto the plane. I just know it was unusual. Finally, we were actually on our way to Kenya in Africa.

LuAnne met us at the airport when we arrived in Kenya. She had made arrangements for us to stay at the Wycliffe guesthouse and while we waited to pick up our luggage, she told us her plans for our next adventure—a genuine African safari! At this time in LuAnne's life she was traveling around the world, and although she really didn't have a traveling companion, when she stayed in youth hostels she usually met up with other travelers and if they were going to the same place, they traveled together. The group she was with at this time was all going on the safari together. Lu was the oldest person in the group, although she looked like the youngest. And then when we came we added a whole new dimension: old people!

After all the luggage had been taken off the plane it dawned on us: we had gotten on the plane but our checked suitcases didn't make it! The next plane from Pakistan didn't arrive for a week. We hadn't yet learned to carry a change of underwear and other necessities in our hand luggage, which was very limited to not much more than a purse. We arrived on Sunday evening and were leaving on the safari early Monday morning. Coming from the Philippines where it was very hot and humid, we found it cold in Kenya, and we didn't have any clothes except what we were wearing. The Wycliffe staff and friends were having a meeting that we decided to attend. Someone had found out about our dilemma and announced to the audience that we needed underwear, sweaters and other miscellaneous items. When the meeting ended, I think every person in the audience must have gone home and brought back to us everything we needed. No matter where you are in the world, the family of God is amazing.

The company that LuAnne's group hired to take us on the safari had sleeping bags, tents, food, a van with a driver, a guide and a cook— everything we could possibly need, except for a few personal items. The sleeping bags were called body bags and made in such a way that you couldn't even turn over on your side to sleep. The tents were really tiny and two people could sleep in them on the ground if they barely moved. Unfortunately, it poured rain our first night out, but we did have a meal and got our tents set up. I think there were eight of us in our group, plus the staff. Dick and I had our own little tent, and Lu was in another tent. If we were desperate to go to the bathroom we had to struggle out of the confining sleeping bag, crawl on hands and knees to the door of the tent and step outside, where we could confront a variety of wild animals. It was also raining and windy. We tried not to be desperate!

We were jetlagged and very tired, so Dick and I went right to sleep. Sometime later we were awakened by someone crawling into our tent and lying down between us. LuAnne whispered, "Don't worry, it's just me. Our tent blew down in the wind and I need to sleep here tonight." There wasn't a lot of sleep that night, but the next morning the young people were talking about the lion that came to our camp. They were really frightened until they finally figured that it was just someone in our tent that was snoring—me! I can't sleep on my back without snoring. They did think that a real lion might hear me and think it was another lion to investigate. Although there were no lions that night, a hyena was seen going through our camp.

After that first traumatic night the weather cleared up and our guide knew just where to take us to see most of the African animals. Dick had a video camera and got some amazing photos: a mother cheetah with her four babies, zebra and a couple of lions stalking a wart hog and her babies, then killing one of the babies. As soon as they killed the warthog, several small lions came rushing out to have their dinner. I didn't like seeing this, but we were in the van (which had an open top so we could stand up and have a perfect view), and we were told how lucky we were to see these things. Besides seeing all the animals and tribal people, we had great meals and wonderful times around a campfire at night.

Dick and I were new at traveling with young people like this and we wanted to get acquainted so we began asking questions. We wanted to know more about their lives and where they came from, and they were very open. Lu took us aside and informed us there was an unspoken rule that they didn't ask what each other did for a living. There was a reason for this. Traveling like this made everyone equal. If they didn't know someone was a doctor and another in the group hadn't finished high school, then they could be equals and they wouldn't be put into categories. Since we didn't know any better we broke the rules.

Some years earlier Dick had a skin problem on his face that could have turned into cancer but the Dr. put powerful medicine on his face and it turned terribly red and blotchy. He looked awful, but he still needed to go to work and there was no way to cover it. People just stared at him and he really wanted to tell them what it was. He wanted to talk about it rather than have people wonder what was wrong with him, but he never felt free to tell them if they didn't ask. I remembered this when we were with the young people in Africa.

One of the boys from England had really bad looking scars all over his arm and hand, so I questioned him about it. No one else had ever said anything to him and he was very happy to talk about the serious explosion that caused burns and these scars when he was a small child. The factory worker with her boss from Australia and the college graduate from Japan also had their stories to tell. The results became a time of sharing and laughing and crying around the campfire. All the self-imposed barriers came down. We became friends.

—⁓—

Dick and I had a scheduled flight to Zimbabwe to visit Jon and Cher where Jon was a pilot with MAF (Mission Aviation Fellowship), so we had to leave the group early. Once again, LuAnne had given us a wonderful and unusual adventure. As I mentioned earlier, I was never very adventurous, but the Lord helped change my attitude. With an attitude change my life changed and I could not only accept adventures, but they became an almost daily part of my life. I have been emotionally stretched. I've experienced anger, hurt, frustration, fear and concern as well as fun, joy, love and excitement. But I have never been bored.

Our plane trip from Kenya to Zimbabwe was unforgettable. The luggage was placed on open wire racks above our heads, and as the plane lumbered down the runway, we were sure it could never make it off the ground. It seemed to groan and moan and shake from side to side, but it did take off and we told the Lord we would try not to get on any planes like this again. However scary the takeoff was, I still remember the delicious meal they served us. It was one of the best we ever had on any flight in the world.

Jon was there to meet us when we arrived. Cher was also there, but she couldn't go into the secured area like Jon could. She had to stay in the lobby of the airport. Since Jon was a pilot and had his uniform on, he took us through immigration and customs without any problem. In 1997 Dick and I had our 50th wedding anniversary. As a special gift, LuAnne wanted to bring us to Bosnia where she was working at the time. This was soon after the horrible war there and Lu was working with UMCOR, a humanitarian organization, on a UN project to rebuild war-damaged homes. Most people would consider this a rather unusual place to celebrate our anniversary, but we wanted to do it! Besides being with her, we were excited to see her fascinating work of trying to resettle internally displaced people back into homes they had lived in before the war. She also wanted us to help her take a van from Bosnia to Albania to be used in a new feeding program for street kids there.

It certainly wasn't the safest place in the world. There was destruction everywhere. LuAnne was working in the field at the time when her office was destroyed, buildings burned, workers beaten and mobs going crazy. When she returned and saw what was happening, she sent her assistant away with the car and hid behind some bushes to take pictures of the situation.

Some men saw her, chased her and tried to take her camera away. However, Lu was not about to lose her precious camera without a fight and she managed to keep it by giving them the film. They didn't want the world to see what they were doing. Lu had already passed one roll of film to someone else to protect, so she did save some great photos. She escaped unharmed and saved her camera, but she had to be transported to the United Nations Army Camp in order to be safe. This was the political climate where we were going for our 50th wedding anniversary gift from LuAnne.

It's easy to forget the horrors of war unless we have seen it first hand. Even then, time will erase many memories. But I don't want to forget, because when we forget we often allow it to happen all over again. One man basically instigated the war in Yugoslavia between the Serbs, Croats and Muslims, and he was able to stir up hatred because of past experiences that had never been forgotten or forgiven. Unless there is total forgiveness, which is often impossible without God's intervention and help, there will always be an undercurrent just waiting to boil over in revenge and retaliation.

All wars are horrible and useless, but this one seemed worse than usual because it pitted neighbors and friends against each other. From one end of the country to the other we saw terrible destruction, but the most devastating sight of all was the graves. Hillsides were covered with fresh graves, and in the cities, parks and churchyards were now cemeteries.

There was hardly a family anywhere in this country that wasn't affected and hurt in the war, often by former friends and neighbors.

I should probably start back at the beginning of this trip. Dick never liked to do just one thing at a time, so we usually combined several projects together when planning anything. Chris Fox did all the work for the first part of our trip after we landed in England. Chris was the wonderful lady who made our first trip to Eastern Europe possible when we went with the Begbies and Jesse. This time she drove us to Croatia where we were asked to do some videos for a special group who were working with victims of the war. These people were able to purchase three buildings and were now either using them or repairing them. The buildings were named Life Center, Peace Center and Hope Center.

Life Center was used for special seminars, meetings, teaching sessions and retreats. It was like a small hotel with bedrooms, a restaurant and a larger meeting hall. The Peace Center was for emotional healing and it was mostly used for women and children. Every person there had lost a husband or father, both parents or some other family member. Some of the women had been raped and the children had been traumatized as they saw their fathers murdered, sometimes by a neighbor who had been a friend before the war.

The stories we heard and the children we talked to kept us in tears most of the time. The workers here were incredible and were filled with so much love and wisdom from God, we could only watch in amazement. Hope Center was still under construction, with the vision that pastors could come here to be revived and taught how to help their people. It would be similar to a seminary where they could live for several months. At all of these Centers they tried to bring people from each of the different groups together for reconciliation and forgiveness.

I met a Croatian man and had the courage to ask him how they could make neighbors and friends kill each other. His answer: "Soldiers would come to a home and tell the husband that if his neighbor wasn't dead by morning, they would be back and kill all of his family." Then he continued by telling me that they taught people how to kill by taking them to a pig farm and having them slit the throats of the pigs. We also went to a refugee camp, which was another moving experience. This was probably much nicer than the refugee camps in Asia and Africa, but every where we went we heard and felt the anger and hatred, unless the people had Jesus in their hearts and had forgiven their enemies and those who had hurt them. After a few days of visiting Croatia and taking videos for documentaries, Chris drove us to Bosnia to leave us with LuAnne and then she drove back to England. Now began more adventures with our youngest daughter.

I wish I could say that all adventures are fun. This isn't true! Some adventures are educational and informative. Pain; physical, emotional, spiritual and even financial is sometimes included in the mix of adventures. Fear and sometimes terror often accompany us on life's journey of adventures. This is where attitude makes all the difference in the world. As individuals we all seem to see the same scene from difference perspectives. The passing of time also has a way of changing our view on experiences.

Somehow Lu managed to borrow a pickup truck so she could take us to a small village where she was working on trying to get some Muslims back to their homes. Serbs would attack a Croat village and drive the people out, then move in and take their homes. This caused the Croats to find a Muslim town to invade, again driving the people out and taking their homes. The Muslims then had to find a place to live, so the cycle continued all over the country. The United Nations was trying to reverse the problem and return people to their own communities. But so many of the homes had been destroyed or damaged and the people were so disoriented and upset, that they really didn't know what they wanted. This was why they attacked the foreigners who came in to try and help. Lu's job was to decide which homes would be repaired and how much money could be donated for the work. This also caused anger and jealousy if someone thought their neighbor received more help than they got. Instead of being grateful, they rioted!

Yugoslavia was a beautiful country, but because of the Communist control for so many years, it hadn't advanced like the Western world. The Communists had been able to keep peace among the Serbs, Croats and Muslims, but as soon as that control was lifted the revolution started with a fury among the different factions. Although the country was stunningly beautiful, the roads were terrible and it seemed like most of the places we went were in and out of mountains.

The village where LuAnne took us was quite small, but it did have a mosque because it had been a community of Muslims. I wondered how people could even find some of these villages to attack them because they were hidden in the hills with almost impassable roads. Although there was awful destruction everywhere, there was one Serb couple living here. No one else. LuAnne was working with this family. They were not living in a real house, but had made a makeshift place as their home. There was no electricity and no water since the village well had been contaminated. We were amazed that anyone could live here, but they were ingenious in the way they collected rainwater, raised a garden and seemed to be fairly comfortable. They were really happy to see her again. Lu always had a way of making friends with people. While she talked with the people we walked around the area to see what had happened. LuAnne strongly warned us not to step on anything, like a piece of wood or cloth, etc., because of the danger of land mines. We walked through a house where it looked like the family there had simply run away, leaving everything behind. Beds were unmade, toys scattered, dirty dishes and clothes were scattered everywhere. The house was totally ruined. Many of the people had not been able to escape and were killed. We went into the empty mosque, but had to be very careful where we walked because of the real danger of land mines there. It appeared that every building in this village had been damaged or destroyed.

When we went back to find LuAnne, the woman had prepared a special treat for us of grapes and homemade beer. They had been able to salvage a few things from the various houses and had saved the grape vines. Now they were serving us. We felt guilty taking anything from their meager supplies, but they were wonderful and so thrilled that we had come. We couldn't refuse their hospitality, but it was a struggle for me and I also really hate beer. Thoughts of any kind of sanitation were pushed out of our minds, and we just enjoyed the fellowship. Although they wanted us to stay all day, we had to get back to Lu's office because we were to leave for Zenica with another couple, in a pickup truck.

I can't remember why we had to go at night, but at the last minute we had to take a different route than originally planned because two towns on the way were having disturbances and were considered a possible danger. So now we had to travel on narrow, treacherous roads over the mountains in the dark. It was really scary for me, and it seemed like we were right on the edge of bottomless cliffs much of the time. We could hardly see what was ahead and the road not only had big ruts and holes, but also was washed out in places. This was not one of my favorite adventures, but we eventually reached our destination (still alive!) where we were given a bed to sleep in.

The next morning we went on to Sarajevo. This city was in the news almost every day when the war was in full swing. Like so many of the cities in Yugoslavia, it is in a valley surrounded by mountains that were occupied by the enemy. This made them sitting ducks, and they were constantly under attack by shelling. It seemed like every field, park and churchyard were filled with graves. Many of the buildings were just empty shells. There were two distinct areas in the city, the Croats and the Muslims, but it was no problem crossing over between them. The Serbs were the ones in the surrounding mountains and responsible for the destruction. We were here for a couple of days, and Lu read to us about the "Siege of Sarajevo." It was unbelievably horrible!! But now it was fun to walk around the city and stop to have coffee or chai tea and pastries at the little cafes with their outdoor tables.

The leader of the Serbs and the one who started all of the trouble— Slobodan Milosevic—was hiding out in a small town in the mountains. It was very difficult to find the men who were considered war criminals and bring them to justice because they were in hiding. LuAnne decided we should go to this town, so we caught a ride with an American Croat. We could only go so far with him because he was a Croat, and the Serbs were in control of this small town. So we took a taxi into town. There wasn't a lot to see or do here, and it was time for us to get back to Sarajevo. It was sort of a spooky little town, anyway.

There was too much tension and clear rules about Croats crossing into Serb areas, so we couldn't get a ride. We tried hitchhiking back to an area where we hoped to get a ride with someone going to Sarajevo, and we finally made it. For a couple on their 50th wedding anniversary, it seemed a bit unusual to be hitchhiking. It was a "first" for me because my Dad forbid us to hitchhike when we lived at home. The one taxi we took cost us a fortune because only certain people could go certain places, and they took full advantage of this by charging whatever they could get.

Our next stop was the city of Mostar. In most of these cities, there was an "old town" and then a new section with more modern structures, roads, etc. Again, as we came closer to the city, the fields were filled with fairly fresh graves. The older part of the city was charming, although every place in the area was seriously damaged. There was a river running through the middle of the city that previously had an old stone bridge (a special landmark of Europe) crossing from one side to the other to unite the city. But now the city was divided, with the Muslims on one side and the Croats across the river. Under Communism, they seemed to get along fine, but now the whole country was involved in the deadly conflict. After more than 400 years, this beautiful landmark was totally destroyed by the Croats in one day. Since it was very important to be able to cross the river, the United Nations had built a temporary bridge in its place.

There is an old wisdom:
When you wage a war, you hope to be better off afterwards.
Then you wish that your enemy shall be worse off afterwards.
Later you are gleeful that your enemy isn't any better off.
Finally you wonder why everyone is worse off.
(But this wisdom is remembered only afterwards.)

We were eating lunch in a lovely café overlooking the river when we saw something happening nearby. Upon investigation, we discovered they were having a big ceremony as they raised a huge stone of the destroyed bridge from the river. This was in preparation for rebuilding the bridge, and since it required special equipment, U.N. soldiers did most of the work. The raising of this stone was very significant, and it was to be the cornerstone of the new bridge. People were hoping it would help bring reconciliation between the Muslims and the Croats. However, there was also the question as to whether the Croats would allow it to stay. This was a fascinating and historic event, and we unexpectedly had the privilege of witnessing the celebration.

Later we were taken to a lovely bed and breakfast home on the Muslim side of the river. This was an interesting and unusual family, because it was a mixture of both Muslim and Croat. Sauna, the mother, took us to a beautiful room with a balcony terrace that had a wonderful view of the city. She seemed really happy to have us there and soon appeared with an afternoon snack of coffee, a dessert and what looked like a glass of water. However, when we started to take a drink of the "water," we almost choked to death. Our eyes were watering, it was hard to get a breath, and we felt like we were on fire. We were so glad Sauna had left the room and didn't see us race to the sink, spit it out and try to put out the fire.

The rest of this drink went down the sink and we were afraid it might burn holes in the pipes! Apparently the people make their own drinks like this and live through it!

Our time in this mostly Muslim home was delightful. We were served a wonderful breakfast on the terrace before going on a tour of this part of Mostar. Every building we saw looked like it was made from a polka dot material. However, the "polka dots" were bullet holes and the buildings mostly skeletons. This city had also been a sitting duck for shelling from surrounding hills. Another book Lu had us read was called "Welcome to Hell" and was an account of what happened in Mostar.

I don't think LuAnne realized that she was driving a van with a Croatian license plate until someone told her it was a very dangerous thing to do in this part of the city. Although the war was officially over, there were still surprise attacks almost everywhere.

While Lu was at work, Dick and I had a wonderful experience. When we were working with our friends, the Begbies of Crossroads Mission in Hong Kong, we had helped prepare a container to go to Bosnia. This particular container just happened to arrive in Mostar shortly before we arrived and the man in charge of the mission organization receiving it was a friend of LuAnne's. We were privileged to go with him when he delivered toys, clothes and equipment to a children's home.

We saw some of the contents still being unpacked and heard stories of where things had already gone or would be going soon. People who had lost everything were now receiving furniture, clothes, kitchen supplies, etc. It did not bring back loved ones who were lost, but it did bring some hope out of total despair. This huge container that we had helped fill was now changing lives. And we got to be there and even help deliver some of the goods. This was another improbable gift from God, and even more wonderful was the story we heard of reconciliation from Lu's friend.

The people were sitting in a large circle around the room and the message had been all about forgiving. This was no ordinary group of people, but Christian Serbs, Croats and Muslims had come together in this one place. There had been a time of worship, and yet you could feel the tension and mistrust. Then one person from one of the factions got up and went to someone in a different group, got down on his knees and began sobbing while asking to be forgiven for what their people had done. Before long the room was filled with the cries of forgiving and being forgiven. One woman just couldn't forgive because her husband had been brutally murdered in this war until someone mentioned how Jesus asked God to forgive those who were crucifying him. It soon became evident that the Holy Spirit was dealing with every person in the room, and before long the circle was complete with arms linked together in sobs, hugs and praises to the Lord.

Even though the Communist government had been able to control the people by force, when that control was lifted, the unforgiving spirit that had been festering for many years broke loose in violence and destruction of both lives and property. And now, unless they could forgive, we heard and felt and saw even more hatred building into plans for revenge. The longer people keep their anger and don't forgive, the bigger the explosion will be someday. It begins to show in faces, and you can hear it in the voice. God offers everyone forgiveness, but we must offer it as well.

We had one more night to stay in the lovely bed and breakfast home, and once again Sauna showered us with kindness. After a special breakfast on the terrace, she insisted on showing us how she made burek, which is similar to apple strudel and is one of the foods we raved about. She was sure that I could make this when I got home, but after watching her work, I was convinced otherwise. Sauna took some flour and water and made a medium size ball of dough about the size of a croquet bell. I probably could do that much, but what came next was awesome.

She took this ball, placed it on her large dining room table and began to roll it until it completely covered the table like a tablecloth. Although paper-thin, it didn't break or crack. It's a little hard to remember exactly what came next and the proper order, but now she insisted it was my turn to be involved. All this time I had been watching in amazement while Dick took pictures. I got to do the fun part: putting fillings on the pastry. There were three kinds of fillings: fruit, meat and vegetable. I really can't recall how she put it all together, but after it was baked, we had a wonderful assortment of burek, enough to make a delicious, balanced meal. When LuAnne came with some friends to get us, it didn't take much to persuade everyone to stay and eat what we had just made.

It was time for us to leave for Croatia and Dubrovnik (Mostar is in Bosnia), but it was hard to leave the new friends we had come to love. We spoke different languages, but had learned to communicate with gestures and love. I still have a lovely red brass vase Sauna insisted I must take so that I would never forget her.

———⁓———

Dubrovnik is a beautiful, unusual and very old walled city, directly on the coast of the Adriatic Sea. This was another adventure LuAnne had planned for us. There was damage from the war, but not as bad as in many other places. The rest of the world pleaded for the city to be saved. There is no place like it anywhere and it's a favorite tourist attraction for many nationalities. It took us about two hours to walk around the old city wall, which was about two kilometers, and much of it juts out into the sea. There was so much to see and spectacular views. At times we could see inside homes and courtyards. The city itself is wonderful, with cobbled streets and small specialty shops.

Dubrovnik seems to have a history of everyone wanting to claim her as their own. She is actually part of Croatia, but in 1991 Dubrovnik was attacked with a siege that lasted seven months, even though she had been demilitarized in an attempt to prevent her from ever becoming a casualty of war. The Serbs claimed her and 56% of her buildings were damaged in some way as she sustained 650 hits by their artillery rounds. However, she is still part of Croatia today.

After leaving Dubrovnik, we had a long drive over bumpy and narrow roads until we arrived at a small ferry that went to one of the numerous islands along the coast of Croatia. We explored small towns, strolled the lovely beaches, ate delicious strudels and watched a big ferry dock. One of the experiences Lu had planned for us was parasailing. She had even made reservations for us, but it rained most of the morning, so we were told to come back later. It did stop raining in the afternoon, but there was also a strong wind and high waves, so they didn't want to take us on LuAnne's new adventure.

When Lu first revealed her plans for us, I was pretty apprehensive, but decided I was willing to do it as long as she got lots of photos that I could show people and prove we did it. I actually was relieved when they refused to take us, and I'm not sure it was the winds and high waves that made their decision to cancel our reservations. They probably used it as an excuse because they thought we were too old for parasailing. LuAnne never thought we were too old for anything, and we took that as a compliment!

We had an early ferry to catch in order to go to Split, which was one of my favorite old cities. I wanted to stay there all day, but LuAnne felt we should be on our way, and she wanted to stay at the Life Center that night.

—*m*—

Our main goal now was to deliver the orange van to Albania. Albania was not that far from Mostar, and it would have been so simple to just cross the border there, but because of the war and all it involved, there was no way we could get across that border into Albania. Because we couldn't cross the border from Bosnia into Albania, we had to drive through Bosnia, Croatia, Slovenia and Italy and then cross the Adriatic Sea by ferry. It was a much longer trip, but we saw parts of the world we never would have seen otherwise and we had an extra week or more with our daughter. Slovenia had been part of Yugoslavia, but managed to become its own nation before the wars began. This was one of the most delightful places we had ever been, with ancient castles and churches, lakes and mountains and charming villages with markets and flowers. Every town was clean and free from the devastation of war. In one place we even climbed a church tower with over 200 steps. It was so wonderful that we hated to leave, but we had a job to do.

Traveling with LuAnne was always interesting. In one place, she had high-powered friends who put us into a first class hotel and fed us gourmet meals. Other times, all she wanted was some place cheap to stay and all I wanted was something clean. Often the "cheap" was not clean and the bathrooms were not only far away, but very dirty. This didn't bother Lu, but it did bother me. I would have been glad to pay the extra money, but Lu wouldn't hear of it. We often stayed in Youth Hostels, which were pretty nice and at least clean. Driving along the coast of Italy was a rather frightening experience. Most of the cars wanted to go much faster than we could go and were nearly on top of us, blaring their horns and flashing their lights. I wondered if we could survive. We decided we had time to go a more scenic route and tried the road near the sea, but it was a disaster, so back to the wild freeway.

We spent a day in Venice, and although we had been there before, it is a fun place to go. There are no cars at all, only boats on the "streets," and lots of walking. Many little shops had good food, but no place to sit down. If you wanted to sit and eat, you had to pay extra at every place except McDonalds.

Although we liked to eat the local food in each country, we finally got tired enough to sit and eat at McDonalds in Venice. That's the nice thing about McDonalds almost any place in the world. They are consistent and dependable. They even have free bathrooms!

It was finally time to go to Bari, the town where we got on the ferry to go to Albania. Although we had business to take care of, we did have some time to look around Bari. We found a walled castle, and then came to an interesting old section of the city where a festival was taking place. There were hundreds of people and it seemed like most of the buildings were churches, some were actually 10 centuries old. It was such a fascinating place, and as we were walking we came to a small back street where older women were sitting at small tables making all forms of pasta by hand. As we walked past them, each one warned us to watch our bags. They informed us there were many thieves and often on motorcycles. As they rode past people, they grabbed purses, bags, etc. and were gone before anyone could catch them.

Although we hated to leave this area and thought we had plenty of time, we decided to be safe and get to the ferry early. This turned out to be a wise decision, because paperwork for the car seemed to take forever, especially since everything was in a language we didn't know. It helped when one of the ship's crew spoke English. He was very friendly, especially with LuAnne, and he did help us with the paperwork and then finding our way around the ship. We had reserved seats, not rooms. It was extremely crowded, the area had freezing cold air-conditioning, and the trip across the Adriatic Sea took eight hours. Throughout the night the English speaking "friend" kept coming around to try and get LuAnne to come with him to his cabin. The ship left about midnight and arrived around 9:00 a.m. the next morning. The idea was that we could sleep all night, but it was just an idea, not reality!

Upon arriving, it took us most of the morning to clear customs. However, we did get through much faster than most of the people. This was because of the language barrier. Our ignorance of what they wanted from us was so frustrating that they just kept waving us on to the next person. We were finally able to drive from this port city of Durres to Tirana, the capital city of Albania.

—*᠊ᜣᜣ*᠊—

However bad we thought other roads were, the roads here were far worse! And there was garbage everywhere. But the most shocking sights were the wrecked cars along the sides of the road. These cars were just skeletons, with nothing left except the bare bodies, and there were piles of them everywhere. We were told that when Albania finally opened up to the rest of the world, everyone wanted a car. It was easy for unscrupulous people to come in with cars that looked good but were really junkers. There were very few car mechanics in the country and no parts for replacements. So the cars were just abandoned by the side of the road. However, they were totally cannibalized until there were only shells remaining.

We finally arrived in Tirana and met Shawn and Catherine, the couple we were delivering the car to. (Shawn is British and Catherine is from the U.S.) As we were having coffee at a nice international hotel, we witnessed a rally in the street. This seemed to be a regular occurrence. After we parked the car, the final time for us, Shawn and Catherine took us to the place they had arranged for us to stay. This was a wonderful, clean, inexpensive, home and the owners were friendly, loving and charming people. They couldn't seem to do enough for us.

After getting settled, Shawn and Catherine took us to a large museum and castle located far up in the awesome mountains above the city. The museum gave us a great lesson on the history of Albania. Although the roads were unbearably bad, we had a really great time and saw plenty of old ruins, castles, villages and magnificent scenery. We even had time for some souvenir shopping and we learned a lot, not only history, but also what it was like under Communism and a totally atheistic government. We were there shortly after they gained a form of freedom.

Although our large private room cost only $5.00 a night, our hosts insisted on serving us tea, fruit and a delicious warm coffee cake. Since they had grape vines, they also served us homemade grape juice that had fermented and turned into some kind of wine. We didn't speak the same language, but we managed to communicate and had a special time of fellowship. Their two children were delightful, and their high school daughter, Dorina, is brilliant. In addition to Albanian, she is also fluent in English and French and can get by with German and Italian. Not only that, but she is an excellent musician. In order to have enough money to give the children music and language lessons, their father worked at three different jobs, seven days a week and only made about $650 a month. We left extra money and I gave the mother my gold bracelet. But they didn't want to take from us; instead they wanted to give to us. In our travels, we found this was so often the case. The people who had the least were the ones who gave the most.

The next day Shawn had a meeting and needed to check on some of his projects in another area. He had helped build and furnish several health clinics with the help of churches and organizations in England. Once again, we saw destruction everywhere. And as in Yugoslavia, the people had destroyed their own country. No one really understands why this happened, especially when they ruined new health clinics that had been built for their benefit. This was not like the war in Bosnia and Croatia, and there weren't the massive killings, but what they did seemed totally unreasonable to us.

On our way to another city we stopped for something, and a mini-bus filled with too many people hit us from behind. Nobody was hurt, but it caused quite a delay in reaching our destination. Shawn had a committee meeting with some important people, so he asked a doctor if she could show LuAnne, Dick and me the hospital nearby. This experience still haunts me.

As we entered the four-story hospital, the smells were so overwhelming that we wanted to back out before we even began. The doctor explained that they hadn't had any water for four days, with no sign of any coming soon. This is a good place to let your imagination run wild, and it wouldn't begin to catch up with the actual situation. There couldn't possibly be any pretense of sanitation. We were shown the X-ray room, but nothing worked. They did have a room for surgeries, but the big light hanging over the operating table didn't work either. The ugly, dirty-looking paint was chipped off the walls, and tiles on the floor were either broken or missing.

Our guide showed us the small area where they kept supplies. A tiny cupboard for medications was almost empty, and the space for bandages had a stack of rags. I think all of the bedding was already on the beds. We didn't see any extra anyplace. We went from floor to floor and saw the rooms with patients lying on dirty sheets full of holes. For warmth, it looked like they were using old worn out army blankets. One large room seemed to be for children and someone had tried to make it more colorful, with brighter paint on the walls. Each mother sat beside the bed of her sick child, but they had nothing! The look on their faces was one of total despair.

Then we were shown where babies were born. We were interested to learn that most of the doctors were women. There was one male doctor, and he was in the maternity area. They had one incubator, and it actually seemed to be working because it had a tiny baby in it. They offered to let me hold the baby, but I was afraid for him to be out of the protection of the incubator. It was probably the safest place in the hospital. When we came to the end of an agonizing tour, the doctor who was our guide faced us and looking straight into our eyes simply said, "Can you help us? Do people know? Do they care? Will you forget us too?" When we came back to the United States, we tried desperately to communicate what we had witnessed. We looked into organizations that sent free medicines and supplies around the world. But even when others wanted to help, it all came to a dead end, because the

Albanian government didn't want outside assistance and made it impossible to send help.

We did care! We didn't want to forget! We tried to help! The whole country of Albania, with the messed up roads, buildings and cars, and the despair everywhere made us sad and we didn't know what to do or how to help. They needed Jesus, but the government had totally rejected God and left the people with no hope. However, we loved the people we met, and especially the family we stayed with. Once again we discovered communication without words. There is the language of love that crosses all barriers. Actions help, like hugs, drinking tea together, sharing time, small personal gifts. And somehow people seem to know when love is genuine. We became friends, even without words.

We wanted to tell them that God loved them and sent His Son so they could have peace and hope and joy and eternal life. That's hard to do when you only have a few hours and no words. We have prayed that someone would go and live there and be able to share Jesus.

—~~—

We had a schedule to meet that required us to leave the next morning. This turned out to be a most interesting and unusual day. It was one of those times for an attitude of liking new adventures. I don't really want to go through it again, but it is a remarkable memory to talk about. After a delicious warm coffee cake with hot tea, another gift of love from our hosts, we set out walking several blocks to Shawn's office. We were loaded with our luggage and sloshing through a heavy downpour of rain. Everyone in the office was bogged down with meetings and deadlines to meet, so no one could take us to Durres, the town where we got on the ship back to Italy. Someone stopped long enough to take us to the bus depot, where we could get public transportation for the long ride back to the docks.

As it turned out there was no bus like we had imagined, only a "mini-bus" similar to our jeepneys in Manila. This small bus was made to carry about 10 people and that was crowded. But people kept coming until there were 16 of us (plus luggage and all sorts of other things) crammed into the vehicle. If it hadn't been so miserable and dangerous, it would have been funny, and it certainly gave us an experience to remember. They brought in some stools for the extra people to sit on, but since there wasn't room, it was like having someone sitting on your feet and leaning into your lap.

The rain had not let up at all, and we soon discovered that the roof had holes. Although we were already soaking wet, we were soon even wetter. Apparently some of the people had been in this kind of situation before, because someone opened up his umbrella to avoid being rained on. The windows wouldn't stay rolled up, but this was OK because once we began our journey, most of the passengers began smoking. There were far more men than women. LuAnne and I might have been the only females. Our little bus did have a windshield, but no windshield wipers, and so the driver had his head out of the window most of time. He needed to see where we were going and hopefully stay on the road without hitting anyone.

The driver had been told to take us as close as possible to the docks. He did this, through back alleys and deep mud paths. We made it to the ship, and we didn't have nearly the problem getting on this time, since we no longer had the car. We met the same man who spoke English, and once again he sought LuAnne. We were late leaving, about 2:00 p.m., and we wanted to sleep because we were going to have an all night train trip in Italy. The ferry didn't arrive in Bari, Italy until about 10:30 p.m.

It took so long going through customs that we almost didn't make it to our train connections. This was our separation time with LuAnne. She was going to Venice and then back to Bosnia. Dick and I were headed for Rome and a plane trip to England. We had about 10 minutes between the train departures. Ours went first and even though we ran, we almost missed it. We hardly had time to say goodbye to Lu, and we were really concerned for her. We had been warned many times that Italy was not a safe place for tourists traveling like this. At least there were two of us, but LuAnne was so small and loaded down with luggage and expensive camera equipment, she could hardly go to the bathroom. Situations like this kept us talking to the Lord about our children. LuAnne always seemed to need special prayer.

When we got on the train we couldn't find a seat at first, but eventually found a place where two girls were spread out sleeping. We woke them up to ask if we could sit with them, and they were kind enough to accommodate us, even though one of them seemed to have the flu and felt terrible. They were Americans from Sun Valley, Idaho. Since I grew up in Idaho, we had a few minutes of interesting conversation before the conductor came and informed us that we didn't have the right kind of tickets for this place. He sent us to another car, but every seat was taken and we had to stand.

It has always been hard for Dick to stand very long, so he finally found the conductor and paid more money so we could ride where the girls were. However, by now those seats were gone. We finally did find a couple of seats, but at every stop more people got onto the train, and it wasn't long before we were wedged in so tight we could barely breathe. Because of the warnings, we planned to sleep in shifts so one of us could keep track of our luggage. I don't think I slept at all, and it was one of the longest six-hour trips we ever experienced before arriving in Rome about 6:30 a.m.

By this time all we wanted to do was sleep, but we had to find a place where this was a possibility. So we did the most normal thing for 6:30 in the morning. We got a cup of coffee and a roll and simply relaxed a few minutes before beginning our search for a bed. We thought this would be easy, since we had a book that told us where to find clean, inexpensive rooms near the train station. However, every place on our list was full, except for one that we couldn't get into until 7:00 p.m. All we really wanted was a bed, but finally decided to go back and take what we could get. Of course, it was no longer available. We spent most of the day just trying to find any place and ended up paying over $100 (which was very expensive at that time), and we wasted the entire day. We were discouraged and had hoped to do some sightseeing while in Rome, even though we had spent time there several years earlier. After eating, we went to bed early. Sometime in the night I began coughing, and it really hurt.

Our charter plane didn't leave until later in the day, so we got up early, checked our bags at the train depot and took the Underground to the Coliseum area. This is such an impressive and interesting place with so much history. We only had a little over an hour before we needed to pick up our bags at the train depot and head for the airport. This involved taking an Underground train to the end of the line and then catching a bus to the airport. Even if we had enough money for a taxi, we didn't want to trust our lives to their wild driving. We had been very skeptical of taking a chartered plane to London, but it turned out to be very nice in every way. We arrived in London about 4:30 p.m.

After taking several trains, we arrived in Woking where Maureen Reid met us at the train depot. Bill and Maureen had made a special room just so they could keep missionaries and friends from around the world who were visiting London. This was a wonderful haven whenever we were there, but now I was really feeling sick. I ached and hurt all over and it was so difficult to breathe that I couldn't sleep. Dick stayed awake and prayed for me most of the night. I began to think maybe I had the fast-acting pneumonia. The next morning Dick was so concerned that he phoned Yvonne in Oregon and asked her to call the church and alert the prayer chain to pray for me. It seemed like I started getting better almost immediately after this, and by the next day I felt fine. We had a few days in England to visit friends and spend a day in London before leaving for the U.S. and home.

There was some unrest and violence in England at this time, and the Northwest Airline office in London had been bombed a few days before we were to leave. We were flying on Northwest and security at the airport was very tight. After checking at the airline counter and finally getting rid of most of our luggage we went into the waiting area to relax and do some last minute shopping for gifts for the family. Suddenly over the loud speaker, we heard Dick being paged. When he stood up to go find out what was happening, several stern looking men in uniform came and surrounded him. By this time, everyone was looking at us and the men spoke loud and clear. They asked Dick, "Is this your brief case?" Dick was shocked because he hadn't even missed it, but now these men had it in their possession.

When he acknowledged it was his, Dick got a very loud and serious reprimand from these officers. Evidently he had set it down at the Northwest counter and forgot to pick it up when we left. Because of the recent trouble at the Northwest office in London, these men had been called in to see if the briefcase was a bomb. They planned to take it out someplace and shoot it, or something like that, to make sure it didn't explode in the airport. But it did have Dick's name on a tag, so they decided to check and see if they could find Dick first. This was all very embarrassing because everyone in the area was watching and listening. The briefcase had all our important papers and money in it. It would have been a disaster if they had destroyed it or we had lost it.

After a nine hour flight to Vancouver B.C. and then several hours layover, we finally arrived in Portland, Oregon where some of our other children met us. We had traveled by plane, ferry, car, truck, taxi, van, mini bus, train, the underground and used our feet to walk and hitchhike. Without the Lord helping me have a somewhat relaxed and adventurous attitude of going into the unknown I probably would have been in panic and fear much of the time and missed the joy of the extraordinary experiences we were having with our daughter. LuAnne had given us another adventure that we could never forget!

And now it's time to hear from LuAnne herself:

Lessons Learned From a Typhoon:
Write Better Journals

Once again, I've decided to try a blog while I enter a new phase of life. The only way this will work is if I don't worry about how well I'm writing, but simply write short notes on my observations and thoughts. So bear with me on bad writing and grammar and consider these the scribbled notes from a journal.

With that said, however, I will try to make my musings better than my journals of the 70's, which read more like telegrams. A few years ago as I was packing to move to Saudi Arabia, I found the box with all of my old journals dating as far back as elementary school. The one that most interested me was from a trip I took to visit my brother and sister-in-law, Jon and Cher, in Micronesia in 1979. I decided to take a small inter-island freighter from Palau to Guam — the only girl and the only "passenger" on the ship (other than crew). I was 21 years old.

On the first night out, we were heading straight into the path of a typhoon crossing between Guam and us. The captain turned slightly off to the east, hoping to miss a direct collision, but it caused the small empty freighter to rock precariously as massive ocean swells hit the ship on its side. Eventually, we turned into the waves, and if you've ever seen the movie "The Perfect Storm," you will know what I saw from the bridge looking out into the darkness: troughs so deep it felt as if we were diving straight into the ocean and walls of water so massive and steep that I was certain with each one that we would not make it to the top.

I was terrified. I knew I was going to die. I didn't want to die. I pleaded with God that I was too young, that no one in my family knew where I was (not even Jon & Cher at that point), and it would cause such agony for them. After a short time of stomach-churning terror, I had an epiphany. The fear I felt would not change anything. I was still going to die. So I had a choice. I could continue to give in to the debilitating fear, or I could let it go, sit back, and enjoy the ride. And what a ride it was. Nothing man-made could compete with this. I watched in awe and wonder at the fury of nature, the magnitude and power of the Pacific Ocean in a typhoon and felt that I was getting a glimpse of something incredible before my death. It was thrilling.

Since I didn't die, it remains for me a powerful lesson on how my attitude can change everything even in the worst of situations.

And so, when I found the journal with the story of the storm, I read it excitedly, eager to be reminded of my exact thoughts at the time of the epiphany. I don't have it here to quote exactly, but it went something like this:

"Got into a big typhoon. Very scary. Next day it was sunny. Laid out on the roof to sunbathe."

All I can say is that I will try to elaborate a bit more this time around."

So now, more than 30 years later, after enough experiences to fill several books, we have one of LuAnne's less adventurous stories, which she titled:

No Fear

Yesterday, as I was about to leave in a rattle-trap tin can of a car with engine trouble, for a village about 20 km outside of Bunia, my brother Jon commented to me, "Well, it's not a boat in a typhoon." It took me a moment to get that he was referring to my previous post and was trying to say that this potential adventure was nothing by comparison.

It did, in fact, turn into a bit of an adventure, although not life-threatening. Of course, anything in

Congo can turn into something dangerous in the blink of an eye and apparently, some people were worried.

I wanted to photograph a seminar by a local Congo group called L'OEIL that brings ex-militia groups from opposing tribes together to teach forgiveness and reconciliation. I've been hired by MAF UK to take photos for their monthly magazine. It's on a per-day basis, and next week I'll be flying to a town quite a bit west of us to shoot a seminar. Knowing how things go in Congo, and that anything could happen to disrupt this assignment, I wanted, on my own and without pay, to see the one taking place at a village outside of Bunia, just in case. So a local pastor involved in the seminar said he would arrange a car to take me out if I would pay for petrol. We were to leave at 1:00 p.m. It was supposed to take about 20-30 minutes to get there (I think really bad roads).

By 2 pm I began to think something had gone wrong. I finally got a text message from pastor Emmanuel saying that the first car had broken down and he was trying to find another. By 3 pm, I got him on the phone and suggested that we cancel. It was getting late. "No, No!" He insisted it was going to work out and hung up on me. Finally around 3:20, he pulled up in front of our gate. The hood was open when we came out and they were trying to put water in the battery. The car, a severely dented green Suzuki, was having trouble with the engine dying. The pastor was genuinely excited that I was coming and that he'd managed to find a car and driver. Jon didn't want me to go. It was late and he insisted that I must be back by dark. 6:00 pm at the latest. And so, Jon said his line: "Well, it's not a boat in a typhoon."

And here I will digress a bit on the African perception of time. The pastor said it would take us about 20-30 minutes to get there. He assured Jon that he could have me back by 4:30. It was now 3:30. There and back without staying to shoot anything, just might get us back by 4:30. Jon pointed this out to him. In reality, it took us 50 minutes to get there, and that was after we took 10 minutes to buy petrol. So in fact, we didn't get there until 4:30. I shot for an hour, the pastors ate some food quickly, and we left about 5:45. We drove for about 15 minutes when the engine died at a soldier's checkpoint.

I checked my cell phone and surprisingly I had a signal. I was able to text, but not call Jon. He had already sent me a text asking if everything was OK. It was already nearly dark, on a small dirt road in what felt like the middle of nowhere. I should have been a bit scared, knowing even a tiny bit of the horrifying violence that has happened in Congo, but I wasn't. The only thing I was worried about was my camera, which I tried to keep hidden in the car under a sarong.

For the next 20 minutes, text messages were flying back and forth. When my cell phone battery started to die, we used the pastor's. In the end, it was arranged for a mechanic to come out by motorbike. Jon insisted, "I am coming anyway!" But he didn't know how to get there. So the pastor arranged for another guy to meet Jon at the house and come out together, showing him the way.

When Jon arrived, I asked if he was upset and he replied, "No, no! I love this sort of thing!" He proceeded to pass out drinks and snacks to all the men (now numbering eight) from a cooler he had thought to bring. Eventually the mechanic managed to get the engine going and we set off back home, this time in Jon's nice car. We arrived home around 8:30 pm.

So no, it wasn't even remotely the same kind of adventure as getting caught in a typhoon on the ocean. But I did think about fear and how pointless it would be for me to give in to that, even though I had every reason to feel it. Nothing bad happened, and no energy was wasted on fearing the unknown.

During one of LuAnne's times back in Newberg, she was asked to exhibit some of her photos for a special event. Something had to be written about her and since she hated talking about herself, Yvonne's husband, Walt Everly, volunteered to do it.

LuAnne Cadd loves traveling

And she loves people. She also loves photography, so what you see here is the obvious outcome of someone who pursues her interests with a serious passion. But LuAnne doesn't just like traveling; she has an insatiable craving for adventure, a trait that causes admiring awe in some people and causes others to assume she's lost her mind – the latter being her mother.

Her aversion to boredom probably developed while growing up in the Philippines during the Marcos martial law era. She has subsequently worked on a 1.5 million acre cattle station in Australia, ridden across half of Africa on a motorcycle, worked as a photojournalist on an opposition newspaper in apartheid South Africa and traveled the "gun run" between Mozambique and Malawi with her sister Carolyn during a civil war (generally LuAnne travels alone because her idea of luxury accommodation is a $3/night bat-infested hovel). She has been chased by rioters in Bosnia while doing humanitarian work, held off attackers in Pakistan while armed only with a Swiss Army knife, and again in Paris stood ready to defend her honor with a very intimidating cheese knife.

Initially LuAnne was a self-taught photographer, learning on the job as a Location Scout in the L.A. film and commercial industries for 13 years. Eventually she decided to get serious about photography and in 1992 earned a Journalism degree with an emphasis in Photojournalism at San Francisco State University. (Her successful operation of technically complicated photo equipment is itself an accomplishment considering she is not in any sense of the word a "detail" person. This is the same woman who, when I was teaching her to drive in 1976, turned the wrong way onto a one-way street because – and I quote, "I don't look at signs".)

In 2004 LuAnne returned to school and earned her Master's in teaching at Western Oregon University with the goal of teaching at an international school. In 2005 she moved to Saudi Arabia where she taught English, Digital Photography and Yearbook at an international High School in Dhahran.

While her photojournalism training provided the basic skills she needed, it is the years of traveling and cultural experience that have honed LuAnne's ability to take photographs that pull the viewer in and make them feel like they have not only shared the experience, but gotten to know the subject. And that is the most appealing kind of photography, after all, that takes the viewer to some far off place they can't go themselves and introduces them to new people, customs and culture.

Many of the photos in this exhibit were taken during LuAnne's years living and traveling in the Middle East. In an age where most media information about Arab countries is highly politicized, it is refreshing to see photos that are focused on everyday people, the kind of people we would be if we lived in those places.

Walt Everly
(Envious brother-in-law)

LuAnne has spend most of her life traveling and living overseas, starting from age four. At one point in her life, she traveled around the world solo for 16 months.

After three years at university, LuAnne came back to the Philippines for a year and ended up as a co-host on a weekly live variety show.

LuAnne has lived and worked in South Africa, Bosnia, Saudi Arabia, DR Congo, and most recently Kenya where she traveled to MAF programs worldwide.

For three years, LuAnne worked at an international school in Saudi Arabia teaching English, Photography, and Yearbook. Here she is with her Yearbook video team.

LuAnne, Jon and Cher, and their son Josh and his family have lived in Africa for many years, which has given LuAnne a family overseas.

CHAPTER 20

ADVENTURES WITH DEATH

During my devotions one morning, I happened to read in the Bible I Thessalonians 4:13, **"And now I want you to know what happens to Christians when they die so that when it happens, you will not be full of sorrow, as those who have no hope. For since we believe that Jesus died and then came back to life again, we can also believe that when Jesus returns, God will bring back with Him all the Christians who have died."** I was afraid God gave me this scripture because my tiny grandson, Josh, was to have a serious surgery. We had been praying continuously for him. At the time we were in the Philippines teaching at Faith Academy.

The others left for school, but since my class wasn't for three hours, I stayed home to write. About 9:00 a.m. Dick walked in the door and I asked, "Why are you home now?" He simply replied, "I came to see you." But as I looked at his face, something seemed wrong and I questioned, "Are you feeling OK?" In return, he asked me, "Are you feeling strong?" My heart almost stopped. "Did Joshua die?" Dick quietly answered, "Not Josh, Honey." Without even thinking I said, "My Dad! Did Dad die, Dick?" Dick nodded and we sat on the bed, crying together in unbelief. We hadn't known Dad was sick. I don't know why he came to my mind.

Dick told me all he knew. "Your brother, Harold, tried for several hours to phone you here at the house, but he couldn't get through. So he tried Faith Academy and finally consented to talk to me since you weren't there. Your Dad had surgery last week and was doing fine, but for some reason his heart just stopped today. Josh is OK, Honey." Suddenly, the morning scripture came back to me.

I had always heard that God's grace was sufficient when we needed it. I wondered if it would be for me when death within my immediate family was involved. But God has assured us, "My grace is enough; it's all you need. My strength comes into its own in your weakness." (From II Corinthians 12: 9 in The Message) Since my Dad died, several in my personal family have gone to be with Jesus, and I can say, "Yes! God's grace is enough!" It hasn't taken away the tears and the pain. It hasn't made me stop missing them. It hasn't kept me from being lonely at times. I still love and miss them, but I have peace, and I have hope, and I even have joy. I am probably more thankful for the rest of my family and friends than I have ever been. Jesus not only helps our attitude about life, but our relationship with Him can change our attitude about death and can give us hope. Without hope, there is no reason for existence. GOD has made it possible for us to have hope when we believe and trust what the Bible says in John 3:16, **"For God loved the world so much that He gave His only Son so that anyone who believes in Him shall not perish but have eternal life."**

I didn't have to deal with death again in my immediate family for several years, but the inevitable did come. I remember lying in bed beside Dick one night and thinking how totally content I was with Dick there beside me. I thought, "I don't ever want this to end," but just as quickly my mind told me that wasn't a possibility.

———*m*———

One morning, Oct. 3, 2005, we were planning a trip to a town nearby to do some banking and other errands. Yvonne was on her way over to go with us. I went into the bedroom to see if Dick was ready to go, and he was slumped over the chair. I was alarmed and asked, "Honey, what's wrong?" He replied, "I don't know." Those were the last words I heard him say. Yvonne arrived and called 911. They asked if we knew of any particular problem because it didn't seem like a heart attack.

That was when I remembered about the abdominal aneurism. Earlier, a specialist in our area had told Dick that he had seen them larger and they hadn't broken, and he had seen them smaller and they had ruptured. But he felt surgery was not the best option for Dick at his age, and he felt Dick was better off to leave it alone. Dick had already made up his mind that surgery was not an option. The doctor did say, "But I will warn you that if it does rupture, you will die quickly." That's what Dick wanted.

The guys who came with 911 thought the aneurism was probably the problem, so these thoughts were going through my mind as we were on our way to the hospital. By this time, Dick was unconscious. Yvonne called Carolyn from school where she was teaching and she came within minutes. Someone driving past our house had seen the 911 vehicles and informed our grandson Josh, who also came within a few minutes. My other children were all overseas.

Dick had signed papers saying he didn't want life-support in case something like this happened. After a quick examination, the emergency room doctor informed us that there was nothing they could do. The aneurism had ruptured and Dick would probably live only a few minutes more. The hospital staff left us alone with Dick. We all told him how much we loved him and that he was the best husband, father and grandfather anyone could ever have. His life was a total success and after we kissed him, we released him to Jesus. Yvonne said, "Dad, you're going to have a lot better day than we'll have!" This is so true. When someone has a relationship with Jesus, what can be better than going to be with Him? But for those of us telling them goodbye it's very painful. This is one of those adventures we would rather avoid, but it's also one that we will all experience.

When we came home from the hospital, my house was filled with family and friends. They wanted to make sure that I wouldn't be alone at this time, although they gave me all the privacy I needed.

I went into Dick's office and the first thing I saw lying on his desk was a big folder. It had a note with clear instructions on the top: "To be opened when I die." Once again, my thoughtful husband had made everything as easy as possible for me. He had all the important papers I would need, as well as his desires for a memorial service. Dick wanted this to be a celebration, and he had chosen joyful songs of praise to God.

All of the family wanted a video of Dick's life to be shown at the service, but Dick was the one who made videos. We had all of the equipment needed, but no one knew how it worked. So two of my grandsons, Josh (Jon's son) and Damon (Yvonne's son-in-law) found instruction books and set out to tackle a job they had never even thought of before. This was not an easy task, and they spent day and night for almost a week working on a 10-minute video. They did a remarkable job.

It actually was a rather unusual memorial service because Dick was very much present through recordings of the Four Flats (World Vision Quartet) and the videos we had made in the past. The quartet furnished the prelude music, and a video had been made when our family put on an evening of music a few years earlier. The opening song was of Dick leading our family in "O For A Thousand Tongues," and then after a few introductory remarks by my brother, Harold Antrim, our family sang "Soon and Very Soon" with Dick directing again. One of the most interesting parts was when Dick led the audience (on a video), praising the Lord and singing one of the songs he had chosen, Everyone stood and sang with Dick: "*All Hail King Jesus, All hail Emmanuel. King of kings, Lord of lords, Bright Morning Star. And throughout eternity, I'll sing Your praises, And I'll reign with You throughout eternity.*" It couldn't have been more appropriate.

Josh and Damon's video captured so much of Dick's personality, talent and love of life. During the sharing time, there were tears, but also times of laughter and joy. The other three quartet members (Ron Crecelius, Norval Hadley and Harlow Ankeny) were present, although about three weeks after Dick died, Ron joined him in Heaven. Dick's memorial service ended with him singing "My Tribute" – to God be the glory! I will always miss him, but I know we'll be together again some day. God gave us 58 wonderful years of loving and working together here on earth, the greatest family anyone could ever hope for and more adventures and awesome experiences than we had imagined or dreamed possible. The best part is the joy we had in our relationship with God through Jesus Christ.

We had faced near-death experiences numerous times in our family over the years, but near death is not the same as actual death. It was not easy losing Dick, but I had so much to be thankful for. Hope has a way of offering joy at a time when it would otherwise be impossible. And great memories bring light at times of darkness.

———

However, one thought has stayed with me since our first child was born: parents should not outlive their children! Unfortunately, that choice does not belong to us. Our many marvelous and memorable adventures with our fourth child, Yvonne, also include some we never would have chosen. But with every experience in life, God has been present with strength and peace. So adventures with Yvonne are sprinkled with a mixture of sadness and joy, but always covered with hope and trust in the Lord.

From the day Yvonne was born, we often quoted Mary Poppins: "Practically perfect in every way." Dick and I often wondered, "Where did she come from? Who does she take after? How did we get her?" Her hair was a beautiful bright red like three of the others, and in that respect she was the same. But Yvonne was an unusual child. She didn't seem to know what it meant to be selfish. She never demanded, insisted, begged, or even asked for anything for herself. Instead, she gave! Actually, she wasn't totally perfect. When she was two, she found a ballpoint pen in my purse during a church service and wrote all over my new white leather jacket. As with all of our children, we learned to love people more than things.

For me, having a baby was synonymous with moving. We moved shortly after Carolyn was born, just before Jon came, the day we brought Steve home from the hospital and a little ahead of Yvonne's arrival.

When the quartet moved from Oregon to California, Mary and I were expecting our babies very soon. We desperately needed to find a doctor. Since we were so near the delivery dates, most doctors wouldn't have anything to do with us. But we finally found a sympathetic doctor. Yvonne's birth was special. I had a spinal, which took away all pain and I relaxed and enjoyed the thrill of watching her arrival through mirrors. In those days, there was no such thing as natural birth and husbands being present.

Yvonne had to grow up too fast. She was the baby of the family only 19 months before LuAnne came along and required special attention. Yvonne talked and sang constantly, but it took a lot of concentration to figure out what she was talking about. After the ice cream man went by one day she said, "Bread man all gone Mommy." I responded, "Yes, Honey, the ice cream man is gone," to which she distinctly replied, "Me can't say ikeem man."

Because LuAnne needed so much care, Yvonne began watching a lot of TV. In California, children's shows ushered in each day at 6:00 a.m. and they continued enticing little people until past bedtime at night. One day we realized Yvonne was addicted to the television set and sucking her thumb went along with the problem. Her thumb wasn't in her mouth the whole day – just 90% of the day. We tried every method known to remove it and keep it out, but nothing helped. One day we took the children for a checkup with the doctor. When he saw Yvonne sucking her thumb he had a private little chat with her. He convinced her it was bad for her, and from that day on she never sucked her thumb again. Instead she sucked her two fingers! This continued for a few weeks, but one morning she came out and announced clearly to all of the family, "I'm not going to suck my thumb or fingers anymore." That was her decision and she never again had any part of her hands in her mouth.

Yvonne seemed fragile. Even inoculations made her desperately sick and dosages had to be cut in half. She was the kind of child you wanted to assist and love and protect. But just when you thought she was helpless and dependent, she suddenly surprised everyone with a strength rarely seen in children or even adults. While still in grade school, I often found her in the living room reading the Bible at 3:00 a.m.

From the time she could write, she showered us with notes: information, asking forgiveness, humor and always love. One evening I got a note about some money she had borrowed and was paying back, with love. Then she wrote a note to Dick saying she loved him too and we were the best parents in the world, "but I don't owe you any money." The final note was an apology for anything wrong she had ever done, and "please forgive me for anything in the future, because I am tired of writing so many notes." But notes continued to come. Her first consideration was always of others.

Like a lot of young people, Yvonne's prayers weren't always profound, but were certainly effective. When we brought our special singing group to the U.S. in 1974, we often sang in public high schools. We couldn't do a lot of spiritual songs, but we always invited the students to our evening service, which was usually in a church. Sometimes this created a problem because high school kids filled the auditorium and didn't leave enough room for the regular church members. Probably most of the young people had never been in a church before, but they were a great audience even though this was a spiritual concert. Our choir members were always available to visit with people after the service.

After one of these concerts, Yvonne met Marisabel and wanted to tell her about Jesus. When the janitor finally turned out the lights, they simply stepped outside. However, our hosts for the night were waiting and we had to go with them, so Yvonne gave her new friend the "Four Spiritual Laws" booklet and promised to pray for her. Marisabel said she wanted Jesus, but would pray at her home alone. Yvonne was disappointed and she wanted to be sure this happened. On the way to where we would be staying that night, Yvonne got a terrible stomach ache, but instead of bemoaning the pain, she prayed, "Lord, please don't let my stomach ache go away until Marisabel makes her decision to trust in Jesus. If I keep this terrible hurt, I'll remember to pray. But just as soon as she accepts you, please take away the pain. That way I will know about her decision." After about two hours of interceding, the agonizing pains suddenly left and Yvonne was convinced God answered her prayers for Marisabel.

Yvonne's boyfriend in high school was the son of a missionary doctor and his mother was a nurse. He tried to convince Yvonne that she should be a nurse, so that if they got married they could work together as a team, but Yvonne wasn't sure. She wanted to find out if this was really what she wanted to do. So after graduation, she stayed an extra year in the Philippines and spent some time working at the mission hospital her boyfriend's Dad had started.

After helping with the birth of a baby, Yvonne wrote to me, "Well, today is my birthday! And I've decided that on every birthday, it's not the kid who should get presents, but their mother. After all, she's the one who went through all the pain on that day, not the kid, so why should I get all the glory for simply appearing in the world. Happy Birthday, Mom! (Now can I get my driver's license?)" This was accompanied by a beautiful single pearl necklace as her birthday gift to me. The hospital experience convinced Yvonne that she did want to be a nurse, and she was even willing to take chemistry, a subject she was afraid she couldn't do.

Yvonne attended George Fox College, focusing on pre-nursing classes, took nursing courses at Samford University in Alabama, then finished her RN program at Oregon Institute of Technology in Klamath Falls, Oregon. While in college,

Yvonne met a musician, Walt Everly, whom she married on Dec. 17, 1977. During her career as a nurse, Walt and Yvonne went to the Philippines where she worked for two years providing nursing care for low-income families and jail inmates. She started a clinic for babies in a squatter area near where we lived and taught the mothers about sanitation. It was during this time that their first daughter, Miriam, was born. After they moved back to the U.S., Walt became a computer specialist while Yvonne worked part time in both gynecology and general practice clinics. They had two more daughters, Hannah and Megan. Yvonne loved taking care of people and their physical needs, although she found it difficult to watch when the doctor gave her own baby a shot.

Yvonne's notes continued to come and delight us. Since Dick's birthday was the day after Valentine's Day, one of her notes (after studying in Alabama) read:

"HAPPY VALENTINE'S DAY! HAPPY BIRTHDAY DADDY! (Sorry they will both be late.) I want you all to know how much I love you and miss you. I think I've got the greatest parents in the world and the neatest brothers and sisters (even adopted ones) and wonderful sister-in-laws! I love 'ya'll' so much! Daddy, aren't you getting tired of being 39?"

Yvonne's positive outlook on life could turn any situation into an adventure. Her love of travel took her to many countries around the world and one of her favorite activities was to plan another trip. After Dick died, Yvonne claimed she was the one who would take care of me the rest of my life.

However, in 2002, while working for a clinic in Newberg, Yvonne was diagnosed with breast cancer. This became a battle for the next few years, with both victories and setbacks. At one point, Yvonne expressed some of her feelings in the following article.

Centering Down
By Yvonne Everly

After dealing with breast cancer for five years I thought I was an expert in traumatic events, but last summer I discovered there's always room for improvement, so to speak. I had already been on an emotional roller coaster for several months after the discovery the previous autumn of the cancer in my bones, liver, lymph system and lung, followed by several months of chemo and then my relief as the cancer appeared to retreat. Six months later, though, I could tell something was wrong again and feared the worst. The roller coaster started up again: schedule the doctor appointments; order the scans; wait for the insurance approval; have the scans; wait for the doctor to see the results, then wait for him to get back to you. Anyone who has dealt with a serious illness knows how frustrating and frightening it is having to wait for the process to plod slowly along. It all takes so very long, giving you more than enough time to worry and fret over the what-ifs, to imagine all the worst-case scenarios. Lots of time for fear to take root and grow.

One of my lifelines was Paula, a sweet, young wife and mother with the same diagnosis as mine. From opposite coasts, Paula and I lived parallel lives as we coped with bad news, with treatments, fears and setbacks. We spent hours and hours together on the phone, crying, laughing, celebrating and hoping together. I hit bottom the day I called to see how she was doing and her grieving husband told me she had passed away. In all my life as a Christian I have never experienced such a crisis of faith; I was overwhelmed by feelings of betrayal, confusion, loss and hopelessness.

While in this darkness, a dear praying friend brought me a Beth Moore study called "Believing God." Beth's intent in this study was to lead us to the place of believing God for who he is, not what he does. She explained that when my faith in God depends on what he does for me I am attempting to be in control.

When God doesn't "perform" to my expectations and desires, then I exercise control by no longer believing in him. But if I believe God and trust him because of who he is, then no matter what my circumstances are I can still believe in his goodness and love. Fear and panic have no place where God is in control. "The Lord is my light and my salvation—whom [what] shall I fear?" Does this mean I no longer have moments of doubt and anxiety? Let's just say I'm still working on this, some days more than others. But I am finding that when I praise God and thank him for who he is, when I yield control to him, when I lay down my expectations and demands—his peace really does take over.

"I am still confident of this: I will see the goodness of the Lord in the land of the living. Wait for the Lord; be strong and take heart and wait for the Lord." Psalm 27: 13-14 "You will keep him in perfect peace, whose mind is stayed on You, because he trusts in You." Isaiah 26:3

Yvonne seemed to get better and even took another trip with her sisters to Guatemala, but there came a day when she wrote the following letter:

Dear Friends and Family,

I need to get this news out to many people so in spite of the fact that I'd like to talk to each of you individually, this seems to be the only practical way to do it. Most of you know that I was diagnosed with breast cancer in 2002. After a mastectomy, chemotherapy and reconstruction surgery, I've been followed by an oncologist and have felt great. Since there are no reliable breast cancer blood tests to go by, the follow-up is mainly symptomatic—if you have pain, it is followed up with appropriate tests. So when I developed pain in my shoulder and sternum recently, many tests were run. It was discovered that my cancer has returned and has spread to most of my upper bone structure, lymph nodes, neck and a spot on my liver. Although the doctors are reluctant to give a prognosis, it is clearly not a good scenario.

This week I had a port-a-cath (permanent IV line) inserted in the anticipation of starting chemotherapy in the next week or so. If this cancer turns out to be the same as before (estrogen receptive), then there is a newer chemo drug that is more specific to target it.

As you can imagine, this has been a difficult road to travel — one we had hoped to avoid. My personal concern has been for my family — besides our two daughters who live here in town near us (one is married, the other a freshman in college), our youngest daughter (15) is spending a year attending Faith Academy in the Philippines where I went to school. Another concern is my mother who is still recovering from the loss of my father and my younger sister who lives in Saudi Arabia and feels frustrated at not being able to be here to help.

Even though this has not been public news until now, we've already seen an outpouring of love and concern from those who knew. Those caring acts and prayers have held us up when things have looked darkest. We will continue to need wisdom as we face each new challenge.

In an effort to keep everyone informed, I hope to be able to send out periodic updates. This will save me the effort of repeating myself dozens of times. If you would like to be included on this update email list, please let me know by sending a short note to that effect. Only those I hear from will be put on this list so nobody gets extra emails they don't need. We appreciate your prayers at this time.

Yvonne (and Walt) Everly

It hardly seems appropriate to call this section on death an adventure. Usually we expect to have an unusual and exciting time as we plan our adventures, although there are times when an adventure involves danger and the unknown. And attitude still plays an important part in any adventure, even suffering and death. I've heard it said that this type of experience can either make us or break us. We can become better or bitter.

Years ago I read a book titled: "But God. . ." When we allow God to be involved in our adventures and attitudes, He makes a difference. Everything can look hopeless, "But God. . ." enters the equation and everything changes. Roman 8:28 has probably been quoted more than any other verse in the Bible (except John 3:16). The translation I know best (King James) says, **"And we know that all things work together for good to them that love God, to them who are the called according to his purpose."** After telling how God's Spirit is helping us, praying for us from our wordless sighs and our aching groans and keeping us present before God, The Message assures us, **"That's why we can be so sure that every detail in our lives of love for God is worked into something good."**

We may not be able to see or feel how any good could ever happen again, but when we trust God we can have peace and hope. This morning during my special time with the Lord, I was reading from Psalms in The Message. I just happened to open to a page where I had written quite a lot beside one part of a Psalm. I was curious about what I had written some time ago, so I read what the Bible said before I read my comments:

Bless our God, oh peoples!
Give Him a thunderous welcome!
Didn't He set us on the road to life?
Didn't He keep us out of the ditch?
He trained us first,
passed us like silver through refining fires,
Brought us into hardscrabble country,
pushed us to our very limit,
Road-tested us inside and out,
took us to hell and back;
Finally He brought us
to this well-watered place.

I wrote: *"I feel like this is what happened to Yvonne! We could only stand and watch! We always called Yvonne our family's angel. Maybe she really was. So I've asked God why she had to suffer so much, and He said, 'I know how you feel. I sent my Son to help people, and He had to suffer and die a horrible death. But He brought salvation to the world and now is in Heaven interceding. Yvonne's life also has a purpose.'"*

Yvonne depended on prayer, and she had assurance from friends around the world that they were praying for her. As a family, we continually pleaded with God to heal Yvonne. However, there was one particular woman, Lecia Retter, known to be an unusually powerful "prayer warrior." Lecia became a very special friend to Yvonne, and Yvonne constantly leaned on Lecia for strength and support. Lecia's daughter, Paige, had this to say about Yvonne:

Yvonne Cadd Everly is the strongest and most capti-vating woman that I have ever met. Her exceptional talents in music were drawn out at a very young age, and when she sang, you could feel the sun radiating from the deepest part of her innermost being. Yvonne's beauty was exquisite. You could sense the passionate work of her maker as your eyes fell from her flowing red hair, through her peaceful gaze, into her wide, genuine smile and settled on her flawless complexion. You couldn't help but be drawn to her in the same way that a child is drawn to the fragrance of a new season. Yvonne could stand silently and people would flock to her.

My mother adored her most of all. She was, almost, perfect. For as long as I can remember, Yvonne has been a warrior against cancer. Its first place of attack was her breast, affecting only her body, leaving her soft heart unscathed. The tears and painful nights, this round, didn't last long as some. They came and went and were soon replaced with shouts of joy and a vic-torious, vivacious pink wardrobe. But the blueprints were already being studied and a new battleground was closely watched, preparing for its most important slaughter of all. We shielded Yvonne with prayer, but the fight against brain cancer was overwhelming to all of us, especially my mom. It spread throughout her entire body like a waterfall, seeping into every crack and sparkle. Yvonne's husband, three daughters and son-in-law watched her outer beauty fade into baldness, dizziness, frequent illness and a swollen face so big that she was barely recognizable, her smile almost hidden. Her lover held her as she cried day in and day out, and we all silently counted the days that she had left.

Yvonne Cadd Everly passed into the arms of Christ, leaving her spouse, daughters and a brand new grandchild who she never even got to hold, behind. My mother lost one of her closest friends that day, and I watched it shred her emotions from the inside out.

As humans, we will always have the opportunity to witness a loss, but we have to pay attention to how it affects us. I looked on as a friend died, but everything causes an emotional reaction of some sort. Don't go through life without pausing to review your steps and blessings. What are you taking for granted?

It was devastating to see our beautiful daughter suffer and watch how cancer destroyed her body. For seven years she fought this disease, and there were times when she seemed to be totally free from it. But Yvonne described having cancer as being like having an elephant in your living room. Even though everything else seems normal, it's impossible to forget about and ignore that elephant. When that elephant decided to step out of the living room and take over the house, all we could do was to watch and pray and be available.

Yvonne eventually needed a full time caretaker. LuAnne was teaching school in Saudi Arabia, but she came home to be with her sister. All of us wanted to take care of Yvonne, but because of children, jobs and serious obligations, it was LuAnne who moved in with the Everly family and was available full time. Yvonne and LuAnne had always been extremely close, being only about a year and a half apart in age. LuAnne was not only efficient and meticulous in every detail of Yvonne's care, but she cooked, cleaned, did the laundry, took Yvonne to the endless doctor appointments, and always loved, always cared! Walt had to continue working, but he moved his office to just a few steps away, where he could be near when needed.

One of the activities that Yvonne really enjoyed during the cancer period was to help serve meals at the community kitchen in one of the churches in town each week. She was the one who drew our whole family to work there for Thanksgiving dinner one year instead of indulging in a huge meal at home. I continued to take Von there every week as long as she could walk. She had also saved enough money to take her family on a Caribbean Cruise and made all the arrangements and reservations even when all hope of her recovery was gone. She wanted the family to have good memories. And so they went, even though there were apprehensions about how much she could handle, especially when she insisted on going parasailing and doing other activities that required some strength.

Yvonne's oldest daughter Miriam and her husband Damon had adopted an adorable four-year-old boy. Isaiah and Yvonne instantly bonded and spent every available moment together reading, playing and cuddling. When Miriam found that she was pregnant with a baby girl, Yvonne was determined to live long enough to see her granddaughter. However, God had other plans.

We had told the doctor that we wanted to know about how much longer he thought Yvonne would be with us, because her brothers wanted to come home from Africa and Asia for time together. I will never forget when he took us aside and said we should tell them to come as quickly as possible. Before long the whole family had moved into Yvonne's or Carolyn's home (which was next door), in order to be as close as possible. Yvonne belonged to a Women's Bible Fellowship, and someone from this group brought dinner for our whole clan every evening for two or three weeks. This was a beautiful gift, since no one really felt like cooking.

Another special gift came from one of the young women in the Women's Bible Fellowship. It appeared as a story about Yvonne. AJ Schwanz wrote:

> Instead of talking about how I did or did not love all today, I'd rather focus on a woman who is known for her love.
>
> When I first attended Women's Bible Fellowship, I hadn't participated in a group activity for some time, and I'm certain I had spit-up on my shoulder. I was late, having to sneak in and take a seat up front at a table with women I didn't know, which almost had me run for the hills, but then women started sharing about how their summers were. One woman stood up and talked about her breast reconstructive surgery and how women had thrown her a party when it was done, complete with a cake shaped like a boob. My two thoughts: I can't believe these pillars of the church community are talking about things like boobs—they must be real people after all! And if they can talk about boobs within five minutes of the gathering starting, then I can be okay here.
>
> This wonderful woman had had cancer, fought it, won, and then had a relapse, recovery and another relapse. And now she's within days of leaving us physically. Our women have prayed over her, the church community has prayed over her, friends have experienced insomnia and deep soul groanings over her suffering and imminent passing. She is a woman I did not know well personally, but she embodied warmth and acceptance and love that only comes from knowing Christ. She persisted in praying for everyone, loving them even

if they didn't appear to want to be loved. She walked with people through hard times, and she allowed us to walk with her through these past years of pain.

I'm sure I saw her as a tyke. Her uncle was my childhood pastor, and her family was known for their musical abilities, so I'm sure they came to my church and performed. Such beautiful harmonies I've heard her family blend together, most recently as they've sung hymns and songs of praise to her in her sun room to help ease her pain and do the thing they seem to love best: worship the Lord together.

This evening an update was given stating that she now has the 'death rattle,' a sound in the chest present hours or days before passing. To think that a body capable of creating such beautiful sounds is now involuntarily giving off that kind of noise: I don't want that to be the last thing her family hears! But then I realize that it's only for a short while and hopefully their memories of her past songs, words, actions—the natural hum of her true self will reign dominant as she'll be singing as she was created to with the other saints. And I hope, oh I hope, her family and loved ones will feel that hum in their daily lives, because you know she'll be interceding like nothing else. Lord, transform that rattle into a hum; thank you for letting Christ love us through her; may we continue with the melody today and everyday.

More than anything in the world, Yvonne wanted to help others and have her life be an influence for Jesus, but she often felt like she had failed. However, the phone calls, emails, letters and cards from around the world, indicate that her desire has been fulfilled, with changed lives, because of her life. Here's a message one person sent to LuAnne:

Subject: Yvonne

LuAnne, my name is Lena Davis McClellan, and I have spent the evening looking at your very touching pictures of your sister, Yvonne. I am saddened to hear of her death. Yvonne and several of the girls from Faith Academy, Madri-Gals & Guys, spent many days at our house at Clark Air Force Base in the Philippines. Yvonne and Leah Eaton, along with the Madri- Gals & Guys played a major role in my finding God and living in His light. Tonight, as I listened to the songs that you sang on the sun porch with Yvonne, I thought back to the days when Leah, Yvonne, Joel and Dave all sat around my dining room table eating candied apples and wondering why Leah never puckered when she ate the skin of an orange. I looked at each picture that you have posted and I cried many tears, not just of sadness and of tender days gone by, but also because I too have just finished fighting a tough battle with colon caner.

You captured Yvonne's smile and her love of life, the love between two sisters, the love and sadness between a mother and her daughters and the tenderness between a man and his wife. Your pictures are priceless. I will miss Yvonne and pray that God will wrap his loving arms around her family members and comfort them during this difficult time. In His love, Lena

I don't think it is possible to ever stop missing Dick and Yvonne. Every day something happens that reminds me of them. It might be a song, or a photograph, or a job I can't do that they always did for me. Often as I play the piano during my worship time, I "hear" Dick singing one of his favorite songs, and tears flow freely. But it's OK. Tears can be healing. Often it's a reminder to pray for others, but more than anything, I am so thankful for the time we had together and the assurance that we will have even more time when we meet again with Jesus in Heaven. As Christians, death is not the end. I can declare with confidence that trusting Jesus makes a huge difference in our attitude toward death.

CHAPTER 21

CONTINUING ADVENTURES

How do you close a book like this when life continues on? And life does continue as long as we still have breath. We have the freedom to choose. We may not have a choice about our circumstances, but we do have the freedom to choose how we will respond. That's our attitude. We don't have the freedom to decide the results of our choice, but again we can choose our attitude. I live just a block from a beautiful retirement community. My brother and his wife, my sister, and my cousin live there. My parents lived there, as well as other relatives. I have many friends who make this their home. I am often asked why I don't live there. It's a choice I have made. At one time Dick and I considered moving into one of the apartments, and we asked different people how they liked living there. Here are some of the various answers we heard:

> "I might get used to it someday, but it's not easy."
> "It's where I ought to be."
> "I was really looking forward to being here, and I love it."
> "I'm old, and I don't have much choice."
> "I will try it for a year and see if I like it."
> "I couldn't be happier."
> "My family thinks this is where I belong."
> "People are wonderful, and it's a good place."

"The rooms are too small."
"Too many rules and not enough freedom."

Dick expressed to one woman that he didn't think he could survive in such a small room. Her reply was the best we ever heard and showed how the right attitude brought total joy.

This is like a dream. I'm living in a mansion, a palace. I have my own bedroom and private bathroom, with someone to do my cleaning. And then I have access to so many incredible areas. There's the library, personal chef, exercise room, pool and coach. Friends live close enough to see every day and the gardens, walking area, and lawns are beautiful. If I am sick, I have a nurse on call at all times and a doctor visits regularly. I'm just across the street from the University where I can attend classes, concerts, plays, basketball games and all kinds of activities. I can get free help with my taxes, can make friends with students and get all kinds of advice. I have banking service and can attend church here if that's my desire. I even have movies. I can't think of anything more that I need or want. I feel like royalty!

Some people live in a tiny one-room apartment, while others live in a palace—all in the same place, the same environment, the same opportunities, the same advantages. Attitude makes the difference.

I was visiting in the special health care center one day, and almost everyone I met had a frown on their face and was shuffling down the hall. It was rather dark and dreary. Suddenly it was like someone turned on the lights. One woman had the biggest, brightest smile and greeted me with joy in her voice. She was a ray of pure sunshine that lit up the whole area.

Yes, choosing the right attitude is the key to opening the door to a life of amazing adventures. If we have trouble turning the key, we have assurance of help simply by asking from the one who made us and loves us. John 3:16 tells us that, "God so loved the world that He gave His one and only Son, that whoever believes in Him shall not perish, but have eternal life." And Ephesians 3:20 assures us that "God who by his mighty power at work within us is able to do far more than we would ever dare to ask or even dream of — infinitely beyond our highest prayers, desires, thoughts, or hopes."

I love to remember that God has told us, "I am holding you by your right hand—I, the Lord your God—and I say to you, don't be afraid; I am here to help you." (Isaiah 41:13)

FREE GIFT – MUSIC CD and DVD DOWNLOAD

Please visit **http://helencadd.com/download.html** to download your free copy of:

- **Music** from the young Cadd family, and the Madri-Gals & Guys.
- **Video** of the Four Flats Quartet and The Cadd Family Concert.

MUSIC

The music is a collection of songs from the young Cadd family from 1966, and the Madri-Gals & Guys from 1970, 1974, and 1976:

Cadd Family

1. I Have Christ in My Heart
2. Praise the Lord
3. Little Drummer Boy
4. Sing Your Way Home
5. Supercalifragilisticexpialidocious
6. Thank you, Jesus
7. He Touched Me
8. God Is Love

9. I Found What I Wanted
10. This Little Light of Mine
11. I Wish We'd All Been Ready
12. Follow Me

Madri-Gals & Guys

13. Get All Excited
14. Who'll Be a Witness
15. For A Thousand Tongues
16. Put Your Hand in the Hand
17. On a Wonderful Day Like Today
18. Ballad of St. Peter
19. What You Gonna Do
20. Jesus Took My Sins Away
21. The Meeting in the Air
22. There's a New Song
23. He's Everything to Me
24. My Tribute

VIDEO

The video is a combination of songs from The Four Flats Quartet and The Cadd Family Concert. The quartet made a video for their families, and it was produced in the George Fox University Media studio in 1984. The guys not only sang, but also told numerous stories of their adventures together. I have included mainly their songs.

After almost 11 years apart, all of the Cadd family came together from around the world in 1995 to Newberg, Oregon. All of the children were now grown with families of their own. Requests began to come for a concert, which we thought would be fun, so with only one week to prepare, we gave a performance at Newberg Friends Church to a full house. It was a great experience for our family since we could include not only our children, but also grandchildren. It was not filmed professionally, but simply as a family memory.

CPSIA information can be obtained
at www.ICGtesting.com
Printed in the USA
FSOW02n1609130616
21489FS